Becoming a Social Worker

by Yodit Betru, LCSW, DSW

Becoming a Social Worker For Dummies®

Published by: **John Wiley & Sons, Inc.,** 111 River Street, Hoboken, NJ 07030-5774, www.wiley.com

Copyright © 2024 by John Wiley & Sons, Inc., Hoboken, New Jersey

Media and software compilation copyright © 2024 by John Wiley & Sons, Inc. All rights reserved.

Published simultaneously in Canada

For general information on our other products and services, please contact our Customer Care Department within the U.S. at 877-762-2974, outside the U.S. at 317-572-3993, or fax 317-572-4002. For technical support, please visit https://hub.wiley.com/community/support/dummies.

Wiley publishes in a variety of print and electronic formats and by print-on-demand. Some material included with standard print versions of this book may not be included in e-books or in print-on-demand. If this book refers to media such as a CD or DVD that is not included in the version you purchased, you may download this material at http://booksupport.wiley.com. For more information about Wiley products, visit www.wiley.com.

Library of Congress Control Number: 2023949836

ISBN 978-1-394-20087-0 (pbk); ISBN 978-1-394-20088-7 (ebk); ISBN 978-1-394-20089-4 (ebk)

SKY10061004_112723

Contents at a Glance

Table of Contents

Introduction

Have you ever considered social work? You may have gotten this question from other social workers or career coaches when you talk to folks about your aspirations. People ask this question because social work is a gem of a profession, and many people don't know much about it. That's where this book comes in.

In *Becoming a Social Worker For Dummies*, I have the immense pleasure of talking to you about a profession that not only offers the deep satisfaction of knowing that you're doing good in the world but also provides numerous career options and opportunities. I know this because I've had an amazing career doing work that matters, work that tries to make the world more equitable, and work that compensates me well. Yes, you read correctly: Social workers can earn a very good living and do it while making a difference!

Becoming a Social Worker For Dummies is unique in that it gives you foundational information about the subject of social work *and* tips and tools that practicing social workers use to be successful. Social workers, like other helping professions, love acronyms, programs, and jargon. This book cuts through all that mess and gives you the information you need in an organized and accessible way.

About This Book

One of my many roles is serving as a social work college professor and program director. When I meet with prospective students, we talk about why they should choose social work as a profession and why they might choose my program. In this book, I give you the information on why you should consider social work. If you want to come to my program, well, good for you! But there are many wonderful schools of social work and many career options and educational paths.

Becoming a Social Worker For Dummies introduces you to the field of social work practice in three distinct ways:

>> It gives you an overview of a career path in social work and the daily life of a social worker.

>> It gives you an introduction to the helping process and foundational knowledge on issues of justice and equity as the building blocks for the profession.

>> It gives you information on specialization areas of social work practice such as trauma, mental health, addiction, health care, community organizing, leadership, and international social work.

The chapters define terms and definitions, giving you context and some background information on the topic so you have an overall sense of it. Where possible, I use real-life examples to illustrate what this looks like in action. I've worn many hats as a social worker, and in my role as an educator I get to have lots of contact with practicing social workers and community organizations. My goal for this book is for you to feel like you have access to the topics in the way that I do and for you to be able to explore more if you want to look deeper into a specific area.

I use a social justice and a strengths-based framework in this book. This is because the field of social work addresses social problems by helping people who are hurting and by addressing the conditions that are causing the hurt. We do both. We ask the fundamental questions, "Why is this problem showing up this way, with this person/community, at this time?" and "What have we done in the past to address it?" These questions show that we're curious about the person and the condition. We don't blame or ascribe fault to the person; we want to know what happened. Social work is also a field that looks at capacity — how people and communities have thrived and coped, and what we can do to join this process. You see these themes throughout the book.

Within this book, you may note that some web addresses break across two lines of text. If you're reading this book in print and you want to visit one of these web pages, simply key in the web address exactly as it's noted in the text, pretending as though the line break doesn't exist. If you're reading this as an e-book, you've got it easy — just click the web address to be taken directly to the web page.

One note on the book's title: Social workers would never use the word "dummy" to describe someone. But the *For Dummies* series uses the term irreverently — it's tongue in cheek. Dummies readers are bright and capable — they just need to get up to speed quickly and easily on a subject they're beginning to explore.

Foolish Assumptions

As I wrote this book, I made some assumptions about you, the reader:

>> **You may be taking an introductory course in social work.** If so, this book can help clarify some topics and areas that may seem intimidating, like areas around social justice or nuanced topics like addiction.

>> **You may know you want to be a social worker, but you're not sure which career path you want to take.** If so, this book can help you explore the diverse areas of practice in social work and help point you to career tracks you hadn't considered. Perhaps you only saw yourself working one-on-one with people and you're discovering that you may like group work or community organizing. Maybe you were curious about international contexts and global social work. Or maybe you're interested in macro or community practice but you aren't too clear on what kind of work that involves. This book can help clarify these areas for you.

>> **You may be interested in the helping professions in general and want to understand what social work offers.** If so, this book is for you, too.

Icons Used in This Book

Throughout this book, icons in the margins highlight certain types of valuable information that call out for your attention. Here are the icons you'll encounter and a brief description of each:

TIP

The Tip icon marks tips and shortcuts that can help you do a professional task more easily.

REMEMBER

The Remember icon marks information that's especially important to know. To siphon off the most important information in each chapter, just skim through these icons.

TECHNICAL STUFF

The Technical Stuff icon marks information of a highly technical nature that you can skip over if you're short on time.

WARNING

The Warning icon tells you to watch out! It marks important information that may save you headaches.

Beyond the Book

In addition to the abundance of information and guidance related to the social work profession that I provide in this book, you get access to even more help and information online at Dummies.com. Check out this book's online Cheat Sheet for an overview of the social work profession, the helping process social workers use to make change, and educational paths and jobs you can have as a social worker. Just go to www.dummies.com and type **Becoming a Social Worker For Dummies Cheat Sheet** in the Search box.

Where to Go from Here

This book is organized so you don't have to read it from beginning to end — you can skip around to find the information you need, letting the Table of Contents and the Index be your guides. Not sure where to start? If you're curious about the day-to-day work of a social worker, head to Chapter 15. Looking for foundational knowledge about social work? Turn to Chapter 1. Want to find out more about social work specialties? Part 2 has the answers you need.

I wish I had found the field of social work sooner and that I hadn't stumbled onto it. My hope is that this book will serve as a clarifying guide for you and that you get a chance to check out the wonderful world of social work. It's a great area, and it needs good people. Have you ever considered social work?

1

Getting Started with Social Work

Understand the social work profession's values and principles.

Differentiate social work from other helping professions.

Explore the educational path for social work and the specialty areas in the social work profession.

Learn about the art and science of the helping process social workers use to intervene at the individual, group, community, and system level.

Get fundamental knowledge on areas of social justice dimensions of diversity that the social work profession is committed to addressing.

IN THIS CHAPTER

» Understanding what social workers do

» Considering a career in social work

» Seeing how social work differs from other professions

» Setting the record straight about social work

» Getting to the heart of social work

» Considering the skills you need to be a social worker

Chapter **1**

Seeing What Social Work Is All About

Many people are looking for jobs that give them meaning and purpose and that do good in the world. But the path to finding work that meets these criteria isn't always clear — there are so many ways to help. Social work is unequivocally dedicated to doing good in the world.

Maybe you've been looking for a career that matches your interests, and social work has repeatedly come up, but you aren't sure what social workers do or your impression of social work isn't super positive. Or maybe someone has told you, "You should look into social work," and you're finally getting around to checking it out.

In this chapter, I give you an overview of social work — what it is and what it isn't. I also give you a sense of what kinds of work social workers do. If you want know more, keep reading this book! Or maybe this chapter will help you determine that social work isn't for you. Either way, I want this chapter to help you make one of the biggest decisions of your life — which career path to pursue.

Defining Social Work

At social events, I'm often asked, "What do you do?" I beam and say, "I'm a social worker." I don't say I'm a professor, a therapist, or a board member — all roles that are presumably higher status. I proudly say I'm a social worker because I love the profession, what it stands for, and what good it does in the world.

Sometimes, I hear my friends or perspective social work students wonder about their purpose in the world or what kind of legacy they want to leave behind. Other times, I hear people feel really discouraged and hopeless about the state of the world.

This is where social work comes in. Every day I know that my work makes a difference and that I'm doing something that is morally and ethically aligned with who I want be and what I want to do, which is leave the world and the people and systems I interact with better than I found them. Social work allows me to pursue my passion for helping others and the world in a real, practical way. It's not just wishing that things were better — it's enacting change to *make* things better.

So, what is social work? Social workers tackle hairy and wicked problems — what social scientists call *social problems.* These problems are complex, seemingly impossible to address, and entrenched. Think poverty, homelessness, violence, trauma, addiction, and more — problems that seem to have a slippery definition, are hard to measure, seem to exist in society no matter how many ways we try to improve them, and are generally hard to solve. Social work is a profession dedicated to solving these issues because there is a moral imperative to do so and a deep and relentless hope in the fact that humans and structures can change and be better.

According to the National Association of Social Workers (NASW; www.social workers.org), the largest organization of professional members of social workers in the world, the mission of the social work profession is to "enhance human well-being and help meet the basic human needs of all people, with particular attention to the needs and empowerment of people who are vulnerable, oppressed, and living in poverty." We often say social work is a calling — it isn't a job that you clock in and out of. It's often an extension of your desire to do good in the world and, more important, to do better on behalf of and with folks who society has deemed invisible, unworthy, or, in many cases, intentionally harmed.

Social workers are trained to be *interventionists* (people who have the skill sets to break down complex problems into parts and enact change through a thoughtful, scholarly, and scientific process). Yes, social work involves training. You wouldn't imagine a surgeon walking into an operating room without any medical training and saying, "Hey, hand me that scalpel. I have good intentions and really want this clogged artery to be clear." That would be unthinkable! It's the same for social work.

Social workers are trained to understand the potential root cause of the issue, devise a plan of treatment or action, execute the plan, and then evaluate the plan to see if it made a difference. What makes social work special is that it's using this process — what social workers call the *change process* — to help make someone's life better or society better.

Seeing What Makes Social Work a Fulfilling Career

Social work is a very fulfilling career. In my role as a social worker, I meet people at the hardest juncture of their lives and offer not just hope, but real solutions. What could be more important than that? But this work doesn't just happen in a vacuum — social work as a profession comes from a strengths-based perspective and is focused on social justice, and those key principles form the foundation for the work itself.

Seeing people's strengths

The strengths-based perspective of social work looks at each person as unique and imbued with talent and resources that give them the capacity to author their own solutions. This perspective contrasts with medical training, which sees people or society as sick and in need of a diagnosis and fashions treatment without input from the client. Social workers are trained to see the best in people and to help them develop to meet their potential.

The strengths-based perspective informs how social workers engage with people and communities. It makes the work they do inherently hopeful and fulfilling. It allows social workers to see the potential in people, to understand how they've coped and adapted, and it gives people the tools to empower them and their community. This energy and stance make the daily operations of the job joyful and fulfilling.

The strengths-based perspective is also respectful and takes the time to hear from the individual, family, and community before devising a plan for change. Social workers listen deeply and learn how people have overcome adversity in the past and what resources they have available. They take the time to learn about a person's culture and their experiences with oppression. They listen for times when the person and their community weren't heard, listened to, or given support to help address the problem. Social work doesn't assume that the person is automatically at fault or is so deficient that things are beyond repair. Social workers devise help collaboratively, with the goal of giving the person and community agency and control to make decisions for themselves.

As a social worker, I'm in business of hope. Early in my career, I worked as a school-based social worker at a school that was under-resourced and fairly chaotic. I was told by one of the coaches in the school to only focus on the "good" children and to devise a plan for getting the "bad" ones out the school so they stop disrupting everyone. I was shocked by this advice. Our job was to help all kids — especially the "bad" ones. After all, they're the ones who need the biggest champions! So, I made it my mission to make sure each child knew they were valued and that their families and circumstances mattered. I also decided to hang out with other folks who shared my values (because my supervisor and training told me that I couldn't do this work on my own) and joined a community that's committed to serving all kids. I loved getting up every day and working with children, the school staff, and the kids' families. Even when it was hard, it was good work.

Focusing on social justice

Another central reason that social work is a fulfilling profession is that it's concerned with making the world more equal and just. One of my social work friends often says, "I got into social work because I kept seeing people hurting and not getting what they need. I thought, 'Wait, that's not fair. That's not fair.'" In essence, social work is committed to making the world fair for everyone. That may sound naive and idealistic, but it's the truth. Social workers think about basic human rights, who has the opportunity and access to live out the rights afforded to them, and what we need to do to improve their chances.

The work of manifesting social justice is a rigorous but deeply fulfilling process. It requires curiosity, self-reflection, *applied learning* (where you apply in the real world what you've learned in the classroom), and thoughtful action. Just as people and community problems are unique, so are solutions.

BRINGING YOUR TALENTS INTO YOUR WORK

Social work allows you to use your talents and gifts to come up with interventions, policies, and resources. For instance, if you're a creative person who loves the arts or music, you can devise your work so it includes those elements. You can specialize and get training that incorporates what you love and apply it to the population you want to work with.

For example, the director of a shelter for families who have experienced violence wanted to make sure that the families had access to a garden and creative space; they wrote a grant asking for support to fund this initiative and got it! Another social worker wanted to make sure dance and creative movement were accessible to families with low funds. She partnered with a local organizations and secured a site, hired dance instructors, and created sustainable programming so kids could grow in their dance skills until they graduated from high school.

If you're like me and you aren't really the creative type, but you are relational and a bit of a nerd, you can do the work that fits you! I use my skills to provide therapy, build community engagement and partnerships, and educate the next generation of social work students.

Differentiating Social Work from Other Helping Professions

Many helping professions are dedicated to helping people, specifically within human services. If you want to be of service or do good as part of your vocation, you may be weighing which path you should take. Maybe you aren't clear what differentiates the various academic majors and their associated professions. For example, what's the difference between psychology, sociology, human development, and community organizing majors? What makes a social work degree and career path different from these tracks? Can anyone who wants to do social good call themselves a "social worker"? (The answer to that last one is no.)

In the following sections, I introduce you to a variety of helping professions so you can see the difference between those jobs and social work.

The bottom line of all the following information is this: If you're interested in therapy, you can do social work. If you're interested in social problems and the conditions that create problems for people, you can do social work. If you want to be an activist who organizes and actively disrupts harmful systems, you can do social work. A social work degree enables you to quickly find a job doing exactly what you want and gives you greater flexibility in the workforce.

Social workers

Social workers usually have a bachelor of social work (BSW) and/or master of social work (MSW) degree. They must attend a school that is accredited by the Board of Accreditation of the Council on Social Work Education

(CSWE; www.cswe.org). The education usually involves coursework on human development, understanding and working with diverse populations, as well as skills classes that focus on teaching specific intervention skills like group work or grant writing.

In addition to the coursework, you do extensive internships that are 500 to 1,000 hours long. The internships are considered classroom in the community, where you get to apply your coursework to the population or community you're interested in serving. You can choose from a variety of sites for your internship, like mental health clinics, schools, shelters, hospitals, government, and community centers. Because social work focuses on the person in the environment there are many career opportunities (turn to Chapter 19 for some examples).

Similar to psychologists, social workers can do *clinical work* (work that involves assessing and addressing individuals' or groups' psychosocial challenges, often within a broader social and environmental context) or *therapeutic work* (work that is directly tied to addressing mental health conditions). A person who wants to pursue therapeutic work as a social worker needs to earn an MSW. After completing the MSW, you must do 2,000 to 3,000 hours of supervised clinical work (the amount varies from state to state). The supervised clinical work usually takes about two years. After completing those supervised hours, you have to pass the licensure exam.

TECHNICAL STUFF

Some social work positions are filled by people without social work degrees because the organization hiring needs workers. In other instances (for example, child protective services), social workers should exclusively be the people hired for the work. Due to staffing storages, many counties hire folks who have a background in humanities or social sciences and do extensive training to try replicate social work training. They even offer full scholarships for their employees to get educated in schools of social work.

Psychologists

The career path that is most often confused for social work is psychology. Psychology is the study of the mind and how people behave. Psychologists are interested in understanding the mental process, brain function, and the behavior of individuals. When people think of psychologists, they're usually thinking of *clinical psychologists* (people who treat mental health conditions and what they call *abnormal psychology*).

The American Psychological Association (APA; www.apa.org) requires a doctoral degree as the educational requirement for a psychologist. Training usually involves four to six years of graduate school training.

There are subbranches of psychology that focus on areas like the function of the brain and how a person understands and processes information, the development of a person across the life span, and how people are influenced by group dynamics or their workplace.

TIP

What's important to note about psychologists is their focus on the individual person — how the individual person thinks, behaves, and interacts with their environment. This is different from social work because social workers always think of the person in the context of their environment. The environment influences the person and the person influences the environment, even when considering their mental health and behavior.

REMEMBER

A psychology background and degree aren't as flexible as a social work degree. If you choose to major in psychology, you should be prepared to earn a doctorate if you want to do counseling.

As a young person, I found the idea of doing four to six years of doctoral studies in psychology daunting, so I pursued the MSW degree, thinking of it as a shortened path to becoming a therapist. What I discovered along the way was that the social work degree allowed me to do the clinical work but with a strong emphasis on understanding a person in the context of their environment. It taught me that I have to address issues of justice and equity even in therapeutic work. Plus, the MSW degree allowed me to have other roles, like doing advocacy work or school-based work, which a doctorate in psychology wouldn't have enabled me to do.

Sociologists

A sociologist studies social behaviors and interactions among groups and society. They look at things like education, race, and gender, and study and understand how policies and programs address inequities within these issues. Unlike social work, there is no internship or applied part of a sociologist's educational path.

REMEMBER

The internship experience is key to the social work profession, and robust accreditation requirements must be met. Higher education is a costly investment, and the internship is an essential part of the apprenticeship process.

Sociology is primarily a study of social problems. Social workers also look at social issues and then take the next step if they're devising an intervention to address the inequity.

Sociology is another field that gets conflated with social work. One of my sociology professor friends likes to tell people that he worked as a social worker as part of his background because he did some community-based work and wants to have street cred. I always correct him and say, "No, you weren't a social worker. You were a sociologist who was hired to be a case worker." It may seem like I'm being persnickety, but I'm protective of the social work profession because people who aren't trained in our methods think it's a matter of semantics or words — and it isn't.

Community organizers or activists

Community organizers or activists may identify with the mission and vision of social work but may not be formally trained as social workers. These folks may be deeply committed to communities but not too caught up on labels or what they're called.

Some social workers do community-based or macro-level work and have a specialization where they're taught how to do effective organizing, brokering, and targeted activism. They've also trained in collecting data and conducting analysis that they can use to make or influence policy changes. Social workers are taught tangible skills for organizing — they don't just fall into it or do it as they go along.

Dispelling Myths about Social Work

When I announced to my family that I wanted to pursue a degree and career in social work, they were apprehensive about my future because they had misconceptions about the profession. They thought I was nice person but worried that I was choosing a career where I would be poor and take children away from their families. I'm guessing that when you tell people that you're interested in social work, you might get a similar type of reluctant support. If so, this section is for you! Here, I outline the top three myths about social work and bust the misconceptions about the profession.

Myth #1: You're taking a vow of poverty

Choosing social work as a career is not synonymous with living a life of poverty. On the contrary, a social work degree is one of the most flexible when it comes to career opportunities. Plus, it gives you the chance to earn a good living in a job that is personally fulfilling.

According to the U.S. Bureau of Labor Statistics (BLS; www.bls.gov), the median income for a social worker is $50,390 with the highest 10 percent of social workers earning more than $82,840 per year. Certain positions (such as hospital or government-based positions) have higher starting salaries than other positions (such as crisis workers). The BLS is also projecting that there will be around

78,000 job openings every year in the field of social work. That's more than you'll find in many other professions, and it's growing faster than the average job market. Thanks to the recent introduction of the licensed baccalaureate social worker (LBSW), the demand for social work students is set to skyrocket.

And if you're wondering where you can make a big impact, think rural areas and underserved communities. According to the National Conference of State Legislatures, 37 percent of the population lives in places where there's a shortage of psychologists, counselors, and social workers, and most of that gap is in rural areas.

Plus, there's good news for job security: The Health Resource and Service Administration predicts that the number of social workers will go up by a whopping 114 percent by 2030. So, if you're on the lookout for a career that's not only in demand but also lets you make a real difference, social work should be on your radar!

TIP

Some employers are even offering signing bonuses for new hires! You read that correctly — signing bonuses aren't just for people in the tech industry.

As you grow your role and specialization, your pay will also incrementally increase. For example, maybe you land a paid internship at a social service agency. In a win-win situation, you get hired by the agency for an entry-level position after graduation. You get good benefits and support for clinical supervision (either support to pay an outside consultant to provide clinical supervision for your licensure or support internally in the form of access to an in-house clinical supervisor who is credentialed to supervise for licensure). After two years, you've gotten specialized training in the area of addiction and passed the licensure exam. This automatically bumps up your pay and makes you eligible for roles in midlevel management. It also allows you to start a private practice as an additional stream of income. As you grow in your roles, you're promoted to director and eventually leave the job to be an executive director for a local agency that serves families struggling with substance use. Executive directors have incomes that exceed the $83,840 salary and are often $100,000 or more.

REMEMBER

This career path is not unusual. Most social workers have happy and stable lives and can claim that they do the job because they love it *and* for the money.

Myth #2: You'll only be removing children from their homes

One of the enduring stereotypes about social workers is that they unduly take children away from families. In movies or TV shows, this situation is often depicted as a crying child having their small hands pried from their equally distraught mother. This is followed by the lack of understanding in the depth and breadth of the social work profession. Not only do we not unduly remove children from their homes, but we do so much more.

The truth is, social workers *cherish* the family bond and do our best to support and restore families who are in crisis. Child welfare is an incredibly important part of social work dedicated to identifying and protecting vulnerable children from abuse. This is a critical social function, necessary to prevent child fatality.

That's not to say that children aren't removed from their homes in situations where there is imminent danger. But child removal is the very last option and resort.

Social workers are trained in the strengths-based perspective (see "Seeing people's strengths," earlier in this chapter) and have two important charges: Keep kids safe, and try to preserve and strengthen the family. In the sad event that there is confirmed abuse, a child is removed from the home, but there is a great effort to connect the family to supportive resources. The ideal outcome is family reunification and the safest environment for the child. Federal policies mandate that diligent searches must be done to place children with kin or biological family members when possible. The idea is to place the child in the safer part of the family system while the social worker provides support to the immediate family so the child can return to a safe space.

Social workers work with folks across the entire spectrum of life. We work with infants, toddlers, preschoolers, school-age children, teenagers, young adults, middle-aged adults, older adults, and the very oldest adults. We do the work in many contexts — in health-care settings taking care of pregnant women, in school settings taking care of kids and youth, in community spaces where families and groups can meet, and in government offices where we make policies and enact change. There is an incredible array of work available, and working in public child welfare is one of the many jobs you can hold.

Myth #3: You don't need specialized training

Social work is not charity or volunteer work. It's a discipline of study with specific education and training and with a code of ethics that governs the activities of the profession.

In its early history, social work *was* charity work where wealthy white women wanted to do some good and address issues of poverty and industrialization. They considered themselves to be "friendly visitors." Over time, this practice evolved, and the volunteers began to study the social conditions that created child labor and poverty and became interested in reforming society and how help is given. They conducted research, helped establish court systems to take care of abandoned children, created pension programs for widows, and promoted laws that prohibited child labor and introduced social insurance. Formal methods of training for this type of work started and schools of social work were established.

The first schools of social work were at Columbia University and the University of Chicago. As society evolved and major social issues (such as wars and economic crises) arose, social welfare policies and programs, like Social Security, became incredibly important. These policy developments impacted the social work profession because they made the field very necessary and visible. As pubic aid grew, the need for social workers also grew. Additionally, as the profession grew, specialization in the field grew. Today, social workers make up the largest sector of professionals working in mental health services, in child and family services, and in health care.

Social workers are people who care. But caring is the start of the helping journey, not the end or the only motivator. Clients and systems don't need just hugs — they need policies and people who understand those policies and can create strategies and interventions to make their lives better.

Embracing the Heart of Social Work

The part of social work that is universally respected and appealing to those who care about others and want justice in the world are the core values, principles, and code of ethics. These standards act as guideposts for the profession and the individual social worker. They're particularly useful when you must make difficult decisions that aren't always black and white.

In other instances, they make the decision process very easy. For example, one of the core values of social work is the dignity and worth of every person. Every person is treated with care and respect, even when they do deplorable things. When I worked in a jail setting, I sometimes came into conflict with correctional officers because we had competing values — they often felt like I was too permissive or too soft and being taken advantage of by these terrible criminals. I never saw the people who are incarcerated as throwaways. I saw them as people worthy of dignity, even in this setting, because my training and professional values informed my perspective.

In the following sections, I unpack the values, principles, and ethics that guide the profession.

Recognizing the core values of social work

Values are strong beliefs about how the world should be, how people should conduct themselves, and what kind of conditions the world should be in.

One document that states the values of the American people is the Declaration of Independence. It outlines what human rights look like and the kind state that the United States should be. It states that all people are created equal, that they have the right to pursue a life of happiness, and that they have the right to a representational government. These are big ideals and ones that people hold dearly.

Similarly, professions and professional programs also have values, principles, and a code of ethics that guide their thinking and practice. Social workers have one that they're deeply proud of and would be happy to quote to you at dinner parties. I was delighted to discover them in my studies and found them to be consistent with my moral code and aspirational in how I wanted to practice.

There are six core values of social work. These core values are articulated in the Social Work Code of Ethics published by the NASW. These values are deeply rooted in the history and philosophy of social work, which places a strong emphasis on human rights, social justice, and improving the well-being of individuals and society as a whole. They provide a moral compass for social workers as they navigate the complex and challenging issues they encounter in their practice.

The six core values are as follows:

>> Service

>> Social Justice

>> Dignity and worth of the person

>> Importance of human relationships

>> Integrity

>> Competence

In the next section, I cover the principles that arise out of these values — they shed more light on what the values mean.

Looking at the principles social work is built on

The principles of social work (see Table 1-1) arise out of the six core values (see the preceding section). The principles flesh out the core values.

TABLE 1-1   **The Principles of Social Work**

Value	Principles
Service	Social workers help people and address social problems.
Social justice	Social workers challenge social injustice.
Dignity and worth of the person	Social workers respect the inherent dignity and worth of each person.
Importance of human relationships	Social workers recognize the centrality of human relationships.
Integrity	Social workers behave in a trustworthy manner.
Competence	Social workers practice in areas of competence and develop in their area of expertise.

These values and principles create a road map for how to be our best and ideal selves as social workers. Social workers are dedicated to a life of service — some would say *public* service — with the goal of addressing social problems. This is done by acting with integrity, in a trustworthy manner and with competence. Your clients should be able to trust you to keep your word, do right by them, and connect them with others when you aren't the right person for the job.

REMEMBER

Social justice is nonnegotiable in social work. If you only want to help people or modify their behavior, and you don't want to take their conditions into consideration, social work isn't the field for you. Instead, try another discipline where the person is central and is the only point of concern (see "Psychologists," earlier in this chapter).

Social workers must approach people and systems with humility and respect and believe that relationships are critical for change. Building bridges through intentional relationships is core to what we do. A simple example of this is in the health-care setting. Health-care providers focus on treating the body. When patients are ill, doctors and nurses do their best to stabilize the body and provide a path for recovery. During the COVID-19 pandemic, health-care folks did their best to treat the virus, and isolation or quarantine was mandated. Social workers recognized the need for humans to be connected to one another and devised creative ways for families to see their sick relatives. They advocated for telehealth visits or allowing people to be seen through windows. These practices helped patients recover better.

Accepting social work's code of ethics

The code of ethics outlines how social workers should behave and what the public can expect from them. It's also critical to addressing unethical or egregious

CHAPTER 1   Seeing What Social Work Is All About   **19**

behavior that causes harm to clients or the profession. It's used as the standard for enforcing discipline or adjudicating ethics complaints.

The code of ethics is a guide for ethical conduct and the decision-making process. Sometimes there are competing values, and you must suss out the best things to do given all the information, the limits of the law, agency policy, and social work research and theory.

Good supervision comes into play in this situation to help you with these dilemmas. When I was a school-based social worker, one of my middle-schoolers came to see me because she needed help getting access to pregnancy tests. She didn't want her mother to know she might be pregnant, and she knew the school nurse didn't give out pregnancy tests. I had to make an ethical decision about what I should do. Complex situations like this were something I had to work through routinely in my work.

In the United States, the NASW developed and set the ethical principles of the profession. The principles align closely with the core values of social work. The Social Work Code of Ethics outlines six ethical responsibilities:

>> **Responsibilities to clients:** A social worker is responsible for promoting the well-being of their clients and using strengths-based language they referring to their clients. They should allow their clients to have as much say as possible in their treatment (even if the social worker disagrees with their clients' priorities), to consent to treatment, to have the right to privacy and confidentiality, and to have reasonable access to their own records. Social workers should avoid conflicts of interest and have strong boundaries so their clients are protected. Basically, don't be an unethical jerk who takes advantage of someone in a vulnerable state.

>> **Responsibilities to colleagues:** A social worker is responsible for treating their colleagues with respect, fairness, and courtesy. They should promote cooperative and collaborative relationships among colleagues to enhance the effectiveness of service delivery. This principle encourages social workers to address conflicts or ethical issues with colleagues through appropriate channels, maintaining confidentiality when necessary, and upholding professional standards within the workplace.

>> **Responsibilities to practice settings:** A social worker should ensure that the practice settings in which they work are conducive to providing ethical and effective services. This includes advocating for policies and practices that uphold the welfare and rights of clients and ensuring that the setting provides adequate resources, supervision, and support for ethical practice. Social workers should address any barriers or challenges in the practice setting that may hinder the delivery of high-quality services.

- >> **Responsibilities as a professional:** A social worker should uphold the values, ethics, and standards of the social work profession. They're responsible for continually enhancing their professional knowledge and competence and for promoting the profession's mission and goals. This principle encourages social workers to advocate for social justice and engage in activities that strengthen the profession's influence and relevance in society.

- >> **Responsibilities to the social work profession:** Social workers have a responsibility to contribute to the growth and development of the social work profession. This includes participating in activities that advance the profession's knowledge, research, and ethical standards. Social workers should also mentor and support emerging professionals, contribute to professional organizations, and engage in advocacy to address issues that affect the profession's integrity and effectiveness. A lot of reciprocity and mentorship happens in the profession.

- >> **Responsibilities to the broader society:** Social workers have a profound responsibility to the broader society, requiring them to uphold the highest standards of integrity and professionalism. This entails consistently acting with honesty, competence, and transparency in their practice, while respecting colleagues and diverse perspectives in interdisciplinary settings. However, when confronted with policies or practices that harm clients or contradict ethical principles, social workers must prioritize doing what is right and just, even if it means advocating or protesting to uphold the profession's commitment to social justice and the welfare of vulnerable populations.

Identifying the Stages of the Helping Process

The helping process includes key steps: engaging, assessing, goal setting, intervening, and ending the process.

Engagement

The engagement phase is the first step of coming into contact with a person or situation that needs help. This is the part where you establish rapport and build trusting relationships with your clients. During this phase, you actively listen, empathize, and seek to understand your clients' needs, values, and strengths. People have to trust you or believe that you can help them. Engagement works on that.

Assessment

After you engage the person or situation, you need to gather the relevant information to have a full understanding of where things are now. Whether you're assessing an individual, a family, a group, or a community, there are methods and tools to help you gather the kind of information you need.

This is also where you'll use scientifically or research validated screening or assessment tools or processes to aid you. Social workers deal with complex problems, so you usually need to spend time getting to know the person and system in order to formulate or devise a plan of action to remediate the issue. This, too, takes skills — you'll get better the more you do it and the more support and coaching you have.

REMEMBER

In school, as part of their coursework, students practice doing assessments in class and then are supervised when they do it out in their internships.

Goal setting

The next step is to set mutual goals with your clients. I said *mutual* goals, not goals you want for your client, but goals they want for themselves and that you support.

When I was working with people who were victims of intimate partner violence, I thought the goal was always to sever ties with the abuser and get a new, better life. But what I learned was that most people are in relationship with the person who is hurting them — they want the harm to stop, but they don't always want the relationship to end. I had to respect that and help them devise the best way to be safe and get what they need. Specific treatment modalities teach social workers how to best do this.

Intervention

After the goals are set, you get to the action part. Intervention is what the social worker does to move the client from the problem-identifying part of the helping process to the coming-up-with-the-solution part of the process.

In the example of working with survivors, one common goal people have is to be safer in their homes and have more financial stability. In this case, social workers devise what's called a *safety plan* and talk through the steps the client needs to be more financially stable. I may connect a client to social services, educational programs, and other survivors who are on the other side. I also work one-on-one with them to help them process their feelings about themselves, their partners, and other people in their lives.

If you're interested in *macro social work* (addressing social issues and systems at a large scale), you may do an assessment of the organization. You'll also use a model to identify the needs of the organization and devise a strategic plan to address the gaps and needs of the organization. This process is similar to working with individuals, but your audience is bigger, so the level of impact you have will be larger. That's often the reason people like doing macro or group-level work.

Ending the process

Believe or not, it also takes skills to end the helping process. You need to effectively conclude the professional relationship with a client, which includes discussing their progress, addressing any unresolved issues, and facilitating a smooth transition to ensure they're prepared to continue their journey independently or with appropriate ongoing support. These skills help create closure while emphasizing the client's growth, self-sufficiency, and readiness for change. The end of the process has to be planned, and it's something you'll keep your eye on when you start the helping journey. The goal is for folks to be well resourced and have access to material, emotional, and social supports, ensuring a comprehensive foundation for their ongoing journey. The goal is for them not to need you anymore. Social workers often joke that their goal is to go out of business and for social problems to end. People should be developing strengths, skills, and the capacity to not need a social worker, or at least not need them as much.

Endings take on many forms. Sometimes it's ending the relationship all together — maybe you've connected a family with a resource or another service, and you're no longer needed. Usually, it's an ending for now, and you'll tell your client to contact your later if they need you.

For macro-level work, it may be meeting goals and devising the next step of the work. Maybe you've helped create policy to address a need. The end of the process may be implementing the policy or scaling the policy so it reaches a wider audience.

Chapter **2**

Studying for a Career in Social Work and Choosing a Specialty

I f you're thinking about becoming a social worker, you're probably wondering how much school you're in for and what you can do with your degree. You've come to the right place! In this chapter, I walk you through the various degree options, explain what you can do with those degrees, and even fill you in on how much you can expect to earn. (Money probably isn't your *top* priority — otherwise, you'd be majoring in business and going to work on Wall Street — but you don't have to take a vow of poverty to be a social worker, and you can be paid quite well for your expertise.) Read on for information degrees and potential career paths.

Going to School and Getting Licensed

You have several options for degrees in social work — everything from a two-year associate's degree to a spend-forever-in-school doctorate. In this section, I outline your options and tell you what you can do with each of these degrees, so you can decide which path is right for you.

Knowing what you can do with an associate's degree

If you're just dipping your toes into the social work world or you have a high school education, an associate's degree in social work is a nice starting point. You can earn an associate's degree at a two-year community college.

TIP

Community colleges are easy to access, cost effective, and welcoming to people from a wide range of backgrounds. For most people, community colleges' biggest draw is the lower tuition rate and local access. Given the rising cost of education, starting your education at a community college can be very appealing.

TIP

If you think you might want to continue your education at a four-year college after earning your associate's degree, make sure that any social work credits you earn at the community college will transfer to a four-year college after graduation. Many community colleges have agreements with accredited bachelor of social work (BSW) programs, where all the credits you earn at the community college can count toward your BSW degree.

Associate's degrees are usually earned with 60 credit hours and take about two years to complete. When you earn an associate's degree in social work, you'll learn social work terminology, be introduced to social work values and the importance of diversity, and learn the main theoretical perspective for the profession. You'll take courses on intervening skills, child welfare, community resources, human development, addiction, and diversity. Usually, there is a hands-on component or service project that typically requires around 100 hours of work.

An associate's degree in social work prepares you to work in community and social service agencies, usually as a *paraprofessional* (a trained aide who assists a professional). Paraprofessionals play essential roles in social services or public agencies. They're the frontline folks who work very closely with clients and help carry out the daily tasks of programs. Usually, they work under a licensed professional as aides, advocates, and assistants. Their pay rate is usually hourly and can range from $15 to $25 per hour, plus benefits.

REMEMBER

You can't formally call yourself a social worker with an associate's degree, but you can say you're an advocate with training in social work.

Here are some of the kinds of work you can do with an associate's degree in social work:

>> **Patient advocate:** Work in health-care or mental health-care facilities and help patients get the care they need.

>> **Student aide:** Work in a school-based setting and help provide one-on-one support to students who have developmental or mental-health disabilities.

>> **Case manager aide:** Help clients access care by setting up a care plan, providing transportation to appointments, facilitating access to social services, and assisting clients in making and attending appointments in line with their case management or care plans.

Aides who have an associate's degree in social work play a critical role in the lives of clients. For example, in group homes or inpatient facilities, aides are the folks assigned to be in the unit all the time (in shifts) with the children and clients. They're the ones who keep clients safe, monitor the activities within the space, and alert staff to any emerging issues. They set the tone for the care facility because they're the people who patients spend the most time with. They serve as mentors and emotional supports, too.

In the shelter I worked in and managed, I always tried to hire social work–trained aides because I wanted people who genuinely cared and who had a good understanding of what our clients were facing. Too often, people who have good intentions, but no basic training, come into these kinds of jobs and end up being a very bad fit. They become impatient, cold, or punitive because they don't understand why the clients and patients don't behave better. This is the benefit of having some training — the training explains what can seem like baffling behavior and offer a pathway to address the distressing behavior.

An associate's degree in social work allows you to start working in the social service sector and in community-based work. Even if you can't or don't want to continue on in your education, the associate's degree gets you doing good work with people who need you.

Going for a bachelor's degree

A BSW is the minimum requirement for most social work jobs. The Council on Social Work Education (CSWE) accredits schools of social work starting with the bachelor's degree. If you graduate from an accredited school with a BSW degree, you are officially a bona fide social worker, and you're ready to change the world! You have an extremely employable and practical degree. I say "employable" because you do an intense internship that allows you to get hands-on training; by the end of it, you can do real things like:

>> **Intakes:** The initial phase of client engagement, where crucial information is gathered to establish a client's specific needs and circumstances

- **>> Assessments:** In-depth evaluations to comprehensively understand a client's strengths, challenges, and requirements, providing the foundation for tailored service plans

- **>> Casework:** Providing personalized, one-on-one support and intervention to address individual client needs and goals

- **>> Advocacy work:** The crucial role of advocating for clients' rights and interests within various social, legal, or institutional contexts

- **>> Group work:** A collaborative approach that entails facilitating therapeutic or educational sessions for a group of clients who share common concerns, fostering mutual support, and creating a platform for shared growth and development

I'm amazed by the kinds of work BSW students do and the problems they tackle. They take on homelessness, food insecurity, child abuse, and neighborhood conflicts, and serve as legislative aides. One of my BSW students interned for our local congressman, who eventually became the mayor. They went from taking walk-in concerns from local constituents and organizing listening sessions to being one of the aides for the mayor of the second largest city in our state. Another student who earned a BSW degree went on to earn their master's degree in community organizing and is now themselves a congressman! Both of these folks started out as people interested in helping the community and chose social work as the path. Now they're making changes at the state and national level — all with a BSW degree.

The BSW degree is earned at a four-year accredited program. I keep mentioning accreditation because there are schools that offer degrees in things *similar* to social work (like human development or social science or even sociology), but that's not social work. On the other hand, some schools of social work are housed in interdisciplinary programs, especially in smaller schools, where the degree is under an umbrella of social services. But the degree earned is a BSW and the program is accredited by the CSWE.

The BSW curriculum covers topics on human development, diversity, the fundamentals of social work practice, social policy, research, and skills classes on working with individuals, groups, and communities.

BSW students must also do an internship their final year, lasting a minimum of 400 hours; most programs require 500 to 600 hours of internship. The internship is an immersive opportunity to develop your social work skills in a guided manner. Students are supervised by social work–educated supervisors on-site. The supervisors meet with student interns every week for an hour of supervision where they discuss how things are going, any ethical dilemmas, and the emotional toll of the work. This time is protective and helps students manage difficult cases and emptions that can lead to early rates of burnout.

Social work programs have relationships with local agencies and place students at internship sites that align with the students' interests. Some placements aren't as jazzy but offer payments to entice students to consider a career in an area they might have otherwise overlooked.

TIP

The internships that offer payment tend to be the ones involving child welfare work and work with older adults. Students just don't know how rewarding the work is until they get into it! I speak from personal experience — I was pretty explicit about not wanting to work with children. No thank you, not me, never. Then my supervisor said, "Well, the position you're working in is grant funded and it's ending. We need you to pivot and work with kids. And it will be middle-schoolers." Lord have mercy, not middle-schoolers! I went into the school with a pretend happy heart and I ended up *loving* the work. Those stinky middle-schoolers melted my cold heart. It's even one of my areas of specialty now!

For a BSW student, an internship can require 15 to 25 hours a week (or two and half days a week) over two semesters. This is in addition to having coursework (which can be up to four courses a semester). It's a pretty intense schedule juggling four classes and an internship. Some schools allow students to do *block placements* (intern close to 40 hours a week and enroll in only one course over the course of one semester). Educators tend to like the two-semester option better because it gives a student more time in the agency and the opportunity to experience a whole lot of things and get to do a whole lot of stuff. Similar to dating, agencies can show you their best side for the first couple of months. But when you settle in and give it more time, you get to *really* see what the work and the agency culture are about.

Another benefit of internships is that they are extended job interview and an opportunity for agencies to check out the emerging talent. Most students end up getting a job at the agency site and becoming full-grown social workers with a degree in one hand and a job offer in their inbox.

What kinds of jobs can BSW graduates qualify for? "So many" is the answer. Here are just some of them:

>> **Administrative specialist:** Supports the operation of an organization or department by handling clerical tasks, managing schedules, and ensuring efficient communication

>> **Benefits specialist:** Assists individuals in understanding and accessing various benefits (such as health care, unemployment, or disability benefits) and helps them navigate the application process

>> **Caseworker:** Works with individuals and families to assess their needs, provide support, and connect them to available resources and services, with the goal of improving their overall well-being

>> **Community program coordinator:** Organizes and oversees social programs and initiatives within a community, ensuring that they meet the needs of residents and are executed effectively

>> **Community resource coordinator:** Identifies and connects individuals or communities with relevant resources and services, helping them access the support they need

>> **Counselor:** Offers emotional and psychological support to individuals dealing with various personal or emotional challenges, and provides guidance and coping strategies to help them improve their mental health

>> **Emergency shelter case manager:** Assists individuals who are experiencing homelessness by providing them with shelter, support, and resources to address their immediate needs

>> **Family advocate:** Works with families facing challenges and helps them navigate systems, access services, and advocate for their rights and needs

>> **Family caregiver development specialist:** Supports and educates family members caring for loved ones with medical conditions or disabilities, helping them gain the skills and knowledge they need

>> **Medical social worker:** Provides essential support to patients and their families by assessing their social and emotional needs, coordinating access to resources, and offering counseling and advocacy within a health-care setting

>> **Mental-health technician:** Assists in the care and treatment of individuals with mental health disorders, often in clinical or residential settings

>> **Program specialist:** Manages and implements specific social service programs, ensuring they operate effectively and meet their intended goals

>> **Research assistant:** Supports research projects, collecting data, conducting literature reviews, and assisting in research analysis within the social work field

>> **Residential case manager:** Oversees the well-being and care of individuals residing in group homes, shelters, or other residential facilities

>> **School-based services:** Works in educational settings, supporting students, families, and staff in addressing academic, emotional, and social challenges

>> **Youth support partner supervisor:** Oversees teams of youth support partners who work with youth who need additional supports, providing mentorship and guidance to improve their lives

These positions don't have the title of "social worker," but they typically require you to have a BSW degree. The pay for these positions tends be an annual salary ranging from $32,000 to $50,000. The positions allow you to work independently, carry your own cases, and have incremental salary increases consistent with your tenure at the job. Many child welfare case workers hold BSW degrees and retire with good benefits, pensions, and sustainable income.

TIP

If you're interested in management positions and you want to do the most you can with a social work degree, a master's degree is the best option (see the next section). The good news is, if you have a bachelor's degree in social work, you have an expedited path called *advanced standing* that allows you to get your master's degree in one year.

Earning a master's in social work

The master of social work (MSW) degree is called a *terminal degree*. A terminal degree is the highest degree that you can earn for the profession. For some areas of study, the doctor of philosophy (PhD) is the terminal degree; for others, such as social work, it's the master's degree.

TECHNICAL
STUFF

You *can* earn a PhD in social work (see the next section). But that's a matter of advancing your education for your own benefit or to become a professor or researcher. You can stop at the MSW degree and be at highest education level for the profession.

Similar to the BSW degree, you must attend a school that is accredited by the CSWE. Right now, there are 350 CSWE-accredited MSW programs in the United States — find the full list at www.cswe.org/accreditation/about/directory. You can attend in person or online, and you can do so as a part-time or full-time student. The programs range in cost and can be at private or public institutions or, as is the case with my school, be confusing and be called a "private/public institution."

TECHNICAL
STUFF

Public institutions are funded by taxpayer dollars and are usually less costly than private institutions, which are funded through tuition, endowments, and donations, and often have more independence in their operations. Private/public institutions benefit from *both* taxpayer support and private contributions; this dual funding structure allows the university to offer more affordable in-state tuition but also grants it some operational flexibility compared to entirely public institutions, which are subject to greater government oversight.

The quality of the school is ranked by its research and its general reputation. You can find a rankings list in *U.S News & World Report* (www.usnews.com/best-graduate-schools/top-health-schools/social-work-rankings). Some people choose schools based on rankings, and others choose based on what's most accessible and affordable. There is no right or wrong decision — just do what makes sense for you. In the end, employers only care that you have the MSW degree.

If you're going full-time, it usually takes about two years to complete your MSW degree. If you're going part-time, you can earn an MSW in about three and a half years. And if you have a BSW degree, you can earn the MSW degree in one year.

TIP

Most BSW students go directly from earning their BSW straight into an MSW program. That way they can finish up their higher education in five years and walk out ready to conquer the world with the highest degree for their profession.

The first semester and a half of the MSW coursework is actually identical to what you study when pursuing a BSW degree. (That's why BSW students have shorter MSW coursework. Their senior year is equivalent to taking graduate-level courses and an internship.) You take coursework on human development, social policy, research, diversity, and social work practice and do an internship that mirrors the BSW internship experience — it's about four courses and 16 to 18 hours of internship hours a week for two semesters.

What differentiates an MSW student from a BSW student is that you take higher-level classes that specialize in policy and skills. Most programs have specialization tracks like working in direct practice with individuals and families or a track that focuses on community-based work; some schools even offer certification options within the specialization. Other programs have what's called an *advanced generalist curriculum,* where all students are expected to know things about individuals, groups, and communities — the idea is that you need the tools to intervene at all these levels and not just get siloed into one track.

Most schools offer a specialization and certificates that focus on mental health, children and youth, gerontology, and health care. Those certificate options correspond with the job demands. Social workers are the lead providers for mental health care in the country, so it isn't a surprise that most programs offer a specialization and certificate in this area.

As you progress in your coursework, you'll also progress in your level of expertise. You'll take more policy and behavior classes, and they'll be focused on your certificate of choice. For instance, if you selected mental health as your concentration, you'll take a class on mental health polices and your behavior class will cover mental health issues across the life span. Your electives will be courses that address mental health issues like diagnosis, substance use, work with couples and families, and specific evidence-based treatment modalities like cognitive behavioral therapy, trauma, and group work. You'll learn how to assess, diagnose, and do therapy work — but from a social work perspective, one that is holistic, is focused on the person in the environment, and looks at empowering the individual.

In a similar fashion, macro or community-based specializations also have specialized coursework. The policy courses are focused on organizations and systems. The higher-level courses focus on organizing and nonprofit management. Macro-focused specializations focus on organizing and community development courses or human service work like organizational management and finances. The electives for macro specialization are courses on grant writing, leadership, entrepreneurship, organizing, group work, and sticking it to the man. Okay, that last part is not a class, but my macro-focused students are the ones who quickly rise to be community leaders and executive directors of human service organizations. That's because they have coursework and training that prepares them to do programming, evaluation, fund development, and policy analysis. But this, too, is done from a social justice perspective and is more explicit about its desire to transform systems and structures.

Similar to the BSW degree, the internship is critical for the making of an MSW-trained social worker. In fact, field or internship is considered the signature pedagogy for the profession — that's a fancy way of saying it's the most important part of the educational experience. In 2008, the CSWE determined that field experience would be the signature pedagogy for the profession of social work, stating, "Signature pedagogy represents the central form of instruction and learning in which a profession socializes its students to perform the role of practitioner." The internship apprentices students in the acquisition of professional skills while also immersing them in the profession's fundamental mindset and work practices.

At the MSW level, students who do not have a BSW degree have two internship opportunities, a different one each year.

>> **First year:** The first-year internship tends to be more general and is meant to expose students to the kind of work social workers do. I usually recommend that students do something that they'll most likely come into contact with in their line of work or that addresses one of those wicked problems like homelessness, child welfare, intimate partner violence, or international social work.

>> **Second year:** The second-year placement is more intense and focused and should be in an area you want to work in when you graduate. If you're interested in health care, do an internship at a hospital or community health provider. If you want to do fund development or be a grant writer, intern at a foundation or philanthropy office.

The combined internship hours need to be at least 900 hours and must also be supervised by someone who holds an MSW degree. Students start off by shadowing a worker; then they're given a small amount of work; and eventually they do the work by themselves. This gives them the tools to work independently after they graduate.

After earning your MSW degree, you may want to get licensed. You have two options: licensed master social worker (LMSW)/licensed social worker (LSW) or licensed clinical social worker (LCSW). You can take the exam for the LMSW/LSW license the last semester you're enrolled in school. Some jobs may require the LMSW/LSW licensure; others may just prefer it and hire candidates who have it over those who don't.

The important thing to note is this: If you're interested in doing therapy work in a private practice setting, you *must* get the LCSW license. You cannot work as an independent private practice therapist with an LMSW/LSW. The LCSW license requires clinical experience, and you'll need that before you can treat clients on your own. Yes, you've done hundreds of hours of internship, but trust me, you're in no position to diagnose and treat people without supervision and consultation.

Let me give you an example of how I came to this humble opinion: I graduated with an MSW and got a job in a school-based setting. I had all the treatment manuals on working with children and families and school-based social work. I joined the School Social Worker Association of America. I went to conferences. I signed up for training in structural family therapy and motivational interviewing. Gosh darn it, I was ready for work! I even got all the cool play therapy games and art supplies and paid for all this out of my own pocket. On the first day, I bounced my eager self into the classroom where my first student was, and I called him to me. He happily came to the door and waved goodbye to his teacher. Then he proceeded to sprint and take off. I was shocked as hell. There was nothing in my training that said what to do when your client literally runs away from you! Thank goodness for supervision. I told my supervisor what happened, and she had a good laugh and said, "Next time, make it a race." I wrote in my notebook, "Make it a race." This is why, as ready as you think you are, you need guidance for a while — your clients just may bolt for the door when they see you!

When you're pursuing the LCSW license, you'll need to find a supervisor who can oversee your licensure process. You'll need about 2,000 to 3,000 hours of clinical work (depending on your state), and you'll have to meet with your supervisor on a weekly basis for one to two hours a week. Think of these meetings as therapy for the therapy you're providing. You can discuss hairy situations, ethical dilemmas, or the progress your clients are making. After you complete the required hours of supervision, you'll apply to take the exam. (There is usually a state-level entity that manages the licensure process.) You'll turn in your educational background information and usually your transcript with your MSW degree; they may ask you to name specific clinical classes you've taken to show that you can do assessment, diagnosis, and treatment (this is where a mental health certificate comes in handy). You'll be asked about your supervisor's credentialing and documentation of your hours. You'll pay a hefty licensure fee, and *then* you'll be eligible to take the exam after you get the state-level approval.

There are licensure prep course materials and courses — your school may offer them. I don't suggest sitting for the exam without preparing. But with some good prep, you'll pass it. (Most people do. For instance, in my state, 83 percent of people pass the LCSW exam.) If you don't pass the exam the first time, you can retake it in 90 days.

After you have your MSW and LCSW, you can pursue any sector of the profession. You can bill insurance and work on your own. After a certain number of years (it varies by state), you can even supervise others for their licensure. Occasionally, I do that — it's a big but rewarding commitment.

Topping out with a doctorate

Let's say you practice for a while and you keep noticing something that isn't being addressed by the books or trainers and you keep thinking, "Hey, has anyone thought about this?" Eventually, you may get fed up by the lack of answers or the frequency of bad answers to this thing you're noticing. And you may decide you want to study it yourself and come up with a solution. This is where a doctorate comes into play. A doctorate is an attempt to investigate and answer the problem that keeps on persisting.

Some people know right away that they'll pursue a doctorate and want to be researchers and professors. For me, it wasn't so linear. I earned a doctorate because I was really frustrated by what I saw in the work. I noticed that the children and families I was working with in many different settings had these huge traumas in their lives, but no one was talking about these traumas as the root cause of what was troubling them. I realized I could work in the field for 15 years and eventually lead the agency, or I could get my doctorate, specialize in trauma-informed work, and come up with an approach that addresses people's trauma. And that's what I did.

There are two routes for getting a doctorate in social work:

>> **Doctor of philosophy (PhD) in social work:** People with a PhD are trained to do rigorous research, teach courses, and be thought leaders in the field. They advance the field by asking critical questions about what we think we know and then testing it. They do some of the coolest work — their research can literally shape or move the field forward.

There are many PhD programs in social work. They're usually fully funded by the social work program — meaning you don't have to pay. Students can enroll in programs on a part-time or full-time basis. They can be competitive, with top schools being the most desirable.

Don't look exclusively at rankings and reputation. Consider the individual school and the professors in the school and see whose work you admire and who can mentor you.

It takes anywhere from four to seven years to complete a PhD. PhD graduates can work in tenure-track, research, or teaching positions at teaching or research-intensive universities. They can also work in government settings, research centers, or the military. They conduct research on what informs practice and do data analysis that guides social policy. They're compensated very well and have annual salaries that start at $70,000 and exceed $100,000 as they advance in rank.

>> **Doctor of social work (DSW):** The DSW degree focuses on advanced clinical, macro, or teaching work for practicing social workers. It doesn't have as strong an emphasis on research as most PhD programs do, but it does still require a dissertation. It's much more focused on advancing practice than it is on research methodology.

DSW programs are growing significantly. You can enroll in them on a part-time or full-time basis, in person or online. Most folks who do DSW programs work full-time and get their degree along the way. Their work supports or informs their education. It takes three to six years to complete a DSW, depending on the program and your pace. DSW programs are not usually funded, so you pay out-of-pocket or borrow money to pay for your education.

People who hold DSW degrees are well compensated and can earn salaries that range from $75,000 to $150,000, depending on the level of work they're doing. They're usually already working as leaders in their field and, upon graduation, get a pay raise or more stature in their workplace.

I chose the DSW route because I'm a practitioner to my core. I love practicing or being hands-on with my work. The DSW allowed me to continue to do that and become a scholar of practice. I used what I learned in my coursework and wrote a dissertation on trauma-informed casework.

Considering the Many Professions in Social Work

One of the many benefits of choosing a career in social work is the ability to evolve and grow in your role. It gives you the chance to discover different parts of the helping process, different populations, and do what brings you the most joy. Some people know right away what they want to do and go for it with full gusto. Others' paths change over time.

All I knew was that I wanted to help people and that I liked the mental-health track. I chose my first job based on who was hiring for that role and who paid the best. Then I kept getting more trainings and, if I moved, I would pivot to another role and add a skill set. Now I have a pretty good sense of the work I do and where I want to keep growing.

In the following sections, I tell you about the array of jobs and roles you can have with a social work degree.

REMEMBER

If you have an associate's degree in social work, you can do paraprofessional work for these roles.

Mental-health clinician

Mental health is the biggest draw for most people who go into social work, and social workers provide the most mental-health services in the United States. The main goal of mental-health clinicians is to help people suffer less, feel more empowered, and have agency in their lives. They diagnose and treat people with a range of mental, behavioral, and emotional conditions (such as mood disorders, substance use issues, and eating disorders), as well as people who have experienced traumas. They do this through the therapy process. Therapy can be done one-on-one, in a group setting, or through family work. It can also be done in multiple settings — including private homes, via telehealth, in hospitals, or in group facilities.

A clinician usually has a therapeutic treatment modality they use that's tailored to the population they treat — you wouldn't use a treatment model for kids that you would use with adults.

Here are somethings that you can do with each of the various degrees as a mental-health clinician:

>> **BSW:** You can do initial screenings, take deep psychosocial history, create treatment plans, and make the initial contact with clients and systems. You can run groups and teach people life and clinical skills in support groups. You can't do therapy — only social workers with an MSW/LCSW can provide psychotherapy. The pay range is typically $35,000 to $45,000 per year.

>> **MSW:** You can see folks for counseling, but you must practice under the supervision of someone with a license. The pay range is typically $45,000 to $75,000 per year.

>> **MSW/LCSW:** You can practice as a private practice mental health psychotherapist. Insurance companies reimburse LCSW holders and may have higher

reimbursements for folks who have multiple specialties, like mental health and substance use. The pay varies by insurance provider and can range from $60 to $120 or more per hour.

» **DSW/PhD:** You can be the clinical director for mental-health clinics or do research that impacts mental health. I have colleagues who research mental-health concerns across the life span. They study kids and families with autism, families who struggle with racism, and older adults who are isolated and struggle with gambling. The pay range is typically $60,000 to $150,000.

Behavior health worker

Behavior health is a blanket term that includes the connection between your physical health, mental health, and behaviors. Behavior health specialists look at the factors that contribute to a health condition and work on addressing the gap between prevention and treatment approach. They address issues that bring people to a hospital for care for chronic or developmental conditions that need consistent routine care.

When they work in behavior health, social workers usually work as part of an integrated team and are one of the providers for clients. Depending on their education level, they can act as coordinators and liaisons for services or the one who directly provides the services:

» **BSW:** The major role is coordinating, serving as a liaison, doing casework, and connecting people to treatment providers or clinicians. They're essentially the glue that connects people to services. For chronic or more one-on-one work, they create behavior plans and help clients learn skills. This could mean that you work with a family or child a few times a week and help them develop social skills or behavior modification skills to be more independent. The pay range is typically $30,000 to $65,000 per year.

» **MSW:** Employers prefer behavior health workers to have an MSW because they have more experience with casework and coordination and, in some cases, can do therapeutic work as part of the health work. Employers also get higher insurance reimbursement rates for someone with an MSW degree. The pay range is typically $40,000 to $100,000 per year.

» **DSW/PhD:** You can work with interdisciplinary teams and research ways to help address behavior health issues like addiction, smoking, or obesity. The pay range is typically $60,000 to $120,000 per year.

Medical social worker

Hospital social workers can serve in as many roles as there are specialized units within the hospital setting. They work in emergency rooms, intensive care units, maternity wards, oncology units, integrated health, psychiatric units, addiction medicine, gerontology, and as discharge workers who help connect folks to services outside the medical center. Because hospitals are big institutions that receive some federal funding, they typically offer high salaries.

Hospital social workers can help with crisis situations, provide preventive care, or do highly specialized treatment like working as therapist in an inpatient obsessive-compulsive disorder (OCD) clinic with adolescents.

REMEMBER

What's important to note about the work is the setting — this is place-based work. The work environment and the roles within it determine the kinds of activities you do day-to-day. It's the hospital's turf, and you're allowed to work there.

WARNING

Hospitals are hierarchical, with the doctors on top and other providers below them. If you're going to work as a hospital social worker, you can't get discouraged by that. People will routinely underestimate your value until they realize they need your help. They may have a client who is refusing care or about to hear devastating news, and they need you to help with the relationship. Research is pointing out that the care environment impacts people's health outcomes as much as the medical intervention itself. Social workers are essential part of the team, not an add-on.

Here's what you can with each degree as a hospital social worker:

>> **BSW:** Hospital work tends to be short term and deals with information gathering, crisis management, and referral and linkage. That's what the BSW degree is designed for — intake forms, assessment, treatment plans, and discharge planning. You can do almost all the jobs. The pay range is typically $40,000 to $80,000 per year.

>> **MSW:** You can do the same thing as the BSW, but you can serve in treatment and management roles. If you have the LCSW certification, you have the autonomy to conduct therapy sessions and take on managerial roles, including signing off on your own paperwork. The pay range is typically $50,000 to $100,000 per year.

>> **DSW/PhD:** There is tremendous research being done in health-care settings and with interdisciplinary groups. There are huge health disparities and access to health care, and social work researchers and administrators work on addressing these issues because it's a matter of life and death. The pay range is typically $70,000 to $150,000 per year.

Military social worker

Military social workers provide support and care for military personnel and their families. They can do this either as civilians or as members of the military themselves. If you choose to enlist as an officer and social worker, you must hold an MSW and preferably be licensed. There are two aspects of your role in this capacity:

>> **Military:** For the military role, you must go to the commissioned officer school and pass the basic training for officers. You need to maintain a level of fitness consistent with military personnel, as well as understand the rules, protocols, etiquette, culture, and history of your branch of the military.

>> **Clinical:** For the clinical role, you must have a license. It's preferred that you have one before enlisting for service. If you don't have your license, you'll have a certain period of time to get it and you may even be eligible to spend time in an officer training facility where they'll provide supervision.

After meeting both requirements for the military and clinical part of your role, you can sign a commitment contract that ranges from three to six years. The assignment lengths have bonuses and benefits that increase in range as your commitment increases.

TIP

Start with a short commitment and find out if the job is a good fit for you. You can always sign on for an additional commitment when you're sure that enlisting as a social work officer within the military is the right career path for you.

REMEMBER

Military service members and their families face many challenges on and off military sites and bases, and families need support. Social workers need to understand the environment, culture, and subculture of service life. This means understanding the stages of military training and the stigma affiliated with asking for help and receiving care, as well as managing complicated confidentiality and privacy issues.

Social workers serve this population by providing mental health or behavioral support, social services, housing, or case management. Social workers have a strong presence across all branches of the miliary, especially with the U.S. Department of Veterans Affairs (VA). The VA is the largest employer of MSW-level social workers in the United States. Military social work provides good salary and benefits, including educational benefits and loan forgiveness.

Jobs for miliary social work require at least an MSW degree:

>> **MSW:** Similar to hospital-based social workers, military social workers ensure care through admission, evaluation, treatment, and follow-up. You do this by having expertise in the area of substance use, family advocacy, or child

welfare work within miliary life and disaster and crisis mental health management. You get experience across the spectrum of service provision. You can enlist as an officer of the military and become a leader who provides clinical supervision and training. The pay range is typically $50,000 to $85,000 per year.

>> **DSW/PhD:** The military branches of government and, more specifically, the VA provide tremendous research funding for behavior health issues. Researchers and policymakers use the funding to address substance use, post-traumatic stress disorder (PTSD), intimate partner violence, and family welfare. The pay range is typically $70,000 to $125,000 per year.

Victim services advocate and criminal justice and reform worker

Unfortunately, society is replete with all kinds of violence. Social workers provide aid and support to victims as a critical part of the profession. They can do crisis work where victims can present for services at safe houses, hospitals, or emergency centers. Social workers are on site or on call at these facilities and can provide victim assistance in the form of counseling services for the individual and family. They do advocacy, mediation, and dispute management.

They also provide restorative process for a victim/offender reconciliation program. Social workers can offer programming and support aimed at bringing together victims and offenders in a way that helps them reconcile or find resolution, possibly through dialogue, mediation, or other restorative practices. These programs address conflicts or harm caused by an offense and foster understanding, healing, and, if possible, reparation between the victim and offender. You may be surprised to read this. Most victims of violence know their assailant and appreciate options that vary in their form of getting redress. Some people want nothing to do with the legal system or assailant — they just want to move on with their lives and get protection from the person by not having any contact with them. Others want legal recourse and the fullest punishment afforded by the law. And yet others want a restorative process where they reconcile with the person but with firm boundaries.

For some folks, working in this area means working in prison systems where juveniles and adults face sentencing, justly and unjustly. Social workers are trained to understand the huge flaws in the criminal justice system and understand the implication of the school-to-prison pipeline that disproportionately incarcerates marginalized folks. Social workers who do victim/survivor and criminal justice reform work understand the complex nature of this kind of work. They have the advocacy and clinical skill sets to provide support for this very vulnerable population.

This an area of work that paraprofessionals, BSWs, MSWs, and researchers can all work in:

>> **BSW:** This area is a good place to cut your teeth. You get to do very high-impact work and have a lot of contact with victims, survivors, those who caused harm, those who have been unjustly confined, and other providers. You can do this as a case worker, a crisis counselor, a victim liaison, or as a social work aide in the public defender's office. The pay range is typically $35,000 to $50,000 per year.

>> **MSW:** You can provide individual and group counseling, do programming for survivors or an agency that does this work, or work as an expert in forensic social work and do jail- or prison-based work. You can also do community activism and organize around reform. The pay range is typically $60,000 to $80,000 per year.

>> **DSW/PhD:** There is great research focusing on and addressing violence in all its forms — child, family, interpersonal, and community. There are significant policy implications for this work that social work–trained researchers and policy analysts are influencing. The pay range is typically $70,000 to $120,000 per year.

School social worker

Schools are the most democratically accessed institutions and one of the most important places for social workers to be. Not all schools or school districts have social workers. (They should, but they don't.) All children must have education, and this usually puts them in contact with members of the public. Teachers and school personnel see children every weekday. Schools become de facto parents. Schools are also the place where we start to see issues that can no longer be ignored — issues of hunger, child abuse, exposure to violence in the home or community, and developmental delays.

School social workers help address the needs of the students and their families and work collaboratively with school personnel. Social workers are usually called in to help with truancy and *school refusal* (meaning kids are missing when they should be at school). School social workers work with students who have emotional and mental health needs by doing one-on-one or group work.

I saw kiddos and families for all kinds of things — suicidal kids, kids who had lost a parent, kids who were routinely fighting, kids whose parents were incarcerated, kids who were coming out of a juvenile detention facility, kids who were recent refugees. . . . I also saw families who needed help paying their bills and accessing food, families who didn't understand special education, and families who school personnel could not get a hold of.

School social workers can be hired by the school district or come as part of a contracted agency that provides work. I've done it both ways, but it's better to be hired by the school district so you're integrated into school life and not a visitor who signs in.

Here are some of the ways you can work as a school social worker:

>> **BSW:** You can work as a school-based specialist who works for a social service agency that's contracted to work with schools. You provide clinical screening, recommend and refer for resources, and run skills groups. The pay range is typically $35,000 to $42,000 per year.

>> **MSW:** You can work as a school based social worker employed by the school district with state-level certification. You do assessments, interventions, and home and school visits, as well as run groups and programs. The pay range is typically $45,000 to $75,000 per year.

>> **DSW/PhD:** You can conduct research on school-based interventions, usually in the area of mental health and substance use. You can work on interdisciplinary teams with education researchers, researching social and emotional development and doing school climate work and interventions. The pay range is typically $60,000 to $110,000 per year.

Child welfare social worker and case manager

Child welfare work or child abuse prevention and treatment work is the work most notably associated with social workers. Child welfare workers are the case workers you see depicted on TV. Social work is traditionally affiliated with child welfare work because social work has its origins in developing scientific casework. Child welfare workers work for county agencies and carry out the public federal and state mandate of investigating child abuse.

By federal law, every state is mandated to have a system of investigating child abuse. Believe it or not, there was a time when people didn't believe that child abuse was occurring or, if it was, they thought it was a private matter. Children suffered and died as a result of this. Now we have a public charge to protect children from abuse or maltreatment. Child welfare workers have the daunting task of doing this incredibly important work through case management.

People who routinely work with children are *mandated reporters*. This means that if they suspect child abuse is happening or a child/minor reports abuse to them, they are obligated to report it. Child welfare social workers respond to these calls and do investigations, usually in the form of a home visit; conduct interviews; and do risk and safety assessments. If the abuse is founded (meaning true), a series of decisions are made to determine where the child should be placed, starting with the extended family. Case workers try their best to keep siblings together. Services then are initiated, with the aim of reunifying families. If the services are not sufficient or if the parent is not able to recover within 24 months, the children are placed for guardianship or adoption. These are difficult matters, but children can't remain in unsafe conditions or linger for years in foster care while their parents recover.

Casework involves a deep assessment and engagement process and detailed plan of connecting the person or family with resources. It could mean referral for counseling services or substance use, referral for housing, and putting behavioral health aides in the home to help with parenting skills. Casework can be done with a BSW or MSW degree:

>> **BSW:** You can do classic case management. The pay range is typically $38,000 to $60,000 per year.

>> **MSW:** You can do case management. You can also serve in a management role and provide therapeutic services. The pay range is typically $40,000 to $85,000 per year.

>> **DSW/PhD:** You can research safety, risk, and variables that can help predict abuse. You can conduct investigations of racial disparity in reporting and confirmed cases of abuse. You can develop and evaluate policies and push for equity work. The pay range is typically $65,000 to $125,000 per year.

Macro-level social work

Marco-level social work looks at enacting change at the broader level and thinking about how social work practice enhances humans rights and social, economic, and environmental justice for people and communities. Macro-level social workers are people who work in human service management, in community development, in policy and legislation formation, and in international contexts.

They fall into two career tracks: nonprofit managers and community organizers and social activists. These roles have different foci, and you can differentiate them very quickly. Nonprofit managers are usually wearing business attire, whereas community organizers and developers are almost always in a T-shirt and jeans canvasing, mad about something, or trying to get you to sign a petition or union card. In the following sections, I cover these two tracks and what kind of work you can do in each.

Nonprofit managers or executive directors

Some social workers have their eyes on leadership from the outset of their education. Others are respected in their management roles and are asked to consider leading the entire organization.

As a social worker, you can specialize in human services and organizational management. That means you understand organizational structure and finances, you know how to raise funds, you have a grasp on organization culture and human resources issues, you know how to do strategic planning and mapping, and you're a visible person in the community. These skills are trained and cultivated.

People often say, "I want to start a nonprofit." Well, it takes more than the desire or filing paperwork. It's a serious job, and a social work degree can prepare you for it.

In order to manage a nonprofit, you'll most likely need an MSW degree and many years of experience — usually 10 to 15 years. Because the job is very time-consuming and public facing, the compensation is good. The pay range is $80,000 to $150,000 with some bonuses. If you're thinking that seems like a lot of money, it is, but keep in mind that folks in private industry who do executive-level work start off in the six figures. Executive directors eat, drink, and sleep their work. The salary is a good incentive to keep them going.

Community organizer, activist, or policymaker

Social workers respond to structural inequality by organizing, developing a plan, and enacting change through collective action. They stand toe to toe and face those wicked problems, saying, "We will not let the status quo be the norm!" They don't just make signs and march — they do targeted collective civil and social action. They're taught how to do these things in schools of social work. They study how social movements have come about historically, effective ways to dialogue and use power, and how to leverage relationships and the group process for change. They have skills relating to community mapping and development and policy development and analysis. Some of the work looks at doing assessment and capacity mapping followed by recommending policy action or figuring out how to disseminate policy change.

Don't let the T-shirts fool you. These are some sharp folks who have incredible relational and analytic skills!

One of my macro students works in the area of substance use. They work with an organization that does harm reduction as its approach for treating substance use. Harm reduction policies look at getting people to use substances in the least harmful way. The goal is prevention and treatment, not necessarily abstinence.

They work on destigmatizing substance use through a number of methods, including a needle exchange program. The organization provides free needles to people who use drugs through injection. They're one of the two agencies in the state that do this work. They organize to decriminalize drug offenses and advocate for more holistic policies. This is a big task that is being led by young people who work hard and long.

Organizing, legislation, and activism can be done by BSW and MSW degree holders. The degree to which they're able to engage the various tasks and offices is based on experience. Organizing tends to be grassroots based and less hierarchal. Leaders can be folks who have been in the community for a long time with little to no formal education but with lots of knowledge and wisdom. It can also be community-engaged researchers who do research in a fundamentally participatory manner. The compensation for the different jobs varies by the organization and funding stream, but the pay can range from $40,000 to $120,000 per year.

Chapter **3**

Looking at the Helping Side of Social Work

ocial workers are more than just very nice people. We're professionals who use scientific and humanistic approaches to help facilitate change. This is an elaborate way of saying we don't roll out of bed, put on sensible shoes, and do nice things until we get tired. Doing social work is not a paid volunteer position. It's a profession that gives you an educational background and the best methods for helping or addressing the issues that are hurting individuals, families, or the community as a whole.

TECHNICAL STUFF

When I say we use scientific and humanistic approaches, here's what I mean: The *scientific* approach is based on the scientific method, in which we figure out what's true through testing and experimenting. The *humanistic* approach looks at and values the whole individual. It's the combination of these scientific and humanistic approaches that makes social work unique.

In this chapter, I walk you through the six steps of the process that social workers use to effect change. I also fill you in on the three different levels in which social workers operate — the micro level, the mezzo level, and the macro level. Finally, I introduce the concept of evidence-based practice, which means using the best available research to inform their work. If you're drawn to social work because you know it helps people, but you're not exactly sure *how* it helps, this is the chapter for you!

The Art and Science of the Helping Process

The classic method of training social work professionals involves the *generalist approach* to the helping process, which consists of six steps:

1. Engagement
2. Assessment
3. Planning
4. Intervention
5. Termination
6. Evaluation

You may want to consider tattooing them on your arm to prove your allegiance to the process.

REMEMBER

Each step of the process entails a *theoretical foundation* (an understanding and an overall approach) to the process, as well as a set of skills to facilitate the change. The scientific method of the helping approach helps tease out which part of the process you're in and what you need to do to get to the next step. In the following sections, I cover each of these six steps and what they entail.

THE SCIENCE THAT HELPS GUIDE THE HELPING PROCESS

Social work professionals are trained in multidimensional intervention models and theoretical perspectives. A theoretical framework helps you understand the nature of a problem and formulate possible treatments or interventions. This is good news for a number of reasons:

- **You don't have to try to solve social problems by yourself.** Don't get me wrong, you're very clever — but you probably don't want to shoulder the responsibility of solving hairy problems like poverty on your own.

- **You aren't experimenting on people or communities at the most painful or vulnerable time of their lives.**

- **You can continue to add to the body of knowledge by adding findings or solutions to problems if you choose to work as social work researcher or teacher.**

The major theoretical and practice models that inform generalist social work practice are as follows:

- **Ecological/systems model:** The ecological model has roots in natural science and discusses the relationship between organisms and their environment. The general systems model states that there are interconnected systems that influence and shape a person's life — the systems are located in micro, mezzo, and macro levels. There are loops of influence — systems influence the person, and the person influences the system. Problems and stress come about because of a poor fit between people and their environment, usually around life transitions, poor interactions between people, oppression, and unresponsive environments. Problems are solved when you understand the problems in multiple layers and change the way a person adapts to the distressing things, as well as changing the environment itself. Social work describes itself as profession that helps foster a healthy relationship between a person and their environment.

- **Client centered, strengths based, and empowerment:** These approaches use humanistic perspective and state that people and systems are able to grow and change and are expert on themselves. Helpers should have unconditional positive regard toward the client and systems they serve — you start where the client is and not where you think they should be. Empathy and respect are essential for change to happen. Look for strengths and ways that clients have been successful and highlight and build on those in goal setting. Find ways to empower and resource the people and systems you work with. Actively resist and challenge views, policies, and narratives that demean or diminish the humanity or dignity of the people you serve.

These frameworks help explain human behavior, the factors in the environment that influence how people function, the mutual influence humans have on the environment, and how people can solve problems that ail them and their systems. These theories demystify complex issues. Because of my training in these frameworks, I'm rarely overwhelmed by the nature of the work and can map out a way to find a solution or tell you, "The only solution is to start all over again." (This is the stick-it-to-the-man solution.)

For example, for years, we've tried to address the issue of homelessness by trying to make unhoused people behave better or, as we used to say, "be more self-sufficient." Now we have a more radical and obvious intervention: housing first. Give people free or affordable homes. Quit making them jump through impossible hoops only to have them sit on waiting lists for affordable house for years and years. Build affordable housing or make housing accessible. Quit blaming poor people for being poor. See what I mean by "start all over"? I've studied this issue and worked with people who are suffering because of homelessness for years. We know what works and what doesn't. When you have an untenable situation, you want a social worker there. We have the training to be humane professionals in the worst of conditions.

Engagement

Engaging with the client is the first step of the helping process. This part of the interaction sets the tone for how you'll interact with the client going forward.

You have to consider and attend to many factors when you make your first contact. It starts with you. Clients are trying to figure you out and decide if they can trust you with their most intimate information about themselves. Social workers are trained to examine their lives and understand the complex nature of interacting with different people in political and social contexts. This self-examination is critical because you could be the sweetest and most well-intentioned person and still be deeply offensive and ineffective.

Social work education and training involves getting educated on how people have tried to help in the past and how this help has harmed or moved things forward. This information is important to know because when you show up in a marginalized community and tell them, "I'm here to help," community members may say, "Last time someone came and said that, we ended up getting hurt." You have to approach the helping process with humility, not with a savior mentality.

Engagement starts with understanding yourself, your motivations for why you want to help, where you have advantage and disadvantage (earned and unearned) in your life, and how those advantages and disadvantages impact what you understand about your clients' lives. This usually means you've taken the time to examine how your age, race, ethnicity, gender, sexuality, class, culture, and ability were shaped by how you were raised, where you were raised, and where you are in life now. This self-inventorying builds on your emotional intelligence and allows you to build the all-important rapport.

Here are some questions to consider before meeting a client for the first time:

>> How were they referred to you?

>> Is this one person, a couple, a family, or members of an organization?

>> Is the treatment mandated or voluntary?

>> Where will your first meeting be and how comfortable and private will it be?

>> Will you need an interpreter?

>> Are there things you can glean from the paperwork or other workers who can give you insight into the client's identity, culture, or diagnosis? (This is important in order to convey respect, but don't use this information to form biased beliefs or stereotypes about the client.)

>> Do you have any biases or personal experiences working with this population that I need to be aware of?

>> Can you be objective with this process?

TIP

After you've prepared for your meeting, here are a few tips that will help build rapport:

>> **Ease into the conversation and have a warmup conversation.** Warmup conversations can be simple icebreakers, talking about the weather, or brining up a recent event in the community like last week's big football game. Depending on the culture or the client, the first session may simply be a warmup session where they get exposed to you, and the major work is just showing up.

>> **Clarify your role, your scope of work, and how you approach things.** After a period of warming up, let them know that you've read their paperwork or chart. People can get upset or feel dismissed if they took the time to fill out paperwork or have been seen before and they're asked for the same information over and over again.

>> **Start exploring what their concerns are and what's distressing them.** If you're meeting with a young child, you'll get information about the child's functioning from the parent or caregiver and you'll have to use child-based interventions to engage the child. This is usually in the form of play therapy.

>> **Convey respect and empathy in your verbal and nonverbal cues.**

>> **Ask permission to ask them more structured questions for the assessment phase of the work (see the next section).**

Assessment

After building rapport with a client, you'll enter the assessment phase of the helping process. Assessment is both a process and a product. It's the process of gathering information to help you build a hypothesis of what you think is causing the distress. A result of the process is a written document that details relevant background information and ends with a statement of what needs to be considered as a plan or intervention. Assessment is not a one-and-done deal. It's a valuable step that occurs over and over again throughout the helping relationship. As you know more, you update the information.

TIP

Assessments are initially conducted through a structured interview in one or two sessions, although this is the most formal way to do it. Assessment is context dependent and is determined by where you're working and what your role is. If you're in an office context, it may be more formal. If you're community based, it may be less formal or on the floor with a child and their family. Regardless of where and how it occurs, the interview process covers the following topics:

» Demographic information, including age, race, sex, gender, occupation, sexual orientation, military involvement, and education

» Childhood development, such as meeting childhood milestones, educational opportunities, and any childhood stressors

» The history and current state of the client's physical health, mental health, and substance use or misuse

» The client's interactions with other people and systems, family, faith community, work, health-care providers, the legal system, and schools

» The client's definition of their problems, stressors, concerns, and needs and a description of how they're affecting their functioning, relationships, and emotions

» The client's supports, strengths, and resources

In addition to the questions themselves, screening instruments can indicate the presence of a problem (such as alcohol screening tools that suggest a potential issue with alcohol consumption) and diagnostic instruments that confirm the presence of a specific condition (like alcohol use disorder). There are tools that measure physical health, mental health, and overall functioning. Social workers can administer the tests themselves, depending on their licensure levels, or receive reports from other providers like doctors, psychologists, or school personnel.

At the end of the initial assessment, some work facilities may require a diagnosis. The diagnosis can be around physical health (for example, type 2 diabetes), mental health (for example, adjustment disorder), behavioral health (for example, addiction), or another classification if it's for an agency or community (like identifying food deserts in a community).

REMEMBER

The sources of information at this stage include the following:

» Paperwork on the client or systems

» Interviews with the client and stakeholder

» Observations of the client or system during your time with them

» Tests, screens, or assessment tools

» Interactions with you, their family members, or clients

» How you feel while you're spending time with them

At the end of the initial appointment and assessment, you'll have a sense of what has been going on and your impression of the issue from your perspective and the client's perspective.

What sets social workers apart in their skill set is their holistic perspective on clients — they view themselves as collaborators rather than experts on the individual's life. I've had many students referred to me for services because teachers and school personnel were convinced that the child had problems with anger or attention. After spending time with the kiddo and doing a home visit, I would often discover that it was rarely that simple. Usually, the family was struggling financially, was stretched beyond their capacity, or had suffered a recent loss or trauma. The issue wasn't that the child was angry — they may have been hungry or tired and their parents need more resources or help. In many instances, angry behaviors and emotions stem from an underlying primary issue in the client's life, such as poverty, hunger, domestic violence, or bullying. I would then devise a plan that was consistent with my assessment. If the issue was hunger, I would help provide resources for food. If it was a stressed caregiver, I would spend time figuring out the best supports for them. If it was loss or trauma, I would work on counseling support for the child and the family.

Assessment is a dynamic process. It starts with the first sessions, but if you continue to work with the client or system, you're constantly updating your view of the problem as you move forward with your work. Maybe the issue initially presents as anger, and in your work, you discover substance use. Maybe you think there is lack of support, but you discover there is physical and emotional abuse going on. You incorporate your newfound information and adjust your treatment plan accordingly.

Planning

Planning is the explicit goal-setting portion of the process. The goals should be client-centered and tied to the issues presented in the assessment. Planning and goal setting can seem straightforward, but there is art to it. There are the overall goals themselves, the prioritization of the goals, and the timeline of executing the goals. You may have a goal for a client that's different than what they want, or you may recommend things to the agency or community that are incongruent with their values or perspectives. A goal needs to be congruent with the client's motivation, ability level, and resources. Maximizing opportunity and success is likely only to occur when goals are congruent with the client's motivation, ability level, and resources.

Your client may be coming to you because they've been mandated to do so or because they've chosen to do so voluntarily. How you approach the planning phase needs to take this motivation in mind:

>> **Mandated:** If your client has been mandated to see you, this usually means a court has ordered the treatment — the person will lose their job or a key relationship unless they get treatment. Your client's goal may be to end contact with you. Your goal is to get them to collaborate with you and find a workable solution. Because you're well trained on working with people who are reluctant or resistant, you won't be surprised or dismayed if they're cold or aloof, or genuinely believe that everyone got it wrong and they don't need help. You'll use intervention approaches like harm reduction, trauma-informed interviewing, or motivational interviewing to set goals.

If someone is legally mandated to work with you, the goals will have to include the goals of the system. You can start with the end in mind and agree with the client that the goal is for them to not need you in their life. You can say, something like, "I know it isn't easy being here, and I appreciate your even showing up. I want to work with you and get out of your hair. Let's come up with some goal and steps that will help you and give you back your time. It usually helps if we can come up with goals you think are feasible and ones I think the court will accept." If they agree to that, you can ask them something like, "What are the concerns of the court and what are your concerns?" This can help you tease out where they stand.

>> **Voluntary:** If the person you're seeing has chosen to be there, planning is a bit easier. They're usually more motivated, and they already see you as a resource. You can ask them to prioritize what's bothering them the most at this time. If they're in crisis, you can determine the best steps to help stabilize them. Any goals set should be measurable, time limited, strengths based, and attainable. They should use the language of the theory or intervention you're using. Don't make them basic goals anyone can create or too high and lofty so they set the client up for failure. Clients usually just want to feel better or may express that they feel hopeless and that this may be futile.

In the planning phase, consider yourself the hope coach. By hope, I don't mean wishful thinking — I mean optimism and the sense that challenges are not insurmountable. One of my favorite things that happens in the course of working with someone is when they start feeling better and having lightbulb moments and say, "Wait a minute . . . is this what my life could've been like?" Or the best is when they're a source of hope and encouragement for *other* people in their lives, or they quote you to their friends and family. It makes you feel like a celebrity! If that happens, I correct them and say, "Well, actually, I didn't come up with that quote — it was Freud. But my summary was pretty good, right?"

Intervention

The intervention part of the change process is where you select the strategy for change and start implementing it. You'll use techniques that are consistent with the principles and ethics of social work and match the needs of the client. You'll also use modalities that are evidence supported and within your scope of practice.

If there are gaps in your knowledge or techniques, get additional training. Don't blame the client or tell them you don't deal with those issues.

The interventions can be task oriented and time limited, where you clearly target the problem and develop very targeted tasks. For example, when I was a school-based social worker, I had a child who was anxious about coming to school — drop-off was pure hell for the parent. I used a check and connect model, which is evidence supported, where I had the child identify a school person they liked and trusted. I had the identified school person meet the mom in the parking lot in the morning and help bring the child into the school. This helped the child see some-one who was safe and comfortable as their first contact, and it helped them walk into school with someone they trusted. It also helped the mom not feel guilty or have to pry her kid's fingers off her to get out of the school building. We instituted a reward system where the child got something super special at the end of the week. This took time to work smoothly, but eventually the child eased into the drop-off process. Task oriented interventions like this one are usually used in case management practice, in crisis intervention models, and in solution-focused work.

Other models are phase oriented or use specific steps. For instance, trauma-informed work has phases of treatment: building safety, understanding how trauma has impacted the client's life, mourning, and recovery. Each phase has steps or interventions you use to help the client process that stage.

For instance, I never ask a client to make any changes or do big moves until I've established trust and safety and taught them some skills on managing their trauma symptoms. For some clients, my work just stays in building safety and my interventions are increasing how safe they feel in their bodies, with people, and in their communities. Other clients are ready to do even more work and say, "I want to work through all the trauma symptoms"; in those case, I use a technique that will work best for them. If they're creative or more able to express themselves through art or music, we'll use that. If they're writers, we'll use that. The inter-vention is client centered and specific to them. I also challenge folks and say, "Let's try something that evidence says works even though it's not really your thing." I'll ask them to humor me and then, when it works, it becomes one their skill sets. If it fails, we have a good laugh at the silly thing I got them to do.

APPROACHING INTERVENTION WITH THE A CULTURALLY SENSITIVE MINDSET

Interventions must be culturally affirming and conscious interventions. Much of our base for interventions were normed on the experiences of white Americans and use theories of affluent straight white men. That leaves out most of the experiences of the world. Social work principles require that social workers collaborate with clients of diverse backgrounds and create interventions that affirm and uphold people's cultures. We shouldn't pathologize people in our assessments or interventions.

Many cultures are collectivist and have a wide definition of what constitutes family and how close family members should be. Therefore, in our assessment of individual people or groups, we shouldn't idealize nuclear families or marriages or write interventions that are incongruent with the client's culture or desires.

For example, some families that are referred for services are described as "enmeshed," "gaming the system," or "too closed off." Using a strengths perspective, I note that the family is "resourceful," "connected," or "appropriately wary of outsiders." See the difference? If you were reading the client files that described them in the way I did, you'd be more likely to be open and warm to them as opposed to seeing them as "takers." The family will know that, too. Interventions that are culturally sensitive are anti-oppressive and help people live dignified lives. They also level the playing field so people have a chance at life and their children are better off.

Termination

Saying goodbye or formally ending the relationship is the last phase of the helping process. *Termination* sounds ominous and negative, but in this case, it just means that you've reached the end of the formal helping process.

Endings should be talked about in the beginning of every helping process. Helping the client see what's coming sets the stage, brings awareness, and leaves no room for surprises. You can tell them the process for ending the relationship or service and the contingencies around ending the process sooner than planned. For example, agencies have policies on repeated no-shows or dealbreakers like showing up under the influence. Other times, the contact is time-limited by design, like a discharge planning meeting at the end of a patient's tenure in a hospital setting. With organizations, you may have a time-limited project or deliverable like the grant being submitted, the project being executed, or the policy being implemented.

Endings can be planned or unplanned. The best-case scenario is a planned process, where the ending is seen as successful by both the provider and the client. The client, family, or system met their goal and there is no need for active contact. Examples include when case management goals are met, when client symptoms are manageable and they're in recovery, when the family is operating in a healthy manner and people have good boundaries and roles, and when an organization has acquired the program or service it needs.

You usually talk about the ending session several sessions in advance and discuss how you'll say goodbye. Good goodbyes are healing. You may have a ritual or a celebration. At the end of my therapy sessions with a client, I highlight the ways I've seen them grow, remind them of the skills they've gained, and tell them when they should get back into treatment if they struggle again. Usually, there are tears on both ends. It's a graduation of sorts. It's a beautiful thing to see people do brave things and for them to trust you with the most vulnerable parts of themselves. It's a sweet sorrow to say goodbye.

REMEMBER

Unplanned endings or terminations also happen. They can occur for a variety of reasons. For example, if the client is having substance use issues, coming in and out of treatment is part of the process — I let clients know that relapse is normal and they can always come back. In other cases, the client may just vanish on you, and you won't know why. They may also just not feel like you're a good fit — if so, you can try to help them find another therapist in your own agency, if that's possible. Terminations can also happen because your own life circumstances have changed — you may move, change jobs, or have medical issues that prevent you from seeing the client anymore.

When the termination is unplanned or disruptive, it can leave you with a range of feelings, including anger, sadness, and loss. Paying attention to your own emotional state, getting good supervision, and managing your feelings is important. Otherwise, you can be left with unsettled or unprocessed feelings that can lead you to become cynical, cold, or burned out with your future work.

REMEMBER

Endings are endings for now, for some folks. If possible, you can keep the window open for them to come back for what I call "tune-ups." If you're working with an organization or larger system, the projects and work evolve. You'll take the lessons learned from your current work and adapt them into future projects.

Evaluation

You've done the hard work of engaging, assessing, planning, intervening, and saying goodbye. How will you know if your efforts made any difference? How will you demonstrate to funders or other critical stakeholders that what you do matters?

You measure your efforts through an evaluation process or metrics and point to the data to show that what you did move the needle. Evaluation is not an after-thought or a linear process; it takes place informally and formally throughout the change process, beginning with assessing the impact of your engagement skills and continuing through intervention steps to ensure they align with theory, agency support, and client-centered focus.

Whereas informal evaluations are ongoing, more structured evaluations are essential to validate the effectiveness of interventions and goal achievement, as well as for agencies to secure funding. If the client system isn't improving, it's crucial to identify the reasons. This emphasis on accountability underscores the significance of integrity and competence in the social work profession, ensuring that your commitment to social justice and advocacy goes beyond mere words, ultimately benefiting both you and the client system.

Historically, helping professionals and nonprofit managers used personal anec-dotes or observations to share successful outcomes. Today, personal narratives and insights are valued, but they aren't sufficient indicators of success. In fact, what *is* expected from social workers and service providers is measurable out-comes over time. This is good for social workers and clients — it gives bench-marks for success for the provider and shows progress (or lack of progress) to clients.

There are a number of ways you can evaluate the services and outcomes for a cli-ent, depending on who you're working with:

>> **Individuals:** You can do behavior analysis and measure the frequency and severity of the problem behavior and how it has changed over time. Or you can measure how much the problem is impairing the person's life and measure the changes over time. For example, you might indicate how often they engage in the negative behavior (drinking excessively, more than six drinks at a time) and how that has changed (drinking no more than three drinks at a time). You can also use formal assessment tools, like a depression inventory, and see how the client fares over time. There are scientific tools for almost all kinds of physical health and mental health behaviors. What you hope to show is a decrease in symptoms over time, presumably because of your interventions.

>> **Families and groups:** There are outcome measurement tools specifically for families and groups. You can measure how cohesive the family members are, the amount of conflict they have, and the sense of hope they have. In group settings, members have the opportunity to assess the facilitation skills of the group leader and the overall effectiveness of the group's culture, environ-ment, and cohesion. Typically, pre- and post-evaluation tools with measurable objectives are employed for this purpose.

>> **Organizations:** You can evaluate organizational outcomes by implementing evaluation protocols that assess company culture, accomplishment of company goals, client or stakeholder feedback or satisfaction, and evaluation of the leader. The more complex the system is, the more levels of evaluation you'll need. You'll have to roll out an evaluation plan at the start of the year. Usually, funders have specific outcomes they want companies to achieve, and that often drives how and what agencies use to measure outcomes.

It isn't uncommon for social workers to be slipped a new form for them or their clients to fill out because there is a new stream of income and the funders want something different than what has been traditionally evaluated. It's cumbersome and annoying if it's unplanned, but it isn't unusual.

Where Social Workers Can Provide Help

Now that you know the pathway for the change process, you have to consider what level of practice you'll work in. There are three major categories:

>> **Micro:** Micro social work entails working one-on-one with someone in direct practice. This is the most dominant area of practice for social workers — 80 percent to 85 percent of social workers work in direct practice. The level of influence and your intervention is with one person.

>> **Mezzo:** Mezzo social work entails working with families and small groups. This is where you add layers of complexity to the work and add group dynamics.

>> **Macro:** Macro social work entails working with organizations, communities, and society as a whole. Macro-level work is tied to activism and making changes on a wider scale.

Whether you're working with one person or a social system, the process of providing help through the generalist approach applies. Most people have an idea about what level of practice they want to do. Macro social work students are unequivocal about where they want to impact change — they're the movers and shakers. Micro social workers are also definitive on wanting to make a big impact one person at a time — they're very relational and enjoy getting to do deep work with individuals. The mezzo space tends to be more flexible in their area of interest.

If you want to have a good time, tell a macro social worker that you want them to do therapy work or tell a micro social worker that you want them to do policy analysis. They'll both look at you like you lost your mind.

In the following sections, I cover each level and discuss what the help process and work looks like.

Micro level: Working with individuals

Although social work is thought of as an activist degree, most social workers and practitioners work at the micro level or what is referred to as *direct practice*. Because of this interest, social workers who work in micro practice have training in the life cycle and developmental models. This means they understand what should be in the range of normative functioning for the age range and what factors impact well-being, trauma, and resilience.

REMEMBER

Even if they're working with individuals, social workers operate using the person-in-the environment framework. How are the individuals functioning in their homes, in their communities, and with the systems they interact with? You can't pretend that a child is separate from their family unit or that an adult lives in a vacuum. Context matters — even with one-on-one work.

Children

TIP

The federal government defines children as anyone under the age of 18. That's a big window! People who work with children know that definition is too broad. So, here's how children are categorized by the folks who work with them:

>> **Infants:** Less than 1 year old

>> **Toddlers:** 1 to 2 years old

>> **Preschool:** 3 to 4 years old

>> **School-aged:** 5 to 12 years old

>> **Youth/adolescents:** 13 to 17 years old (see the next section)

So, working with children can range from working with infants (which is really working in maternal health and working with the infant's caregiver to make sure they're stable and have access to care) to working with school-aged kids. We also work with babies on social and emotional developmental skills or work with their parents on meeting their developmental milestones.

For school-aged children, this is the first time they may be seen by the public. Teachers and medical providers are seeing them on a more regular basis. This means that unmet needs or concerns are being raised, giving society and helping professionals an opportunity to mitigate risk and put kids on a better track.

Youth

Youth (ages 13 to 17) get their own consideration because they're so darn special. At this age, brains, bodies, and behaviors are going through significant shifts, and youths require interventions tailored to them. There is a huge difference between a school-aged child and a kid in high school. The issues youth grapple with are identity and social based. They're trying to figure out who they are outside of their family of origin, within their peer groups, and they're attempting to be independent. That's the sophisticated way of saying that they'll keep their parents up at night worrying about their new attitude and friends.

Society is also charged with helping them become responsible adults. Direct practice with youth recognizes the complexities of these dynamics and will design interventions that will help them negotiate their identity, developing minds, and social relationships and status.

Adults

TIP

Adults are age 18 to 65. Work with adults can be broken down into the following phases of adulthood:

>> **Young adults:** 18 to 35 years old

>> **Early middle age:** 36 to 44 years old

>> **Late middle age:** 45 to 65 years old

Work with young adults is the continuation of differentiating from the home base and building the self. Middle-aged adults contend with their multiple roles within their homes, their work life, and finding purpose. This is also the age where health issues began to arise. Late middle-aged folks deal with being sandwiched between generations and wrestling with the impact of their early adult life decisions.

Older adults

Adults over 65 are considered older adults. *Old* or *elderly* is not the language we use to describe adults in this age range. *Older adults* is the term of respect. And like our middle-aged friends, older adults get a range in categorization:

>> **Youngest old:** 65 to 74 years old

>> **Middle old:** 75 to 84 years old

>> **Oldest old:** 85 years old and older

Advances in medical technology and improvements in health habits have allowed human beings to live longer. The number of older adults is increasing, and there is a great need for social workers who specialize in working with older adults. With the aging process, we also see the rise of physical health issues, mental health issues, and chronic illnesses. Social workers can specialize in working with older adults, or what is called *geriatric social work*. They can work with clients and their loved ones and help them navigate the complex issues that come with aging.

Mezzo level: Working with small groups

At the mezzo level, social workers intervene with families and groups. Beyond adding to the number of people they see at a given time, the mezzo level practice adds an additional layer of dynamics. When you're working with a couple, for example, you have the perspective of two separate people to keep in mind, but the couple is the target client.

Think of the different systems as spinning plates — you're the juggler who keeps an eye on all the motion.

Couples

Couples can be considered micro or mezzo level. I think of them as mezzo because they're the duo that makes up a family unit and working with couples requires specialized training that goes beyond micro-level work.

People who present with couple, partner, marriage, or romantic troubles need help managing a number of issues, including conflict, intimacy or sex issues, financial issues, physical and mental health challenges, and parenting difficulties. Social workers can help address the nuanced issues that impact how the two people relate to one another and how they're impacted by the systems around them.

Families

Family work is one of the most classic and traditional spaces that social workers have practiced in. Social work practice has its roots in helping families that have been displaced, under-resourced, or plagued by social ills.

Like working with couples, family interventions consider the perspective of individual family members, but keep the family as the core client. Social workers get training in family-based services and learn how to build trust and with different family members to make the family unit healthier.

Groups

Groups work as an intervention is very powerful. Group work has high impact because individual members of the group have an opportunity to work out their stuff with a range of actual people. As the provider, instead of having a second account of interpersonal reactions, you can see how the client engages with a diverse group of people.

There are a range of types of groups, including task groups, treatment groups, psycho-educational groups, and recreational groups. The social worker must determine the purpose of the group and objectives of the group. For instance, you can have a psychoeducational group where you learn about a topic and explore it as a group, like a group for parents who adopted kids from the foster-care system. Skill-building or therapy groups focus on mental health and behavioral health needs, like a substance abuse group or a trauma survivors group.

Group work also requires training and competency. It isn't enough for you to pick up a workbook, arrange some chairs in a circle, and ask people how they're feeling. Group work requires planning and training in group work modalities.

When group work goes well, it's an incredible tool. People can learn to help themselves and others, and it's wonderful to see. Sometimes people take advice or help better from someone who's in the struggle than they do from the "expert" in the room.

Macro level: Addressing issues on a larger scale

REMEMBER

Social work is concerned with the general welfare of society and the development of people and their communities. Macro social work is explicit about making changes on the highest level. Marco practice has *big* goals, like elimination of poverty, economic justice, and policy change. These goals are achieved through high-level planning, action, and activism. If you want to end poverty, you can target a large system that influences poverty like the education system and enact changes that range from your local schools to federal policies that affect all the schools in the country.

Macro-level practice can occur in communities, organizations, and small groups. Macro-level social workers do a range of activities, including activism, policy planning and analysis, community organizing and development, agency management, and international social work practice. They focus on how power is disrupted and managed and use organizing and activism to bring about change. They mean business.

Community practice is an intervention process that social workers use to help individuals, families, and groups within neighborhoods. The focus is on the improvement of community conditions, as well as the well-being of the people who live in the community. Community development work focuses on the physical and economic environment of a distressed neighborhood. It can help residents maintain affordable housing, have access to public services, build community activism and capacity, increase investment and employment, and improve education. This helps communities have a voice in what happens to them. It gives members of the community a vehicle to organize and be heard by their local government.

Evidence-Based Interventions

The helping process that social workers use to facilitate change should use the best available research to inform the practice. This is called *evidence-based practice.* In the process of doing evidence-based practice, social workers are taught to incorporate scientifically or empirically supported treatments. These are treatment models that have strong research to support the efficacy of the treatment.

Social workers aren't just *hoping* that the intervention works; we have data and evidence that the intervention is effective for the issue we're addressing. There is a hierarchy of how much evidence a particular intervention has based on the type of research that was done to support it. It can range from a true experimental design (strong evidence) to a quasi-experimental design (moderate to low evidence).

The generalist model and the ethical principles of social work practice state that social workers must be diligent about using the best methods and processes to help. You must continually get educated to help your clients and systems have the best outcomes. Earning your degree in social work is the start of the journey — not the end.

Social workers as scientists and researchers

Social workers are not only consumers and implementers of research; they can also *produce* research. They design, implement, and share research that enhances the knowledge and practice of social work. Social work researchers create new knowledge for practice and are considered thought leaders in the field.

Because social work is interested in multidimensional work, social work researchers collaborate with other disciplines. For example, a macro-level social work researcher often collaborates with community members, educators, and other social scientists to conduct their study. They look at lots of factors that impact the system and engage with a diverse range of research partners to design and execute the study.

REMEMBER

What's important about social workers doing research is that social workers are explicit about their commitment to social justice and improving the lives of people and communities. They aren't just curious or ambitious. They're committed to advancing human rights and bettering society.

Social problems that social workers address

What kinds of problems do social work researchers and practitioners address? Big ones. The social work profession is pretty ambitions about what it wants to do and how it sees the world.

In 2012, a group of social work educators and national leaders met to create ambitious but achievable goals called the "grand challenges." These goals are meant to galvanize and organize the profession and create communities of changemakers. The current grand challenges are categorized in three areas — individual and family well-being, stronger social fabric, and just society — with goals under each domain. You can find the individual goals for each of the domains on the Grand Challenges for Social Work website (https://grandchallengesfor socialwork.org). The initiative makes updates annually, but the goals are pretty big and there is healthy debate on what makes it on the list.

Chapter **4**

Navigating Race, Class, and Inequality Issues

All social workers must advance both social justice and equity in their work. No matter where you work and what kind work you do, you must be committed to this core principle of the profession.

Social justice has to do with systemic or legal rights afforded to all people, especially those who historically have been marginalized. Social justice usually involves the justice system and laws. Equity is the equal and fair treatment of all people. An example would be universal rights like free public education for children.

We need both equity (the principle of fairness) and justice (the mechanism of ensuring equity) to have a just world. Advancing social justice and equity is one of the major areas that makes social work stand out from other helping professions.

In the social work helping process, we think about how power, privilege, and oppression impact the advancement of social justice. We consider how these constructs present themselves in how service is provided and how the person or system receiving the help is impacted by power, privilege, and oppression.

Practically speaking, it looks like: Let's say a family is referred to me, as a school-based social worker, for services. I must consider how my own identity and experiences will impact my approach to helping them. I also must consider the family's *layers of identity* (such as their race, class, or disability status) and how those layers of identity impact how they'll think about being referred for services, how they perceive the school, what kind of resources they may have access to, and who decides on the allocation of those resources. If in the course of my work with the family, I see repeated patterns of exclusion or barriers for them, I have to address those issues and not just say, "Oh, man, that's too bad" or "I wish it were better."

In this chapter, I unpack the various components of justice and equity through the lens of privilege, power, and oppression and discuss the application of that lens in two areas: race and class. Chapters 5 and 6 discuss the other important domains and groups like gender, ability, and nationality.

REMEMBER

These topics are central to understanding what it means to be a social worker and something social workers are extremely proud of. We consider ourselves social justice warriors. It's a lofty goal, but it's also what usually draws people to the profession.

Privilege, Oppression, and Power

If you see people as "nice" and helping as just a transactional act of connecting people to resources or services, you'll be limited in your capacity to help. Social workers call these stances *color blind* or *neutral*.

On the surface, these neutral approaches may seem kind — after all, you're trying to increase people's self-sufficiency and resources. Unfortunately, these approaches ignore patterns of exclusion and the dimensions of the person's identity. They also lead to a savior complex for the helper and make people feel like they're receiving charity instead of the support that it's inherently their right to receive. The color-blind stance (which views the helping system as neutral) ignores a significant issue in the helping relationship and process: the issue of authority, power, and access to resources.

When people ask for help, they're in a vulnerable position and at the mercy of the helping system. The helping professional and the system the professional represents (child welfare, for example) hold tremendous authority and power in the life of the client — authority to make decisions about the client and power to share or withhold resources.

When social workers talk about doing "the work," they mean the self-reflective work that social work students are trained in. Social work education teaches approaches to working with diverse populations and systems. The work involves the following three stages of anti-oppressive practice:

1. Education and self-reflection on privilege, oppression, and power.

2. Gaining awareness/consciousness about how privilege, oppression, and power show up in the social work profession and how the social worker can seem like a representative of oppressive systems.

3. Advocacy and activism to liberate people from harmful practices and systems — transferring power back to clients and advancing equity and justice in all aspects of the profession.

If the social worker assigned to a family hasn't taken the time to do what we call "the work" (see the nearby sidebar), they'll see good outcomes for the "good" clients (the ones who are compliant and make progress on the timetable set for them) and bad outcomes for the "bad" clients (the ones who are labeled as resistant, not making progress, and deserving of having their children removed from them).

What's deeply problematic is that the helper's stance and training, as well as the agency culture, aren't factored into whether the client is seen as successful or unsuccessful. This distinction is purely based on the behavior of the client and divorced from the context of the client's life and the system they live in. These approaches perpetuate harm and cause generational trauma. Interventions that were set up to help caused more harm. This is traumatic, unjust, and immoral.

REMEMBER

You can't ignore issues of privilege, oppression, and power because doing so creates more harm. In the following sections, I walk you through all three of these key issues.

Defining privilege

When you think of a "privileged" person or a "privileged" life, that word usually conjures up images of opulent wealth, celebrity, and traveling in luxury. If you're thinking, "This doesn't seem like an area social work is concerned with," you're correct! That's not what social workers mean by "privilege."

When the social work profession talks about privilege, it's talking about what's considered normal, ideal, or the standard. It's also where, to whom, and under what circumstances advantages and disadvantages are awarded. These advantages are given at the individual, institutional, cultural, and environmental levels, and they're shaped by history.

Dominant or privileged groups systematically perpetuate their own cultural privilege to the disadvantage of marginalized groups. Sometimes, they're not overly aware that they're continuing the legacy of disadvantage. Other times they're very much aware and intentionally target certain groups.

Either way, they're okay with their actions because they believe they earned their advantage through hard work — this is referred to as the *myth of meritocracy:* "I earned all of what I have without any help." What we know, of course, is that nobody earns anything on their very own. People get help or are given the opportunity to succeed. Something in the environment — say, access to good schools, mentoring, or referrals — helped facilitate that person's success. Pick up any memoir of someone who made it big, and you'll see that no matter who it was, they were given a shot by someone or some entity — even if they were dirt poor when they started.

Sometimes people's initial reaction to the topic of privilege is to clutch their proverbial pearls and say, "Surely you don't mean *me* or *my* family." They tell stories about how they don't have a mean bone in their body and they were raised to see all people as equal. Or they may talk about their family members who marched on Washington with Martin Luther King. Or they may mention their best friend, who is black, gay, wheelchair-bound, Jewish, and/or an immigrant. Sure, they may have a black, gay, wheelchair-bound, Jewish, immigrant friend — good for them! — but that's just one friend. They may still hold privilege that is unearned and perpetuates dominance. They can drop in and out of their marginalized friend's life at will.

This reaction is understandable because privilege or advantage is often invisible. People don't have to think about their privilege when they're part of the dominant group. They're taught to see themselves as "normal." That way, they can ignore what's going on around them, unless it's blatant or egregious.

REMEMBER

This discussion of privilege is not meant to make privileged people feel guilt or shame. It's meant to bring an awareness of how things are set up in the world. It helps illuminate why certain groups suffer and are persistently disadvantaged.

For example, heterosexual people do not have to "come out" or think about disclosing their sexual orientation. People assume that all people are hetero unless they're told otherwise. It's the burden of the non-hetero person to disclose. Staying with this example, hetero people can perpetuate their own cultural privilege by not having to think about how gay, lesbian, bisexual, or pansexual people feel, live, or are seen by society at large. They can even wear Love Is Love T-shirts or put up an "In This House, We Believe" yard sign and think they've done their part.

In the meantime, sexual minorities suffer from invisibility or violence and have to worry about how families are talked about or represented in their children's schools, how their health-care provider will treat them and what knowledge they'll have about their community, whether their health insurance covers family planning for same-sex/same-gender couple, and whether they're safe in their neighborhoods. These are subjects that heterosexual people take for granted. What you hear from people when you point out this privilege is "I never thought of that." That's by design. It's not because hetero people are inherently cruel or ignorant — it's because society is set up for hetero people and reinforced by social and cultural messages and institutions. When you aren't part of the dominant group, you become an outsider or an "other." You constantly have to ask for adaptations or access.

Staying with example of heterosexuality, emergency contact forms for children may ask for information on the "mother" and "father," rather than from two "parents" or "caregivers." In these situations, same-sex/same-gender couples have to cross out part of the form or ask the school to create a more inclusive form. Even with this request, some schools ignore the request and write in the second parent in as an "other" on the form. This is when parents have to decide if they want to stay at that school (if they have the choice to leave). It's these constant battles that folks in the dominant group don't have to endure. They can go about their lives never having to think twice about a school form.

REMEMBER

Privilege exists on multiple dimensions — individual, institutional, and societal:

>> **Individual:** At the individual level, privilege refers to being considered "normal" or the "ideal" within a particular society. In the United States, this norm is often characterized by being white, male, thin, heterosexual, *cisgender* (where one's biological sex matches their gender identity), able-bodied, and financially secure while adhering to the Christian faith. This leaves out a whole lot people, right?

This concept of privilege can manifest in various ways:

- **Levels of advantage and disadvantage:** Individuals can experience varying degrees of advantage or disadvantage based on how closely they align with this societal norm.

- **Self-perception in relation to others:** Privilege also influences how a person perceives themselves in relation to others. Do they receive the benefit of the doubt? Are they automatically considered smart and capable by default?

- **Perceptions of beauty and civilization:** Privilege extends to how society perceives beauty and civility. It often favors those who fit the norm, reinforcing stereotypes and biases.

An individual's privilege is closely tied to how well they align with the societal norm, and it can significantly impact their experiences and opportunities in various aspects of life.

» **Institutional:** On the institutional level, privilege is how policies are created and enforced for the dominant group. Here are some examples of institutions and how privilege plays out in them:

- **Schools and neighborhoods:** What is a "good" school and neighborhood? How are communities developed, and where are the slums? What curriculum is allowed in schools? How are schools funded and resourced? Who has access to elite universities? Who has the most buffers when there is crisis (like a pandemic)?

- **Financial institutions:** Who can easily get a loan? Who is given notices about credits or special programs to access money for purchasing large items like a home or education? Who is easily given home loans? Who has inherited homes from family members? Who has benefitted from the G.I. Bill (the federal law that provides education and training benefits to eligible veterans and their dependents, aiding in their transition to civilian life after military service)?

- **Law enforcement:** How are policing and surveillance done? Who is seen as a criminal? Who is jailed or incarcerated and how is it done? Who is given rehabilitation versus incarceration?

- **Health care:** Who has access to health care? Who gets special funding and policies to address their needs? How is care given to different groups of people?

- **Access to food and nutrition:** Who has access to quality and affordable food? Are there grocery stores in the neighborhood or places where people can easily access fresh food? Do the food places accept government vouchers for food?

» **Societal:** Privilege on the societal level represents the cumulative result of individual and institutional advantages. This encompasses a wide array of factors, including cultural norms and beliefs (such as the idealization of the nuclear family), which shape our understanding of what is considered normal or ideal. It extends to the way subjects are discussed or depicted in media, including news, films, books, and art. These media tell us who is ideal, normal, and desirable — namely, that we should all aspire to be middle-class families who have Christian values. Privilege is reflected in our perception of beauty and the accessibility of certain ideals, which is usually thin, white, and expressing middle-class values (it usually involves brunch).

Many people, often individuals from advantaged groups, have a hard time accepting that their identity provides them with unearned privilege. They're offended if you suggest that there are other things at play, like laws and institutions that were created to advantage their group and keep others out. When the topic of privilege comes up in my classroom, one of my students shared that they were taught to view everyone as equal and that there wasn't much discrimination in their town because there are so few folks of color. If there were folks of color, they tended to be very professional, like doctors. I asked them to consider how they could live in an exclusively white community when the United States is such a diverse country? Turns out, it's because the town they grew up in was the result of white flight when integration laws were passed. Their life was absent of diversity, with the exception of the model minorities who were welcomed on a case-by-case basis, because it was designed to be a white enclave.

Now, my student's parent's didn't sit them down and say, "Look, we're white extremists and we want to keep other groups out." On the contrary, they raised a kind, conscious, social work student who wanted to give back. But even with a big heart, my student had a blind spot about their own upbringing and its implications. They never questioned why there was such an overt lack of diversity because it really didn't interfere with how they lived their day-to-day lives. They weren't actively against other groups, but they also weren't actively trying to diversify their town.

The fall break can be an intense time for students who go back to their homes after gaining these insights. We have to tell them to take it easy on their families and not blow up their Thanksgiving dinners by telling their families they're all bigots. You don't need to be an insufferable, moralizing dinner guest. There are ways to address this subject in a manner that doesn't alienate the people in your life.

REMEMBER

The family you're born into and the life advantages and disadvantages you face are mere luck. Luck determines which doors are easily open for you and which doors you have to build from scratch.

Understanding oppression: The flip side of privilege

The simple definition of *oppression* is certain groups being subjugated by the dominant group. People are sorted into groups and social categories and are given membership and rights depending on where they land. For example, some people can walk into a space, like a store, and believe that they have the right to be there and to enjoy the space. Other folks walk into that same space and understand that the space is suspicious of people like them. The simple act of walking into a store can be dangerous depending on who you are.

Oppression manifests as a way of thinking about the world, through avoidant and discriminatory actions and through societal structures and norms. It takes power away from people, it deprives them of their rights, it robs them of their material goods (homes and land), and it is violent.

In the same way that privilege opens doors or normalizes someone's reality, oppression closes doors and relegates a group to be outsiders, even if they're technically the bigger portion of the population. Consider states where the majority of the population is nonwhite, but their elected officials are almost all white. This isn't just a fluke — it's because of concentrated efforts to suppress votes and redraw district maps. There is significant investment in keeping decision-making in the hands of a few nonrepresentative people. Oppressive ideology makes the determination on who gets to be centered and who gets pushed to the side. Oppressed people are expelled from participating in society and have to contend with exclusionary rules that tell them to stay away or that they don't exist.

As I'm writing this, a law was recently passed in Florida referred to as "Don't Say Gay." This law bans schoolteachers from introducing LGBTQIA topics to school-aged children (turn to Chapter 5 for more on LGBTQIA issues). This is an example of marginalization. It makes a whole group of people invisible or sick and defines what is "normal." Imagine if there were a legislative proposal called "Don't Say Straight." What would the reactions to a law like that be? People would see it as aberrant and unnatural. Who would even *suggest* such a ridiculous law? The dominant group decides what are the templates and that what they do — which typically looks like the norms of a white middle-class family with a mother and a father — is the universal, the ideal, and the norm.

When the dominant group decides they like aspects of another group's culture and adopt it as theirs without referencing its origins, that's also problematic. The subjugated groups understand they're on the outside and have to decide to capitulate to the dominant group's norms or resist in order to survive.

Oppression is not just a belief or attitude; it's action. Oppressive tactics include the following:

>> **Harassment:** Behaving in a way that creates a hostile environment for a specific group of people, typically based on their characteristics like race, religion, nationality, or disability status. For example, in the workplace, people may demonstrate oppression by withholding support, withholding key information, and creating a hostile work environment. They may over-scrutinize the outsiders' work or monitor their comings and goings.

>> **Discrimination:** Actions, policies, and practices that intentionally create separation or avoid interactions with nondominant individuals, often involving intimidation, the denial of opportunities, and exclusion from social networks,

frequently influenced by historical context. For example, in the workplace, people may withhold powerful positions from the outsiders. The dominant group may relegate the subjugated group to serving as support staff, not the people with decision-making power.

>> **Robbery:** The act of forcefully taking away people's land or place of origin, typically carried out as a form of imperialism and colonization. For example, oppressed groups may have their homes and land taken away from them. The dominant group finds a way to impose itself on the Indigenous group and expel them from their own space. If the government wants to build a freeway through town, which neighborhood will that freeway go through? Not the rich, white neighborhood. Instead, the people who will lose their homes and their cultural center will be the marginalized folks.

>> **Violence:** An oppressive act that inflicts physical or emotional harm or forceful control over others, often with the intention to dominate or harm them. For example, marginalized groups are subjugated to humiliating or stigmatizing acts, openly questioned and ridiculed, and are the target of violence. Women, Black people, and LGBTQIA+ people have been subjected to violence by both the general population and state-sanctioned entities, such as police brutality against civil rights activists or mistreatment of LGBTQIA+ individuals during events like the Stonewall Inn raid in 1969 but through the state.

Looking at power: How groups are sorted into hierarchy

Power is about authority and influence. It's about who has the authority to open or shut the door for people and systems. Power is the mechanism that helps maintain privilege and advantage. Power is when an individual, a group, or an actor (like an institution) imposes their wishes or desires on others. They can create a system that they prefer, even if they face resistance.

There are multiples sources of power. Power can come from wealth, the state or government, social norms, or the collective will of the public. Power is not static — it's constantly moving and shifting — and people are trying to get power, funnel power, and control power. Through power, people and systems try to control the narrative of what is true, real, or accepted.

We saw a live example of this with the COVID-19 pandemic. People had competing resources for information on what was real and what was safe. They had to decide who they believed was giving them accurate information. The usual sources for public health information and guidance were questioned or at odds with President Trump's message to the public. Sources of public health information lost power or were competing for power in shaping public trust. Prior to the pandemic, people who were opposed to vaccinations were seen as on the fringe. During the pandemic, anti-vaccination sentiments were no longer seen as extremist. Anti-vaccination stances were taken seriously and promoted by people in the highest office in the land. This is what power can do — it can move things that were on the side to the middle and it can decenter and marginalize the things that were at the center.

Social workers are trained to understand how power shapes privilege and oppression. People are categorized by their *social identity* (race, gender, age, sexuality, and so on), their *social standing* (status), and their *social power* (how much influence they can exert). The combination of social identity, social standing, and social power determine how much access they have to resources.

REMEMBER

The highest value is given to the people who have dimensions of the categories. The more traits you can check off a list, the more access you have by virtue of belonging in the category:

>> **Social identity:** Male, white, young, heterosexual, thin, Christian, able-bodied

>> **Social standing:** Economically secure, married, educated, homeowner

>> **Social power:** Politician or policymaker, mega-rich, CEO, board member, influencer, collective movements

The more of these traits you have, the more likely you are to have power. You may hear someone say, "I don't know why anybody ever runs for office." Well, now you know. It gives them power and access, and that has momentum. The more you can be in spaces where decisions are made, the more you get to funnel where access and resources go. And many times, people funnel resources to themselves, their families, and their constituents. This is also why representation matters. When decisions that impact a group of people are made by people who have no understanding of the target group, it can be disastrous. You'll see congressional hearing and decisions about health-care options for women being made by a group of men. And nothing changes until a social movement accompanies the social outcry. That's why it's important to have people in positions of power who are as diverse as the country itself.

REMEMBER

Social workers are trained to be self-reflective about their intersecting identities and their social standing because they have power to impact a person's life. What a social worker views as "normal," "desirable," or "good" is shaped by their own experiences of privilege and oppression. They're trained to watch their expectations and reactions because they may think of the client as the "other." And you can't be good to people you see as the other. You don't see their humanity. When there is critical reflection, self-awareness, and consciousness about how privilege, oppression, and power work, you should be motivated to act, resist, and make changes within your sphere of influence. This is part of what it means to be a social worker.

Race and Racism

In 1865, the Thirteenth Amendment abolished slavery in the United States. In 1964, the Civil Rights Act prohibited discrimination on the bases of race, color, sex, religion, and national origin in education, housing, and public spaces. In 2008, President Barak Obama was elected as the first Black American president. Some people thought of his election as the signal for a post-racial America. As romantic and hopeful as that notion was, racism still exists as an endemic problem and as one of the root causes of inequality. In the United States, people of color make less money, have worse health outcomes, die younger, are less educated, have more student debt, and are the targets of more violence than white Americans are.

Why do these egregious disparities exist? Is there something wrong with folks of color? Or are there bad policies that lead people of color to experience life with these harrowing outcomes? Well, it isn't because folks of color have character defects or a poor constitution. It's that they're born into a system where the odds are stacked against them. When they're successful, it's *despite* the societal structures, not because of them.

REMEMBER

Racism isn't just someone holding negative beliefs or attitudes about another racial group. It's more layered than that.

In fact, race is a made-up idea used to justify enslaving people and creating racial dominance over other folks of color. The fancy term for making race up is that race is a *social construction*. People were categorized as inferior and less than human based on physical features and skin color, in order to justify enslavement and white superiority. Pseudoscience was used to quantify these beliefs and helped create racial categorizations in which there was a promotion of the false notion that "white" people were inherently smarter, more human, and meant to dominate and be in charge.

American history and slavery evolved side-by-side because enslaved people provided the much-needed labor of the expanding settlers, and native people were pushed out of their own land. U.S. history is one of colonialism not of settlers. The narrative of settlers being brave and making something out of nothing is not a consensual or agreed-upon narrative by the people who were in bondage or eradicated. Early settlers stole land from Native peoples and created laws that changed people's status from indentured servants to coerced slaves. Enslavement categorized people as property and ensured that people could be passed down to generations as a commodity, like a piece of cattle or furniture. Even after slavery was eradicated, Jim Crow laws were enacted, segregating schools, neighborhoods, roads, and railroads, and depriving folks of color of their voting rights. These laws made sure that all the advantage and resources were allocated explicitly to whites. Even if a person of color served in the country through active duty, individual states created barriers so veterans of color could not access their veterans' benefits.

People who were Black and Brown were categorized as "savages" and "subhuman" by early American settlers and leading medical and anthropologists. Based on these categorization, white "enlightened" scientists lay the groundwork for the philosophical approach that justified the presumed superiority of the white population. Mighty convenient, right? If you need to keep people enslaved to be the labor for your expanding empire and you want to keep the veneer of being god-fearing people, you need some "natural" explanation for this dehumanization. This is where oppressive white ideology in the United States originates. Race-based polices and laws — including Jim Crow laws, the Indian Removal Act, the Chinese Excision Act, and the Black Codes — were created to enshrine this oppression.

But didn't the abolishment of slavery and the passage of civil rights laws reverse racism and its effects? These laws made major and significant changes to advance justice for folks of color, but the enduring legacy of advantage in the United States is one that is based on racial categorization. It manifests on three levels:

>> **Interpersonal:** Interpersonal racism occurs between individuals. This is what people usually think of when they think of racism — a single individual who has prejudiced views or stereotypes and acts on these beliefs and attitudes. They may act on it in small, subtle ways or in overt acts of violence. The small but consistent acts of aggression or invalidation convey acute disrespect and leave the person on the receiving end on high alert. Interpersonal racism may consist of questioning a person's intelligence or work product, singling them out and questioning them for participating in an activity, characterizing behaviors of children as aggressive or in a negative light, or being invisible in spaces (literally looked over, cut in front of, or being told, "Oh, I didn't see you").

   More overt acts of racism rise to needing court or police involvement. They include workplace harassment based on race, denying people access or blocking them from opportunities, and targeting people with hate crimes.

>> **Institutional:** Institutional racism happens at the cultural and societal level where discriminatory practices produce racially inequitable outcomes for

people of color and advantages for white people. It moves the level of analysis from the outcomes and victims of racism to the systems that produce racism. It's historically informed. Yesterday's racism produces today's unequal outcomes.

Here are some examples of institutional racism in three core areas:

- **Schools and neighborhoods:** Jim Crow laws created segregated towns and allowed housing discrimination and denial of home ownership to people of color. They created color-coded maps to indicate level of risk in neighborhoods. They coded communities of color as hazards through the use of red shading — this is called *redlining*. You can literally see the segregation lines drawn up by housing lenders.

  Funding for school districts are based on funds received from local home taxes. This systematically advantages students from affluent (white) neighborhoods and creates disadvantage for folks of color who were denied equal opportunities for housing. According to the U.S. Census Bureau (www.census.gov/housing/hvs/data/prevann.html), in 2022 the racial breakdown of homeowners was as follows:

Race/Ethnicity	Homeownership Rate
White	74.4%
Black	45.0%
American Indian or Alaskan Native	53.4%
Asian, Native Hawaiian, or other Pacific Islander	61.0%
Hispanic or Latino	48.6%

  Additionally, in schools, students of color face disproportionately harsh punishment and expulsion for small infractions compared to their white peers. This impacts graduation rates and the feeling of belonging in schools. School performance influences entry rates into colleges, and the kids from affluent neighborhoods are given access to elite schools.

- **Financial institutions:** In the 1930s, Home Owners' Loan Corporation developed race as one of the categories that could determine desirability of offering a home loan. Black and Brown people were seen as risky and their neighbors as hazardous. Not surprisingly, folks of color were denied access to home loans based on this unfounded discriminatory practice. After banking laws like that were struck down by the U.S. Supreme Court, the federal government still offered less than 2 percent of federal loans to people of color between 1930 and 1960. Folks of color had to resort to and accept discriminatory parallel banking options. They were only offered predatory payday loans, whereas white communities had access to banks and credit unions. Today low-income communities and communities of color still face disparity in equitable access to banking services, and there continue to be high-cost, abusive, fringe financial services like payday lenders, subprime lenders, and "buy here, pay here" auto lenders.

- **Health care:** In 1946, the Hill–Burton Act provided federal funding for public hospitals and long-term care facilities. States constructed racially separate and unequal facilities. Currently, most Americans access health care through employer-sponsored insurance. Among individuals with employer-sponsored insurance, 66 percent are white, 47 percent are Black, 43 percent are Latino, and 37 percent are American Indian and Alaska Natives. Those without employer insurance are uninsured; Black and Latino people are, respectively, 1.5 and 2.5 times more likely to be uninsured compared to white people. When folks of color show up for health care, they receive poor screening, care, and treatments related to major illness and suffering from pain. The cumulative impact of this systemic racism in health care results in people of color suffering and having higher morbidity rates compared to their white counterparts.

At the societal level, messages, images, and beliefs affirm the assumption of white superiority and assumed inferiority for people of color. Nuclear families are considered ideal, and other patterns of families, including multigenerational families and single-parent families, are viewed as problematic. People of color have a more inclusive, more flexible view of families that is often pathologized. Folks of color are depicted as stereotypes or characters in art and film. They're depicted as being conquered, exotic, or playing secondary or servitude roles. Images of the ideal beauty are Eurocentric or appropriate subcultures without giving them credit, like the proliferation of hair extensions or braids among white women. In the meantime, Black women have been reported to human resources or have received harsh judgements when they've worn their hair naturally.

>> **Internalized:** Folks of color can internalize or agree with oppressed narratives about them and suffer emotional and psychological distress as a result. This is *internalized racism.* Racism can produce poor psychological, physiological, and behavior outcomes. Racial discrimination and racist encounters have been linked with weight gain, smoking, substance use, anxiety, depression, lower self-esteem, and even suicidal ideation. These associations don't happen to all people of color, but the wear-and-tear impact of racist encounters can lead folks to internalize their feelings and be constantly stressed. This can lead to physical and psychological burnout. Beyond being a negative feeling, internalized racism has health and behavior costs. People report more health concerns and visit to doctors and miss or avoid work for self-preservation, all of which has financial and social costs.

The discussion of race through the lens of oppression and racism can leave you feeling defeated. The history isn't good. The current state of affairs isn't good. What keeps us in the work or pursuing justice? It's the fact that people of color experience joy and well-being and are not just victims or a collection of heart-breaking symptoms. Through mutual aid and collective action, there is a well-spring of positive actions and movement. Social workers are taught the history of race and racism and its implications for practice. The goal is to ensure that the helper doesn't reproduce oppression but is instead actively working to understand and address disparities that are the result of racial subjugation.

Class Inequality

The United States is one of the richest countries in the world but has one of the largest populations of poverty for an advanced country. Eleven percent of the American population lives in poverty, and one in six children under the age of 5 are poor. This is baffling given America's large economic power and global standing.

Early in its formation as a profession, social work practice was exclusively concerned with the problem of poverty and wanted to alleviate the suffering of people and create a safety net for the most vulnerable. Social workers helped advocate for and create laws such as mother's pension laws, the Social Security Act, and child labor laws. They still continue to push for policies that address economic injustice.

Class inequality deals with understanding the economic standing of individuals and families and addressing their material needs. The profession of social work looks specifically at the most economically disadvantaged people and tries to understand the root causes of poverty and work on abolishing it. One of the grand challenges of social work is to strengthen social protection to eradicate poverty and social disparities. This means helping to reduce extreme economic inequality and build financial capability and assets for all. There is no reason for child and family poverty. We know what it takes to address this problem — it's a matter of building the public and political will to make these changes.

Defining and measuring class

Social class is defined as the economic status of an individual or family. It's measured in several ways:

>> The material goods someone possesses

>> A person's occupation

MONEY AND HAPPINESS

When I discuss issues of class and poverty in my courses about social reform, I start by asking my social work students how much money they need to be happy. I ask them to quantify it in terms of annual income. Their answers vary from $40,000 to $250,000. They always preface their answer by saying they didn't choose the field of social work for the money and don't think money can buy happiness. (Except for the student who wanted to earn $250,000. He was clear about what he wanted out of life.)

I always ask my students to reconsider their disassociation of economic security with happiness. Economic security is tied to advantage and the ability to live a life of non-scarcity. I also remind them that social workers don't take a vow of poverty. You can earn a good wage, have good benefits, and be able to acquire assets and still be a good social worker (see Chapter 1 for more on this subject).

>> A person's *social location* (standing in society, shaped by their social, economic, and cultural traits, and affecting their experiences and opportunities)

>> A person's assets, material goods, and forms of wealth

>> A person's ability to live a prosperous, happy life

Understanding class inequality

Class inequality is the unequal distribution of wealth and the gap that exists between the rich and the poor. The top 1 percent of the U.S. population own 34 percent of all the wealth, and one-third of the population lives in poverty. These are extreme poles of the economic spectrum. What are the causes of inequality?

>> Housing and neighborhood segregation

>> Predatory lending

>> Tax policies that benefit the wealthy

>> Poor government and public institutions

REMEMBER

Class impacts more than your ability to buy the things you need and want. It impacts how tolerable your life is and how you fare psychologically and physiologically. The experience of poverty is associated with adversity and can predict a person's chances for survival, educational attainment, and ability to be socially mobile. The dream of parents is to give their children security. Affluent families can do that — they can transfer their wealth to the next generation. Conversely, poor families stay stuck or trapped unless they use some social mechanism or program to climb out of poverty and stay out of poverty.

Most folks who are poor work and spend an enormous amount of their paycheck, sometimes up to 60 percent, on rent, making weekly decisions on how they'll survive. One crisis or many small crises can unravel any savings or future plans they have. I saw this happen repeatedly to the families I worked with in the transitional shelter I managed. I had a client who worked hard to secure a deposit and first month's rent for a new place. Just when she was ready to move out of the shelter, her car broke down. It made traveling to work nearly impossible, and she had to spend the money she had saved to fix the car. Understandably, this was devastating, and she fell into depression and started to miss work, which meant she earned less. She was eventually able to overcome these obstacles and moved out of the shelter. But for a period of time, she really felt like the deck was stacked against her — and it was.

Looking at the relationship between class, inequality, and life chances

People's economic status in life is shaped by multiple factors and impacts what social workers call *life chances* (the capacity of a person to live a life with more advantages and the ability to withstand or buffer disadvantages). The opportunity to succeed and be upwardly mobile is contingent on many factors. People often mention education as the sole ticket out of poverty or economic crisis. Unfortunately, education isn't enough. Education is *one* of the factors that can help people, but it isn't the sole factor needed to build *social capital* (the advantage you can earn through your relationships, networks, and interactions). Building social capital involves building a new ecosystem where you're in proximity to people in a higher social class and status. Those people can pull you into their social networks. That's the game changer. Maybe you didn't have access to the folks in a higher social class until you went to college and earned a degree. You may have needed both things (degree and access to people) to get access to their resources. This increases your ability to have a better shot at having a more stable economic life.

Family assets and wealth

Wealth and assets can be directly passed down to your offspring. In fact, this is the mechanism for generating more intergenerational wealth. Parents' wealth also determines their children's educational access and outcomes. These mechanisms pass down advantage, as well as reproducing more inequality. The haves continue to have and pass down all that they have, and the have-nots hope that the next generation will be able to fare better than they did.

One of the most important assets that parents pass down to their children is their home. The family home can be kept or sold to generate more income and be used as a down payment for the next home. Unfortunately, access to housing and homeownership are fraught with discrimination and inequality. White people and families were given access to quality homes and loans when banks first began to offer federally backed loans. Folks of color were explicitly excluded from this wealth-generating process. Even if folks of color can buy a home now, they often don't have the benefit of a down payment being given to them as a family gift. They incur more debt in the home-buying process and live on their income. Although they have access to wealth, keeping wealth can be precarious. They're one paycheck or job away from losing it all, much less passing it down to their children. Children born to asset-poor parents are more likely to reproduce their parents' position in wealth distribution.

Educational access

School performance and access to higher education can make a difference in someone's chances in life. However, it's contingent upon many factors going well:

>> They must have access to a quality secondary school.

>> They must score well on standardized tests.

>> They must apply and get into college.

>> They must complete their studies.

>> They should accrue as little debt as possible.

>> They must get a job with earning potential that is higher than what they would earn without the degree.

>> They must keep the job and accrue savings and retirement.

In each of these steps, there are major inequalities for marginalized groups. Their neighborhoods and schools are usually not the most resourced. Students in under-resourced schools have lower test scores and are less likely to take college entrance exams like the ACT or SAT. When they do take them, they score lower on those exams than their wealthier counterparts do. They often go to community colleges, and if they earn an associate's degree, they're able to transfer to a four-year institution. According to the National Center for Educational Statistics, the racial breakdown of students graduating from a full-time bachelor's degree programs in four years is as follows:

Race	Percent Graduating from Four-Year College
Asian	50%
White	45%
Latino	32%
Pacific Islander	31%
American Indian	23%
Black	21%

Moreover, folks of color are not able to consistently build social capital when they go to college. This can be for several reasons, including the fact that they're commuters and often must work long hours in addition to attending school. After graduation, the first job and salary base determine subsequent jobs and raises. For people who have low social capital and return to their hometowns or neighborhoods where there are limited opportunities, they end up making a little more than their parents did, but not enough so that it's transformational and wealth generating.

Work access and success

Income is usually generated by employment. Access to high-paying jobs that allow for savings depend on social context. I keep mentioning social context and capital because who you know matters! Affluent people have closed networks that allow them to get top jobs, get their children into elite spaces, and keep this wealth among each other. It's a social contract. Folks on the margins erroneously assume that their hard-earned education will give them access to choice internships and jobs, but they may not. The job they applied for may be quietly held for someone else within the dominant group's network, and the job posting may have been merely a formality.

REMEMBER

Getting access to a desirable job is the starting point. People need mentoring and access to future opportunities to move up the corporate ladder. Again, working hard and clocking in long hours are not sufficient. People nurture and compensate one of their own well and keep outsiders at arm's length. This is how oppression is maintained for folks who finally make it to the door. But then they're kept in the hallway and told they should be happy they even got that far.

IN THIS CHAPTER

» **Understanding and undoing gender and sexuality**

» **Shaping the nature of language**

» **Affirming and celebrating sexuality**

Chapter **5**

Supporting LGBTQIA+ Individuals

At a very early age, we're given strong messages about what makes a woman and what makes a man — and we're only given these two options. We're also given messages about who we should be attracted to and the kinds of sexual behavior we can engage in. These messages shape our thinking, our behavior, and ultimately what we think about ourselves.

Sexual attraction, desire, and activities typically aren't discussed. But if they are, it's only within the context of defining sexual orientation as marrying or being attracted to someone of the opposite sex/gender. There's no discussion about desire, preference, pleasure, and difficulty in sexuality. These blind spots, overt omissions, and/or harmful messages about gender and sexual norms can signal that people who are *nonbinary* (identifying neither as male nor female) or *non-heterosexual* (not attracted to people of the opposite sex/gender) are outsiders. They have to bring up these core issues of human identity to their families, their social systems, and their service providers (which makes them very vulnerable).

Social workers are trained to work with diverse populations with a range of dimensions. Two of these dimensions are gender identity and sexuality, which are essential components of self-identity. When it comes to this topic, social workers need to:

>> Have a foundational knowledge of the two topics and their affiliated concerns and strengths

>> Understand the developmental process for gender and sexual development

>> Understand the socialization of gender and sexual development

>> Understand patriarchy, hetero-normativity, and cis-sexism and how these constructs contribute to stigma and oppression

>> Learn to be self-reflective and create inclusive holistic practices that affirm people's gender and sexuality

>> Actively resist oppressive and pathology-laden systems of ideas and practices that harm gender-diverse and sexual minorities

In this chapter, I demystify the terminology surrounding gender identity and sexual attraction. I delve into how these concepts interconnect with deeply ingrained norms and biases, often perpetuating sexism and placing constraints on those who don't conform to these standards. As I navigate this discussion, I highlight the experiences of people who fall outside these norms and descriptions, as well as the considerations they would like to have when you work with them. Finally, I wrap up by exploring the practical aspects of a sex-positive social work practice. I discuss the strategies and actions that social workers can employ to create environments that are inclusive, affirming, and respectful of diverse gender and sexual identities.

Breaking Down the Term: LGBTQIA+

Let's start with the basics: What do the letters *LGBTQIA+* stand for and what do they mean? Table 5-1 provides a breakdown of all the letters, along with definitions of each.

REMEMBER

Lesbian, gay, and *bisexual* (or *bi*) are adjectives, not nouns, used to describe a person's sexual orientation or sexual attraction. The proper way to use these terms is to say "a gay man/couple" or "a lesbian woman/couple." Using the words as nouns — for example, "He's gay" or "She's a lesbian" — is problematic. *Lesbian, gay,* and *bisexual* are descriptions of a person's attraction and orientation — they aren't descriptions of the person in their totality. What about the term *homosexual?* That's stigmatizing and offensive, too.

TABLE 5-1   Understanding the LGBTQIA+ Term

Letter	What It Stands For	Definition
L	Lesbian	An adjective used to describe a woman who is primarily attracted to other women or a couple consisting of two women.
G	Gay	An adjective used to describe a man who is primarily attracted to other men or a couple consisting of two men.
B	Bisexual	An adjective used to describe a man or woman who is attracted to both men and women.
T	Transgender	An adjective used to describe a person whose gender identity differs from their sex. A transgendered man was born with female sex organs but his gender identity is male.
Q	Queer or questioning	*Queer* is an umbrella term used to describe people who are sexual minorities. In the past, it was a very demeaning word, a slur. Today it has been reclaimed and is an area of study in academia. If you aren't a member of the LGBTQIA+ community or studying this topic area, it's best to wait until a person from the community refers to themselves as queer before using the term to describe them. *Questioning* is an adjective used by people when they're in the process of exploring their gender or sexual identity.
I	Intersex	An adjective used to describe a person who has a biological variation in which their reproductive or sexual anatomy, chromosomes, or hormones do not align strictly with typical male or female characteristics (for example, someone who is born with a vagina and has testes).
A	Asexual	An adjective used to describe a person who does not have sexual attraction to others or has minimal interest in sexual activity.
+	Plus	Plus is used to describe people who are gender diverse or whose sexual orientation does not fit into being lesbian, gay, or bisexual.

Understanding the Power of Language

Language is powerful. It shapes dialogue and narratives. The individual, group, or social entity that holds the power to name or label things — including self and others — is powerful. Language can define, expand, affirm, and dignify. It can also pathologize, marginalize, denigrate, or make things invisible by not naming them.

When people find a term that speaks to their experiences and captures the fullness of how they feel about themselves, it's profoundly positive. On the other hand, when the terms used to describe a person are nonexistent, limited, or derogatory, it can produce shame and stigma.

Language can help create a road map of what is real and possible. With marginalized groups, language can be weaponized to dehumanize, to evoke disgust or shock, and to incite violence. If I think of you as the "other" and "less than," I can keep you at a distance. This is why people and groups are sensitive about the language used to describe them and their experience.

Language and terminology also shift, and people can be impatient or rigid about these shifts. Folks may want people to adapt and adjust to shifts in language quickly because they see it as a matter of growing and expanding and not limiting people. You have more words and more precise ways to describe someone — why is that so hard to understand? Other people can be deeply resistant to changes in language because of conscious and unconscious bias and because change evokes fear. They may also feel that when they learn something, their work should be done. They may find the speed of change to be burdensome.

The evolution of language around gender identity and sexuality signals a change in perspective about how we're socialized to see gender as a whole. When a person repeatedly misgenders someone — meaning they refer to the person by the wrong pronouns (*he, she, they*, and so on) — they may be doing it on purpose or they may just be conditioned to see the person in the binary. Using the right pronouns isn't just about words — it's about a shift in perspective and how you see the person.

TIP

When I work with clients, I introduce myself to them with my name and pronouns as a standard greeting and protocol. In their intake or paperwork, I ask about their gender and sexual identity and offer expansive definitions for self-description. I don't just ask about it in the paperwork — I talk to them about their gender and sexual identity as part of the assessment and engagement process. I also use their name to refer to them and avoid pronouns until they tell me which pronouns they would like to use. I give overt and subtle signals that I'm comfortable discussing issues of gender and sexuality as the primary issue of concern or contextual information. I don't say, "If it comes up, I'll talk about it." I bring it up and let folks know I'm open and willing. It isn't my clients' job to bring it to my awareness.

As of this writing, the abbreviation *LGBTQIA+* or the umbrella word *queer* are used to describe a person's gender and sexual identity. *Queer* is an umbrella or inclusive word used to talk about gender identity and sexuality. Historically, it was a pejorative, extremely derogatory term used against LGBT people. Starting in the 1990s, the LGBTQIA+ community reclaimed the term *queer* to describe themselves. Today, *queer* is also used by the general public. However, it is important to note that for some people, the term *queer* is still deeply offensive and will never be a word they'll embrace or accept.

A few other key terms to note are the following:

>> **Cisgender (or cis for short):** The word *cis* means "alignment." *Cisgender* means that your gender identity aligns with your sex — for example, you were born with ovaries and a vagina and you identify as female.

>> **Gender expansive:** *Gender expansive* encompasses a diverse range of gender expressions that fall under the transgender umbrella, reflecting an identity stance that extends beyond the binary of male or female or societal norms. It means there are more than just two ways to identify — gender can be *expansive.* I find the notion of being able to have more words to describe people's experience and identity liberating.

>> **Two-spirit:** *Two-spirit* is a term employed by some Indigenous and First Nations communities, primarily among Native Americans, to describe individuals who do not identify as cisgender. Two-spirited folks are deeply respected and held in esteem by Indigenous people and are seen as healers who can bridge spaces. It's important to note that this term is exclusively used within Indigenous cultural contexts and holds significant cultural and spiritual relevance for these communities.

Considering Gender-Diverse Identities and Attraction

For folks outside the queer community, there seems to be the false idea that issues pertaining to gender identity and sexuality are new. You may hear them say they didn't have these kinds of topics, issues, or "problems" when they were growing up. This isn't because gender diversity and sexuality are a Millennial invention; it's because people who identify as part of these communities are coming out, self-disclosing, or sharing aspects of their identity more frequently and at younger ages.

Societal attitudes have shifted to have more favorable views of same-sex/gender relationships, and there is more awareness about gender fluidity. At the same time these shifts are occurring, substantial gender-based violence is occurring and discriminatory laws are being passed. The push for gender conformity and gender oppression promotes gender stereotypes, violence, and abuse for people who don't conform.

To prevent and combat these forms of oppression and promote inclusive critical practice, social workers must have a working understanding of the definition of gender, the socialization and development process for gender development, and gender-affirming practices. They must also grasp the manifestations of oppression, such as sexism, patriarchy, and cissexism, which arise in response to gender socialization and norms. Social workers should be equipped to address these forms of oppression when assisting clients who identify as gender diverse.

Defining gender versus sex

Social workers are trained to look at people in a holistic and contextual manner. This starts by having a foundational understanding of the difference between *sex* and *gender expression*.

People often confuse *gender* and *sex*. *Sex* is a biological term that describes a person's chromosomal characteristics and anatomy. *Gender* is the psychological perception of being male, female, neither, or both. It's how we understand ourselves and how we express that understanding.

Traditionally, gender has been rigidly described in the binary of male or female. Today, it has been expanded so that it's discussed on a continuum from masculine to feminine.

WARNING

There are shifts even in the use of the term *continuum* because gender is still being defined as a continuum on a binary. People want to get rid of the binary all together and just start with a neutral assumption until otherwise told. Some people welcome this idea; others find it to be a huge shift from traditional norms and a violation of their religious perspective. Politicians weaponize this discomfort and make repeated efforts to codify and enshrine gender binary in laws and policies. They also actively fight or oppose policies that attempt to widen the definition of gender.

Gender expression is how a person outwardly expresses their gender identity. This expression can done through clothing, behavior, physical stance, voice, or other cues affiliated with gender. The cues are usually defined as masculine or feminine, but this is changing (along with everything else).

Understanding how gender is developed

Gender is socially constructed, which is a fancy of way of saying that we make it up. Because it's conflated with sex (a person's biological attributes), people think gender is immutable and inherited. When they're having a baby, they might have a *gender reveal party* (where they find out whether they're having a boy or a girl), decorate the baby's room with gender-affiliated colors (pink for girls, blue for boys), and so on.

TECHNICAL STUFF

GETTING A BIOLOGY REFRESHER

Sex is influenced by three things: chromosomes, gonads, and hormone levels. Here's a quick refresher on all three:

- **Chromosomes:** People inherit sex-linked chromosomes from their parents in a specific combination. Egg cells carry X chromosomes, and sperm cells carry X or Y chromosomes. When a sperm fertilizes an egg, it can result in a combination of X and Y fetal development. Typically, the XX combination results in the female form, and the XY combination results in the male form. People who are intersex may have a mix of sex-linked chromosomes (such as XXY), or they may have just one X chromosome (XO).

- **Gonads:** The term *gonads* refers to ovaries and testes.

- **Hormones:** The gonads release the sex-affiliated hormones — estrogen and androgen. Both male and female bodies produce estrogen and androgen.

The combination of chromosomes, gonads, and hormones determine the physical manifestation of sex.

Genitalia are the organs of the reproductive system. Most people are aware of the external genital organs — the penis and the vagina. Breasts are secondary sex characteristics that develop during adolescence. People's comfort with and knowledge of genitalia vary. Most people tend to have a better knowledge of the genitalia they were born with.

Medical professionals refer to reproductive systems as *male* or *female*, but there is a shift toward calling it the reproductive system without the gender qualifier. For example, a person can have a vagina but identify with the male gender and, thus, not be comfortable having their reproductive system described as *female* in their medical charts.

Gender is shaped by culture. Boys and girls are treated differently starting as young as infancy. Babies who are dressed as girls are treated more gently and given dolls to play with. Babies who are dressed as boys are tossed around more and given trucks.

REMEMBER

Who or what shapes gender development? It's a combination of interpersonal, social, and societal factors. Gender roles are learned in childhood and reinforced in other social contexts like schools and religious spaces and society at large. The following domains are some individual and social factors that shape gender socialization:

>> **Parents/caregivers:** Parents/caregivers may interact with children based on their perceived understanding of gender. They may play rough with boys and gentle with girls or dress children in stereotypical "boy" and "girl" colors.

>> **Schools:** Children may be segregated by gender when they play. Girls may be expected to play "house" and boys may be expected to play with trucks. Teachers may be more tolerant with boys' problematic behaviors or reinforce that boys are good at math and girls are good helpers.

>> **Religion:** Religious institutions may prescribe attitudes and beliefs about gendered behavior to children and families. They may reinforce patriarchal notions of male dominance and female deference to male authority.

>> **Media:** Gender roles and expectations are significantly shaped by the representation of male and females across major media. For example, girls and women are valued for their beauty and boys and men for their intelligence.

>> **Service providers:** Across the life span, people show up for services in various settings and must designate their gender as "male" or "female" and get services under those conditions. Medical care is gendered. Mental health care is gendered and if someone needs support navigating gender-based questions, they may be *pathologized* (made to seem like they're a problem) and diagnosed with *gender dysphoria* (in which people are described as being distressed simply for being gender diverse, whether they're distressed or not). Social care is gendered (for example, shelters are divided by gender).

Looking at what it means to be a "man" or a "woman" in society

Gender is shaped by the way we're raised, our interpersonal interactions, and general societal messages. This leads men and women to have attitudes, behaviors, and interactions in a gender-based way. It creates what social scientists call *social norms* or *societal expectations.* These expectations can lead to stereotypes about how men and women should behave, usually in a hierarchal manner disadvantaging women and advancing men. Historically, the social differences between men and women have been centered on the reproductive capabilities of women and the physical strength of men. Even though people aren't hunters and gatherers, the legacy of these roles lives in the gendered division of labor.

REMEMBER

Women are steered toward roles and jobs that are nurturing and value relationships and communal traits, like teachers, nurses, and social workers. Men are shaped to enter fields that are competitive and rational, like doctors and managers. These traits are presumably valued equally, but they're compensated differently. Men make more money than women because nurturing jobs pay less. Even though men and women are in the workforce in equal numbers, women are still expected to do most of the housework.

Consider the image of a male and female couple coming home from work. The woman starts cooking dinner, cleaning, and parenting while the man sits down to watch TV and relax because he's had a long day. You may think this example is outdated, but research shows that women continue to do housework and serve the primary parenting role within a modern heterosexual family structure. Although there are messages about equity between genders, the gender socialization still reinforces these stereotypes.

When people act outside the prescribed gender roles, they can be met with resistance, disapproval, and punishment. For example when girls and women display assertive and inflexible attitudes or behaviors, in contrast to the stereotypes about their being kind and flexible, they're viewed negatively. The prescribed and expected social differences in gender can lead to inequality, and this is particularly noticed among marginalized groups.

Women of color can face dual oppression — one based on gender and one based on race. They may earn less or have less access to resources and opportunities based on their intersectional identity. In fact, the intersectional framework that many social sciences (including the field of social work) use comes from the study of the challenges that black, low-income, women face.

Addressing the patriarchy and sexism

Gender stereotypes are limiting and create a hierarchy of desired traits, with masculine traits on the top and feminine traits on the bottom. This type of hierarchy — where advantage is given to men — is called *patriarchy*. Patriarchy disadvantages women and other gender identities. It has its roots in a society in which wealth was passed down from fathers to sons. The family was a social and economic unit, and men were central players who held authority and power. This structure created a system where men were "naturally" seen as strong, superior, and more rational, and they were meant to be dominant. On the flip side, women were "naturally" seen as soft, more emotional, less rational, and weaker.

Patriarchy is maintained through sexism and gender socialization in the following ways:

>> Boys are raised to be strong and smart, and girls are raised to be pretty and agreeable.

>> The educational system favors boys and tells them they're good at math and science. Girls are told they're good at reading and social skills.

>> Religious and cultural customs reinforce messages that men are the head of households and hold authority in the life of the family.

>> Men and women enter higher education and major in areas that correlate with the stereotypes. Men major in science, technology, engineering, and math (STEM) and business; women major in social sciences and helping professions.

>> People enter the job market where there is a substantial pay difference between the hard and soft sciences. (Think about how gendered the majors sound — *hard* versus *soft*.)

>> Even in the same jobs and roles as women, men are paid more and promoted faster.

>> Women face challenges when they have children and lose economic grounds for leaving the labor market. Men rarely take paternity leave even when they're given the opportunity to do so, and they continue to have the ability to get promotions.

>> Medical and social research focus on issues that impact men the most.

>> Gender-based violence against girls and women is a global problem.

These socializations are societal; messages center the maleness and create a patriarchal culture. When I bring up this topic in class, my students initially resist it and say that society has moved beyond this. They say they were raised to believe in gender equity. Even if that's case, a helping field like social work is gendered and not compensated at the level it should be. And when men enter the social work profession, they earn more and are placed in leadership roles. Men more often choose macro-level social work where they work in leadership and activism; these roles pay more. Even the social work profession is influenced by gender advantage.

Understanding cissexism: The preference for the gender binary

When gender is categorized in only two forms — male and female — it's limiting. Because of the deep gender socialization we receive, some people aren't aware that there are options beyond the binary. If they don't feel male or female, and they don't know there are other options, this can lead to feelings of despair, which becomes even more pronounced with multiple marginalized identities — for example, there is greater severity of depression and anxiety for folk of color who identify as nonbinary compared to white trans and nonbinary people.

REMEMBER

This strict adherence and preference of the gender binary is called *cissexism*. Cissexism favors and advantages cis people and discriminates against and excludes trans and nonbinary people. What does this look like in real life? Here some examples:

>> Assuming that people are only male, female, and cis

>> Using paperwork and policies that refer to people in binary terms

>> Failing to create safe public spaces like bathrooms

>> No federal policy that includes discrimination on the basis of gender identity in a unified way

>> No medical coverage for trans-affirming care

>> No quality or accessible health-care providers who understand nonbinary patients

>> The lack of a consistent comprehensive education on gender and sexual identity in public education

Supporting authentic gender expression

There is great need to provide inclusive and supportive services for gender-diverse people. For social workers, working with a diverse population always starts with self-reflection and critical awareness. Social work students are asked to reflect on how they were raised to think about gender and reflect on the messages they were given about cis and gender diversity. If they say they weren't given any information about this, that's information as well. It speaks to the dominancy of *cisnormativity* (the belief that all individuals inherently identify with their assigned birth sex) — you don't have to think about gender because it's just assumed. Gender-affirming work embraces gender diversity, celebrates all identities, and actively resists harmful or exclusionary practices.

TIP

Here are some steps to create an affirming social work practice:

>> **Critically analyze your gender socialization.** Begin by examining your own beliefs, attitudes, and biases related to gender. Reflect on how societal norms and personal experiences have shaped your understanding of gender. Self-awareness is crucial for providing inclusive and empathetic care to clients.

>> **Get training on how to support authentic gender expression at any age.** Seek training programs and resources that help you better understand and support authentic gender expression across the life span. These resources can be found through online courses, workshops, and educational institutions specializing in LGBTQIA+ issues. Such training will equip you with the knowledge and skills to affirm and validate diverse gender identities.

>> **Get training on a model that addresses transgender development.** Consider enrolling in training that delves into transgender development models, such as Arlene Istar Lev's transgender emergence model. These models provide insight into the unique experiences and challenges faced by transgender individuals throughout their lives.

>> **Create a list of inclusive and affirming medical providers for linkage and advocacy.** Collaborate with local LGBTQIA+ organizations and health-care professionals to compile a list of inclusive and affirming medical providers. This list can serve as a resource for your clients to access health care that respects their gender identities. Make the list readily available, and regularly update it to ensure accuracy.

>> **Celebrate gender diversity.** Encourage a positive and inclusive atmosphere within your practice by celebrating gender diversity. Emphasize the strengths and resilience of gender-diverse individuals. Avoid focusing solely on negative or pathologizing narratives, because this can reinforce stereotypes and stigmatize clients.

>> **Engage in activism when you see harmful, exclusionary, or discriminatory policy and laws being created, debated, passed, or implemented.** Gender and sexual orientation are highly politicized, and there's a proliferation of harmful laws against LGBTQIA+ individuals. Social workers must not dismiss this issue as outside their practice or expertise — they must actively address human rights violations and advocate for change.

Looking at Sexual Orientation and Sexual Development

When the topic of sexual orientation or sexual development comes up, people often think about sexual activity or bedroom behavior. Although that's an *aspect* of the topic, sexuality is about much more than sexual acts. It entails attraction, desire, romance, commitment, expression, and, yes, sexual acts.

Sexuality is important because it's one of the core aspects of being human. We're social beings who are dependent on relationships to live and thrive. Our *sexual orientation* (who we're attracted to) speaks to the kind of people we're drawn to and the kinds of activities that give us intimacy, pleasure, and satisfaction. That's the positive part of the discourse. The sobering part of the conversation is that *sexual minorities* (people who don't identify as having opposite-sex attraction) are stigmatized and targets of oppression. The oppression occurs in two ways:

>> The larger society tries to render sexual minorities invisible by denying that they exist.

>> Sexual minorities are targets of interpersonal, psychological, and systemic violence.

So, sexual orientation is important not only because it's an important part of a person's identity, but because the group needs advocacy, support, and solid interventions. Social workers are trained to examine this area as a core part of their foundational education.

In the following sections, I explain sexual development, what attracts us to other people, sexual orientation, and variations in sexual behaviors.

Understanding sexual development

Sexual development considers attraction, behavior, and identity and how these things develop over time. In sexuality studies, when sexual development is mentioned, people bring up the early psychological theories (such as Sigmund Freud's psychosexual theory), as well as biological and hormonal theories (which say that same-sex and opposite-sex attractions are based on hormones or the way our brains are physically structured and "wired").

REMEMBER

Social workers use the person in the environment to think about development; these are called *biopsychosocial theories.* Dr. Daryl Bem, a prominent social psychologist from Cornell University, applied the biopsychosocial theory to sexuality. He noted that sexual development unfolds through a series of processes and interactions. This contextual perspective on development is valuable because it elucidates the interplay between the environment and a child in the context of sexual development.

Some people may push back and say kids are just kids and they don't really know who they are or who they like until they're older, but this is adults imposing a process on them. Surprisingly, research shows that kids as early 3 years old are aware of their sexual orientation and gender identity. They know who they notice and like and whether that's socially acceptable.

TECHNICAL STUFF

Developmental models help explain how children learn, grow, and adapt. The developmental models for sexual development have these basic tenets and processes: Kids are born with certain temperaments. These temperaments lead to preferences in what they like to do and how they like to play. The play, preference, and expression can be gender conforming or non-conforming. They may develop different feelings for peers. They may develop interest in or attraction to another peer. Around puberty, they may develop attraction, arousal, and sexual feelings.

Understanding the development process and model is very important for intervention. When a person shows up for help and their gender identity is the primary concern, it's important that the social worker understands how this is developed, the social barriers around this topic, and how the person can be empowered. If there is questioning around their orientation or they want to share their gender attraction, you need to understand the impact of homophobia and heteronormativity on this process.

Heteronormativity is taking for granted that people are attracted to the opposite sex and the belief that this is normal. No one has to come out as straight. Here are some examples of heteronormativity:

>> In media, white heterosexuality is seen as healthy, normal, and affirmed.

>> A straight couple can freely express their affection without being gazed at or objectified.

>> Children of straight couples don't have to explain the gender of their parents.

>> Religious institutions, customs, and rituals affirm straight relationships.

>> Heterosexual people don't have to represent all straight people.

REMEMBER

Homophobia is the irrational fear of queer people (in particular, fear of gay men). People act on this fear through prejudiced beliefs and attitudes and through discriminatory behavior. In gender socialization, masculinity can be couched as an opposition to gayness. Gayness can be associated with femininity and softness. Masculinity is policed and performed. It's perceived in clothing, the ability to fight, posture, and mannerisms. These traits are closely policed so people don't get the "wrong" idea about a person who is presenting as not masculine enough. It takes a lot of work! So, when a person has feelings that may indicate they're attracted to the same sex/gender, it may put them at risk of being an outsider and being the recipient of a negative gaze, having to restrain themselves, and having their behavior policed. The stigma around being identified as gay creates internal distress for the person who understands the danger of homophobic sentiments.

When someone is starting to understand their same-sex attraction and wants to share it, this is called *coming out*. The coming-out process can involve feelings of confusion because the person is aware that they're stepping out of a heteronormative world and they may be stepping into a queer identity. They also realize that their attraction may be "bad" because it's nonconforming, and there are personal and social costs to adapting this orientation. A social worker can help a person navigate the contextual issues that shape that internalized homophobia and work to help the person build acceptance and pride. The ultimate goal is to have the client have *identity cohesion*, where they recognize that their gayness/queerness is a positive aspect of who they are.

Knowing what attracts us to others

What are the factors that influence who we are drawn to? What makes someone our "type" or someone we have chemistry with? Is it their looks, personality, intelligence, values, bank account, or networks? What is love?

Researchers have found that the following categories are important to people in a romantic partner:

» Age

» Education level

» Income

» Intelligence

» Appearance

» Trustworthiness

» Openness to life

REMEMBER

There are three components to romantic relationship:

» **Intimacy:** Intimacy is the closeness and warmth partners feel for one another and the bond they share. They value each other and understand each other's needs.

» **Passion:** Passion is physical attraction and sexual intimacy. This is the spicy element of the relationship.

» **Commitment:** Commitment is the decision to stay in the relationship.

The balance between these three components helps the longevity of a relationship. How people are raised, what was modeled for them, and what kinds of resources they have play a significant role in how love is pursued and maintained.

Sexual orientation: Fluid versus static

Sexual orientation refers to the kind of people you're attracted to. As of this writing, here are some of the most recent and common sexual orientation categories:

» **Heterosexual:** Attraction to the opposite gender

» **Bisexual:** Attraction to both males and females

- >> **Lesbian:** The attraction of a woman to another woman

- >> **Gay:** The attraction of a man to another man

- >> **Asexual:** No sexual attraction

- >> **Pansexual:** Attraction to people across a range of gender identities and expressions

- >> **Demisexual:** Sexual attraction rooted in friendship

- >> **Polyamorous:** Sexual involvement with more than one person at a time.

Gender fluidity speaks to how much flexibility people have in being attracted to people. There is some research that indicates women are more flexible in who they find attractive than men are. Women are more varied in who they're attracted to and romantically linked with than men. This may be due to a higher degree of social acceptance or tolerance for women expressing this part of themselves.

In the past 20 years, there has been a shift in the public view of same-sex/gender marriages and people. In 2013, the U.S. Supreme Court struck down sections of the Defense of Marriage Act, which deprived same-sex couples of the right to marry and receive the affiliated financial, social, and economic advantages. Despite this big movement, prejudice and discriminatory policies against sexual minorities still exist.

TIP

Social workers are trained to understand the levels of oppression sexual minorities face. It's our job to create a sex-positive practice. We do this by:

- >> Creating a sex-positive physical space that has indicators of positive support

- >> Having physical objects and messages, such as books and magazines, that are gender diverse and promote sex

- >> Ensuring that our paperwork and policies are gender diverse and sex positive

- >> Being trained in interventions and models that reject cissexism and heterosexism

Variations in sexual behaviors

Sexuality occurs across the life span. It starts with body awareness in babies, curiosity in toddlers and school-aged children, hormones and arousal in adolescence, sexual freedom in young adulthood, stagnation or fulfillment in middle age, and remaining active in older age. Throughout these periods of life, people may have diverse or limited experiences with sex. They usually want to talk about these things but are reluctant or wait for the social worker to bring up the subject. So, it's important for social workers to be aware of the range of sexual behaviors and strategies to address sexual issues. Social workers can also specialize in sex therapy or sex-affirming practice.

When exploring the spectrum of sexual behaviors, from vanilla or traditional to the spicier and more unconventional, it's essential to adopt a sex-positive perspective. This means being open and nonjudgmental about the diverse ways people express their sexuality and being prepared to listen to others' experiences with curiosity and respect. Crucially, always prioritize consent in any sexual encounter, regardless of its nature, to ensure that all parties involved are comfortable and willing participants in their chosen activities.

Here are some basic definitions of variations in sexual behavior that you may come across:

>> **Paraphilia:** Being aroused by nontypical objects, events, or people; examples include toys, feet, or hair. This is a more debated category where people discuss it as everything from fantasy to mental illness to criminal. It must be noncoercive to be healthy.

>> **Bondage, discipline, sadism, and masochism (BDSM):** Being around by negotiated dominance and submissive roles and activities. This can range from fantasy to physical acts of being tied up and dominated. It isn't a form of mental illness, but is considered a healthy expression of sexuality as long as there is consent and no coercion.

>> **Consensual nonmonogamy:** Having emotional and sexual relationships with multiple people. In order for it to be consensual, everyone involved must be aware of the situation and agree to it.

Social workers should recognize the central role of sexual and gender dimensions in people's lives, striving to increase self-awareness, reduce stigma, and celebrate diversity in gender and sexuality. An affirming and sex-positive environment rejects taboos and nurtures personal growth and visibility.

Chapter **6**

Empowering Other Vulnerable Populations

You may have heard the old adage that there are three topics you should never discuss: politics, religion, and money. But social workers *love* these topics! Boy, oh boy, do we love these topics. Have you ever wondered why? Well, it's because, in social work, we think the personal is political. There are no artificial distinctions between taboo topics and non-taboo topics. We want to talk about it all!

In this chapter, I cover two areas of diversity that are important in social work: ability/disability and religion. These areas cover how people identify, their status, and the way they live their lives.

TECHNICAL
STUFF

Often, these topics are covered from the lens of oppression — meaning denied opportunities, stigmatization, and harm. In this chapter, I address the significant areas of oppression related to these topics, but I also come at them from a strengths-based perspective and emphasize the inherent dignity, value, and collective well-being as it relates to these topics.

On the topic of ability/disability, I clarify historical terms and buzzwords like *ableism* and discuss how you can be an advocate for this population. On the topic of religion, I cover the importance of organized religion, significant changes in religious affiliation, Christian privilege, and religious discrimination. I also discuss the inclusion of spirituality as part of a culturally competent social work practice.

Ability and Disability

When most people think about disabilities, they think of physical disabilities and how those conditions limit people, but that's a pretty limited view of a complex subject. Any discussion of ability and disability should include the environment and cultural perspectives that society has about folks with varying degrees of ability and disability. That way, we get at the expectations that people have about folks with disabilities and what society thinks their capacities are.

REMEMBER

In order to define disability, we have to consider where we think the problem starts. If the problem is located at the individual level, it's up to the person with the disability to demonstrate what and how much they need — and then hope that there are supports and structures in place to address their needs. If the problem is located at the social or structural level, then it's up to society to ensure that there are supports in place at all levels so people are given the support they need, without always having to disclose their needs. This shifts the conversation away from disorders and problems and toward what is an asset, an opportunity for adjustment, and a challenge that needs to be addressed materially.

In the following sections, I define disability, look at *ableism* (the notion that people with disabilities need to be fixed and that fully able bodied people are the ideal), and consider what we can do as social workers to be anti-ableist activists.

Defining disability through the four disability models

Defining disability can increase stereotypes and essentialize people with disabilities. *Essentialism* is the notion that some aspect of a person is the whole person, whether it's good or bad. For instance, I identify as a woman. Solely ascribing *all* my experiences and perspectives to my gender is essentializing my womanhood. Similarly, in defining disability and ability, we can further segregate people with disabilities as the "other" and essentialize their disabilities.

So, let me start this section by recognizing that a person's area of ability and a person's level of impairment or disability are just *one* aspect of their personhood. More important, this part of them is *not* a problem — it's the way their body and brain are designed — and there are no value or moral judgments about it. This doesn't mean we don't see or recognize that someone has a disability or pretend that that part of them isn't important — disability is an important cultural and social identity. We just know that seeing the person holistically, offering them culturally competent service, and decreasing barriers to them are important.

Scholarship on ability and disability are housed in *disability studies*, an academic area that is usually multidisciplinary (involving social science, humanities, medicine, rehabilitation, and education) and looks at disability from a social, cultural, and medical perspective. Four disability models describe the individual or societal perspectives and beliefs about disabilities:

>> **Medical model:** This model, which is the most dominant in Western culture, including the United States, presents disability as a problem in the individual. According to the medical model, the disability should be dealt with by the person, their family, and a group of specialized and professional people (like doctors, nurses, and special educators). It usually sees the person with disability as someone who is nontypical or abnormal and in need of professional intervention. The onus is on the person with the impairment to ask for help and to make a case for themselves. The cure is assimilation into "normal" society. If a person needs a wheelchair to be mobile, their condition is what is the problem for them to have access to buildings. According to the medical model, we should try to fix the disabled person's body as much as possible to help them be more like a "normal" person.

>> **Social model:** This model states that disability comes from a society that is inaccessible and biased toward people with certain bodies and minds. It acknowledges that some people have impairments, but the social model challenges the assumptions that these impairments are abnormal or need to be "fixed." The focus shifts from the person to the environment. If someone uses a wheelchair, the lack of accessible ramps is the problem that blocks the person's ability to enter a building. It locates the issue *outside* the person and doesn't see the person as deficient for not being able to enter a building using their legs.

>> **Explanatory legitimacy model:** This model conceptualizes disability through three dimensions — description, explanation, and legitimacy.

- **Description:** The description dimension talks about the activities or the range of activities a person can or cannot do.

- **Explanation:** The explanation dimension talks about how people define disability — for example, medical (it's the person's fault) or social (the problem is society's inaccessibility).

- **Legitimacy:** The legitimacy dimension talks about the values given to the person with disability and whether their condition is seen as "real." For example, someone with chronic pain may not *look* like they need special parking, so they may be judged as not have a "real" or legitimate disability. There is a hierarchy of what is real and not real. People may even become hostile to the person who has an invisible disability.

>> **Disability/intersectional model:** This model combines the medical and social model and adds intersectionality as another dimension of disability. It does this in three ways:

- It points out the problems of the medical model of disability and how it creates inequalities.

- It agrees with the social model and discusses how disability is created by social processes.

- It adds discrimination to the mix — essentially it says, "Hey, social model folks, you left out discrimination."

For folks with multiple marginalized identities, especially racial minorities, the source of injustice is the *combination* of their marginalization. For example, forced medical sterilization disproportionately happened to people of color. The intersectional model also criticizes disabilities studies for primarily focusing on the experiences of white people with disabilities. They argue that white people's experiences have been centered and seen as the voice for all people with disabilities, despite the fact that most people who have disabilities are people of color. Therefore, there needs to be a model that addresses disability and intersectionality.

TIP

The social work profession is not aligned with the medical model — it's too narrow and focuses too heavily on dysfunction rather than function. But government-sponsored insurance and benefits, such as Social Security Disability Insurance (SSDI) and Supplemental Security Income (SSI), use biomedical definitions to determine a person's eligibility for benefits. These systems define a person as someone

> . . . who, because of a physical or mental impairment expected to last at least one year or to result in death, are unable to return to any of their past jobs or to do any work that exists in the national economy at a level in which they could do substantial gainful activity.

Social workers help people apply for programs like SSDI and SSI by adhering to this medical model, even though we know it's limiting.

TIP

Most social workers would say that they have a social model orientation and deeply consider the structural context for what access and services aren't easily made for folks with disabilities. The disability/intersectional model is an emerging one that social workers are starting to recognize more. It's more nuanced than the social model and explicitly adds multiple layers of identity as being significant to understanding how a person's disability status impacts their life and ecosystem. It'll probably be the prevailing model in the near future.

Looking at ableism at the individual, institutional, and cultural levels

Someone who has hearing loss may see their deafness as a strong positive identifier and be very proud of their deaf community; they may attend a school or program for the deaf, use American Sign Language as their key communication tool, and be proud to have hearing loss. If it comes as a surprise to you that someone who's deaf may be *proud* of their deafness and not aspire to be part of the hearing world, that's because you're looking at the world from an ableist perspective. (Don't worry — you're not alone. Most of the world is right there with you.)

Ableism is the notion that people with disabilities need to be fixed and that fully able-bodied people are the ideal. In this example, it would mean that someone with hearing loss has a problem and it should be fixed.

REMEMBER

Ableism is a form of oppression that stereotypes and creates prejudice, discrimination, and social oppression directed toward people with disabilities. At the heart of these types of oppression is an idealization of a physical, mental, and emotional type of person. The idealized norm values people's bodies and minds based on a made-up idea of what's "normal." This notion is very problematic and costly on the individual, cultural, and social levels.

REMEMBER

Here are some ableist assumptions that non-disabled people hold:

>> Non-disabled people have the ultimate knowledge on both disabled and non-disabled people.

>> Disability is a loss.

>> There are similarities between different disabled people.

>> People with disabilities are interchangeable.

>> They know what it's like to have disability because they've faced a temporary lack of ability themselves (for example, having to use crutches after breaking a leg).

In the following sections, I walk you through the individual, institutional, and cultural levels of ableism.

WHAT ABOUT THE AMERICANS WITH DISABILITIES ACT?

The Americans with Disabilities Act (ADA), enacted in 1990, was a landmark civil rights law for people with disabilities. It prohibited discrimination toward people with disabilities in many areas of public life. It provided protections for people with disabilities and required that places like schools, courts, public transportation systems, emergency services, and social service agencies give equal opportunity and accommodations so people with disabilities can benefit from the services these places offer.

Despite the ADA, folks with disabilities still have poor access to health care, face infrastructures that are inaccessible, aren't given full information or choices in their treatment plan, have their conditions seen as a problem and a deficit, and are met with health-care providers who are incompetent or hold biased or prejudiced beliefs about them. This results in poor outcomes and, for some, early death.

Why does this level of oppression exist? For a number of reasons, but one of the most important is ableism.

Ableism at the individual level

At the individual level, people make judgments and values about a person based on the following dimensions of stigma. Depending on how much or how little a person displays these dimensions, the level of stigma increases.

>> **Aesthetics:** What the person looks like and what reactions their physical presentation elicits from other people. The reactions can range from no reaction at all to pity, horror, and disgust, depending on the condition, culture, and country.

>> **Concealability:** How visible the disability is and how much disclosure the person with the disability needs to provide. Is it a visible or invisible condition?

>> **Disruptiveness:** How much the disability interferes with social interactions.

>> **Origin:** Where and when the disability developed. Was the person born with the disability? Or did the disability develop later?

>> **Peril:** The perception of danger or threat that the person with the disability has to others.

>> **Pity:** Whether the disability is pitied by society. People who have disabilities that are pitied receive less harsh reactions. They may face a saccharine response that can be infantilizing, or they may encounter an overtly hostile response.

When non-disabled people feel like the disability status of the person with a disability doesn't interfere too much or cause too much of an inconvenience for them, they can respond with mild stigmatizing reactions such as pity. Conversely, if they feel threatened, inconvenienced, or displeased with the disability status, they can engage in punitive and discriminatory behavior. For instance, if a person has a schizophrenia diagnosis, but they can conceal it, people may not have any reaction at all; if the person discloses their diagnosis, people may say things like, "I couldn't even tell you had it" or "You're so brave and inspiring" or "You're the healthiest sick person I've ever seen." This is particularly true for chronic conditions.

TIP

These responses imply that if you *could* tell they had the condition it would be a bad thing. They may also imply that the condition is negative and that the person is bravely weathering it.

If the person with schizophrenia *can't* conceal their condition and has behaviors such as talking out loud or being mobile in a particular way, people may feel threatened and do something punitive like call the police to have the person removed from a public space. The person may be perfectly safe and just living their life, but the perception of them as a threat can cause a great deal of harm to them. On the whole, non-disabled people hold negative views and attitudes about people with disabilities, and this impacts how they interact with and provide assistance to people with disabilities.

Ableism at the institutional and cultural level

At the cultural and institutional level, people who have disabilities face ableist interactions and systems and incur significant negative health and well-being outcomes. This is because of the social stigma affiliated with a person's disability status. People with disabilities are erroneously seen as less equal and/or part of an inferior group.

Stigma is based in historical oppressive notions that viewed or treated disability as a moral affliction or punishment from god. Disabilities were seen as preventing people from being productive members of society. People with disabilities were seen as needing to be segregated and confined to institutions or prisons.

These views were adopted by the majority of people in society and baked into educational policies, medical treatments, housing policies, public spaces, social services, employment sites, and financial intuitions. They impact every sector of society. They reduce the chances that people with disabilities will be able to have lives where they can not only be free of oppression but thrive.

In the following sections, I walk you through some domains where ableism plays out.

EDUCATION

People with disabilities have lower levels of education than those without disabilities. Primary and post-secondary special education programs vary in terms of quality of service and levels of accommodation. They can create a hostile school environment where students who need accommodations are seen as burdens, overly labeled, punished more, and pipelined into juvenile detention centers. Because of these traumatic encounters, people with disabilities are reluctant to enroll in college programs and to disclose that they have a disability that needs accommodation. Many end up not completing their studies. Educational attainment is tied to job attainment and future income. A lower level of education impacts a person's chances of having an economically secure future.

HEALTHCARE

People with disabilities are eligible for Medicaid and Medicare as their form of insurance. Sixty percent of people under the age of 65 who qualify for Medicare don't have it. They may not know they qualify, or they may find the process of applying too cumbersome. Even if they have insurance, they have difficulty finding quality providers who take their insurance or provide quality care.

Medical debt, copays, and out-of-pocket expenses create barriers for people, and they don't get the care they need until it's an emergency. Historically, people with disabilities were institutionalized in jails or medical sites and were subject to *eugenics* (attempts to eradicate people with disabilities through forced sterilization). Today, the medical model views people with disabilities as people who have medical impairments that need medical interventions.

HOUSING

There is a shortage of affordable housing and public housing. This is even more pronounced for people with disabilities who need housing that is accessible. Landlords also discriminate against people with visible disabilities, such as wheelchair users. People who are unhoused or homeless are turned down by shelters who have inaccessible buildings.

PUBLIC SPACES

People with disabilities have had to fight to be allowed in public spaces and have fair and equal access to basic human rights. The passage of ADA, passed in 1990 (see "What about the Americans with Disabilities Act?," earlier in this chapter), addressed discriminatory practices and policies, but there is the lingering social and cultural impact that questions whether people with disabilities can be in public or are deemed too unsightly or frightening.

Prior to the passage of the ADA, cities had what are now called "ugly laws," codes that penalized, jailed, or removed from public people who were considered indecent or had deformities, extreme awkwardness, and handicaps. Currently, these laws have been abolished, but anti-homeless city ordinances and nuisance laws, which displace the public homeless or people who seem to be disturbing the peace, continue this legacy. These ordinances disproportionately impact people with disabilities.

EMPLOYMENT

People who have disabilities and want to work are employed less than nondisabled people are. Employers are less willing to hire people with disabilities, so people give up trying. People who receive income from Social Security are not able to work as a condition of receiving aid. The maximum monthly payout is $794 for SSI and $800 to $3,011 for SSDI. (Imagine trying to live off that amount.) The application process for receiving Social Security disability benefits is very tedious and usually requires hiring an attorney. When you already don't have income, this barrier can be unsurmountable.

ECONOMICS AND FINANCIAL INSTITUTIONS

The poverty rate for people with disabilities is twice the rate of people with no disability. This disparity is even more pronounced for people of color. The poverty rate is tied to educational levels, which are lower for people with disabilities. Forty-eight percent of people who have a disability and are working do not use banks; instead, they use nonformal and more predatory forms of banking like payday loans, rent-to-own, and non-bank check-cashing services. All these forms of banking take a significant amount of the money earned and leave the person with less take-home pay. Additionally, banks give out loans for people to acquire homes and other assets that give a more stable future, but these opportunities are missed when you don't have income and the income you earn is gone in a flash.

Creating an accessible future through anti-ableist activism

What can be done to recognize and dismantle ableism? As with other areas of justice, the work starts with reflecting on our attitudes, beliefs, and position of advantage and disadvantage when it comes to ableism. Social work students are asked to reflect on this topic by answering the following questions:

>> What assumptions do you hold about people with disabilities and the causes of disabilities?

>> Do you think disability is a problem and that people with disabilities need more help than others?

>> Do you believe some disabilities are real and others are made up?

>> What messages were given to you when you were growing up about people with disabilities?

>> Do you have much contact with people with disabilities? If not, why?

>> How do your own background and identity influence how you think about this topic?

>> How does the intersecting background of the person with disability impact how they navigate the world with their disability status, and how will it intersect with your own background?

>> What can you do to dismantle ableist policies?

These self-reflection exercises help address and illuminate personal bias, which can lead to stigma and poor service delivery.

After you've looked at your beliefs and values, it's time to look at how interventions can be accommodating and how systems can work on breaking down ableist structures.

TIP

At the individual level people with disabilities face two major barriers: people not believing them and people giving them no access or inequitable access to care. How can you combat these individual-level or micro-ableist aggressions?

>> **Use person-first language — for example, "a person with disability," not "a disabled person."** Some folks with disability prefer their disability to be acknowledged up front or may refer to themselves as disabled. If they tell you that's how they refer to themselves, change your language accordingly. But until then, use person-first language first.

REMEMBER

Language is always evolving so this may change. Check reputable sites for guidance, including the following:

- **ACHIEVA:** www.achieva.info
- **ADA.gov:** www.ada.gov
- **American Association of People with Disabilities:** www.aapd.com
- **American Council of the Blind:** www.acb.org
- **The Arc:** https://thearc.org

- **National Association of the Deaf:** www.nad.org
- **National Council on Disability:** https://ncd.gov

>> **Believe people when they tell you they have a form of disability even if it's invisible.** The disability may be something like chronic pain or a mental health condition.

>> **Keep invasive questions to yourself, and only ask them as needed in your line of work.** Invasive questions include those that ask how someone came to have the disability, what it feels like for them, or the things they struggle with when the conversation is not on that topic. In casual conversation or the first time you meet someone, you shouldn't immediately ask why the person uses a wheelchair. Also, don't make all conversations about the disability or ask how someone is doing with their disability every time you see them. Think about how you would feel if someone asked about how you're managing your diabetes every time they saw you or thought it was the root problem for everything in your life.

>> **Ask permission before you touch someone's assistive device, like a cane or service animal.** Some people consider their devices to be an extension of their bodies.

>> **Provide accommodations for all people before they ask for it and listen to people when they request accommodations.**

>> **Talk about disability with children and young people.**

>> **Avoid inspirational narratives of disability.** This practice is called *inspiration porn*.

>> **Create person-centered interventions that include the client's preferences and desires, even if they have family members helping take care of them.** Center their voice and desires.

>> **Do not infantilize or talk down to the person.**

>> **Be focused on what the person can do, their strengths, and who they see as their support and community.**

TIP

At the cultural and institutional level, you can be an advocate for people with disabilities in these ways.

>> Remember that the disability community is large and diverse and should not be lumped together as one group.

>> Recognize that disability is not a social problem; it's an identity and a culture.

>> Decrease barriers to getting accommodations in educational settings across the life span.

>> Increase housing stock and affordable housing for people with disabilities.

>> Create programs that help people sign up for Medicaid and Medicare and incentivize health-care providers to treat patients with this insurance.

>> Make sure that public and private spaces are accessible without a person having to ask for it.

>> Increase banking and employment opportunities for people with disabilities.

>> Notice and resist messages that promote or idealize beauty, capacity, and excellence as only for people without disabilities.

Engaging in self-reflection and understanding the individual- and system-level advocacy can go a long ways toward undoing the harm caused by ableist stigmas and policies.

Religion

Religion and spirituality play a significant role how people identify, cope, and live in their communities. People's faith and their faith communities are a dimension of diversity that the field of social work pays attention to in two distinct ways:

>> **We recognize the importance of faith, spirituality, and faith communities in the lives of the clients we serve and incorporate them in the treatment or systems change.** This can be especially important to minoritized groups and to older adults.

>> **We discuss what we call** *Christian privilege* **or** *Christian normativity,* **which is pervasive in American culture.** This can present as many people being oblivious to other faith traditions or people who don't have religious beliefs. In worst-case scenarios, it can lead to religiously oppressing or enacting violence against outside groups.

These topics can feel a bit at odds. We're identifying the importance of religion but also calling it oppressive? Yes and yes. Religion can be a source of strength and a big part of a person's life and culture. It can also be a cultural and social tool that is weaponized to cause tremendous harm. It's complicated — but social work doesn't shy away from complicated or nuanced topics. It's what the work is all about.

In this section, I cover the role of organized religion and the current religious makeup of the U.S. population. I also discuss trends in religious affiliation and the implications for changing affiliation. Then I cover the tension between the freedom *of* religion and freedom *from* religion. I demonstrate this tension in a discussion of Christian normativity or privilege, as well as the role social workers play in addressing and incorporating spirituality in their practice.

Defining religion and spirituality

Entire disciplines are dedicated to defining religion and spirituality. In this section, I define them broadly so you have a baseline understanding.

Religion is defined as a system of beliefs and customs observed by a community and supported through rituals that acknowledge some aspect of a higher power, the divine, or the sacred. Religion usually has a sacred text and moral code of conduct.

Spirituality is more individualized. It's the personal quest for understanding the meaning of life, relationships, and the sacred. Spirituality can be a part of organized religion or not.

People may describe themselves as religious, spiritual, or both — or they may not ascribe to any religious or spiritual practices.

A person's *religiosity* (the quality of being religious) can be thought of as intrinsically or extrinsically motivating to them:

>> **Extrinsically:** For extrinsically religious people, religion can serve as a form of social identity, a means of having status, a social support, a mechanism for passing judgment on what is good and moral, and a form of security. It serves cultural and social purposes.

>> **Intrinsically:** For intrinsically religious people, religion is a means for internal growth, support, and meaning making. It's less social and more personal.

For the most part, both extrinsically and intrinsically motivated religious people live lives in which their religion and faith are central to them. When they face stress or trauma, intrinsically motivated people find their religion to be a source of solace and support but extrinsically motivated people find religion to be invalidating and may feel disheartened or abandoned by the religion that was meant to protect them from harm.

Religion and spiritually matter a great deal to people personally and socially. In the United States, there is constitutional protection to practice religion and be free from religious oppression.

WHO'S RELIGIOUS IN THE U.S.A.?

What does the religious affiliation or religions makeup of the U.S. population look like right now? According to the most recent study from the Pew Research Center (2020), adults in the United States describe their religious affiliations as follows:

Religion	Percentage of U.S. Population
Christian	63%
Religiously unaffiliated	28%
None	18%
Agnostic	5%
Atheist	4%
Jewish	2%
Hindu	1%
Muslim	1%

The majority of people are religious and hope to pass their faith traditions and culture to their children. In their transmission of religion, they also pass down views about life, social issues, politics, surviving, and identity. This can be a great source of comfort and strength, or a tool for isolation, subjugation, and violence.

Seeing how religious identification has changed

In 1990, 90 percent of Americans identified as Christian. It was such a large portion of the population that it was a cultural norm to assume that Christianity was the main religion in the United States. Today, 63 percent of Americans identify as Christian.

Why the change? A majority of adults who no longer identify as Christian moved away from Christianity and have become religiously unaffiliated. Religiously unaffiliated rose from being 5 percent of the population in 1990 to 28 percent of the population today.

People who were raised with a faith tradition (in this case, mostly Christian) are disaffiliating from overtly identifying as Christian to not having a religious affiliation. There seems to be a shift from being religious to being more spiritual.

A few characteristics are tied to the disaffiliation in religious identity and status, according to the Pew Research Center (see "Who's religious in the U.S.A.?"). They name the following characteristics as the variables associated with the shift to religiously unaffiliated:

>> **Age:** People under 30 are moving away from Christianity and not coming back to it. Older adults are retaining their Christian identity.

>> **Education:** College graduates are more likely to be disaffiliated. People with higher levels of education are less likely to be religious.

>> **Gender:** Women are more likely to retain their Christian identity than men. There were no reports on how gender-diverse people affiliated with Christianity, but rigid religious views can marginalize and stigmatize folks in the LGBTQIA+ community.

>> **Geography:** People who disaffiliated after being raised Christian are more likely to live on the West Coast and in the Northeast and less likely to live in the South.

>> **Politics:** Seventy percent of adults who were raised Christian and identify as disaffiliated are Democrats or Democratic-leaning independents. There has been an association between Christianity and conservatism.

People who remain affiliated with a religion report that their faith matters a great deal to them. For a good number of people who are religious, it's critical to them that their children share in their faith practice and grow up affiliated. Their social, cultural, and political views (if politics is a part of their faith) are deeply shaped by their faith.

REMEMBER

People not affiliated with religion are not a monolithic group. They range in terms of what they believe and how they participate in organized or internalized religions. Joel Thiessan and Sarah Wilkins-Lafamme wrote extensively on the this topic and identified four subcategories of people who are disaffiliated: involved secular, inactive non-believers, spiritual but not religious, and religiously involved believers.

People are leaving organized religion and also expressing their spiritualty and faith in individualistic ways. This doesn't mean people are becoming more secular or losing their religion, but they're shifting in how they practice and view religion.

It's also important to note that a growing number of faith communities in the United States do not have congregational practice and do not have a doctrine per se — they have faith practices, meaning they do more than they believe, and the religious affiliation question asked by the Pew poll does not speak to their religious practice. Therefore, they answer "none of the above" when asked about their religious affiliation. So, this poll could be missing out on a whole group of spiritual or religious experiences just because of the way the question is posed.

Those without a religious affiliation also have more progressive politics on social and civic topics like same-sex marriage, abortion, women in the workforce, environmental laws, immigration, and government aid. Conversely, religiously affiliated people may endorse more conservative views of sociopolitical issues. There is a growing polarity between the groups, in which each sees the other as not just holding opposing views but as being problematic.

Combatting Christian privilege and religious oppression

Christian privilege may be a new concept or term for many people. In social work, we use the terms *privilege, advantage, oppression,* and *disadvantage* to talk about how an aspect of someone's identity (like age, gender, race, sex, or sexuality) is shaped or impacted by social forces that offer advantage or disadvantage. The doors are open for some groups and shut for other groups. The opening and shutting of the doors isn't something that is earned — it's a result of social and political advantage that empowers one group over the other. (More information about oppression and privilege in general can be found in Chapter 4.)

REMEMBER

Privilege or advantage is not overt. It's subtle and invisible, and this is by design. Privilege is in the air — it's just the way things are. It's the normal or what we call *normativity.* Groups that are part of the norm or privileged don't have to think about their position or stance because it's a given that their affiliation is the standard or "normal," and it's also the preferred way to be. For example, straight people don't have to disclose that they're straight — it's a given that people are straight unless you're told otherwise. A discussion of religious privilege, specifically Christian privilege, applies the concepts of normativity to an American context. Christian privilege elevates Christianity over other faiths and states that it can have uncontested influence without critique. It holds the assumption that Christianity is normal and what America was founded on.

Some people may challenge this idea and ask: How is a person privileged just because they practice Christianity? Most people in America are Christians, so what's wrong with assuming they are? What's oppressive about someone having a Christian faith and perspective? Aren't people entitled to freedom of religion and worship? These are great questions and ones we unpack in the foundation courses in schools of social work.

There is nothing wrong with having religion or faith. In fact, we want to celebrate what is meaningful and important to people, including their religion and faith practices. People have a right to religion. Where we see oppression and disadvantage is when there is no separation of religion from civic life and non-Christians are asked to endure the Christian worldview and are seen as outsiders or the other if they have other faith traditions or no faith. This goes to the issue of freedom *from* religion. We pretend that the United States is a religiously neutral country, but that isn't the case. This religiously neutral stance prevents people from bringing up religious inequities because they're questioned on the legitimacy of their claims. Non-Christians constantly have to ask for accommodations or out their faith systems, before they want to, because society is organized around Christian norms.

A significant part of the Christian privilege derives from the myth that colonial settlers or the Puritans came here to fight for religious freedom. They *did* come to seek refuge from religious oppression and persecution, but after they got here, they secured religious freedom only for themselves and actively oppressed other religious groups, like Native Americans and enslaved Black people. They even created a hierarchy of Christian groups and oppressed one another. Even in the absence of organized or state-sponsored religion, white Protestant Christians dictated cultural norms, community control, wealth, and passage of wealth from generation to generation. Minorities such as enslaved Black people, Japanese Americans, Chinese Americans, and Native Americans were forced to convert to Christianity and adopt white Protestant traditions and culture.

You might ask, "Isn't that old history? We have religious protections now." Unfortunately, the legacy of Christian privilege is baked into laws and policies, and people still have to fight against religious oppression and discrimination.

Here are some examples of Christian normativity:

>> **The discussion of religious freedom is couched as the conversation about the separation of *church* and state.** The church is the Christian place of worship. Other religious groups worship in synagogues, temples, or mosques, for example.

>> **The Supreme Court has said that people have the right to believe anything they want, but how they practice their beliefs cannot violate political and cultural norms (which are based on white Protestant Christian values).** For example, people who cover their heads or grow beards as part of their religious practice can't participate as service personnel in the military because covering your head or growing a beard is seen as "preferred practice" and not belief. Congress had to pass a separate law to allow civil and

military members the right to wear head coverings. On the other hand, Amish residents were legally allowed to disenroll their children from high schools at age 16, even though it's a federal law that children be enrolled in schools, because the courts found that Amish culture and history are a deep part of colonial American heritage and they deserved this protection. This is an example of privilege.

>> **Federal holidays are based on Christian celebrations.**

>> **Historically, Sunday was the only recognized day of rest from employment because it coincided with the Christian Sabbath.** Saturday was added as a day of rest because of labor movements.

>> **Christian prayers are used during public government and school meetings.**

Here are some examples of Christian/religious oppression:

>> **Jews were fired for missing work to observe the Sabbath.**

>> **The courts allow roads to be paved through sacred and religious Native American lands.**

>> **The Secret Service asked a Sikh agent to shave his beard and not wear a turban while on duty.**

>> **Christian companies are allowed to not offer contraception health-care coverage for their employees.**

>> **Christian graphic designers or bakers don't have to serve LGBTQIA+ customers.**

>> **LBGTQIA+ families are denied opportunities to foster or adopt children based on religious objections from faith-based Christian (mostly Catholic) agencies that child-welfare offices use to contract adoption and foster-care services.**

These examples are from the general population. In social work practice, we see religious oppression show up at the individual, familial, and societal level:

>> **Individual:** At the individual level, children and women may suffer religious maltreatment or gender-based violence based on folks following fundamental Christian doctrine. Sexual minorities face tremendous stigma and attack from faith communities.

>> **Familial:** At the family level, the notion of the nuclear and ideal family is based on the Protestant white Christian ideal of a heterosexual married couple with

children. Other forms of family formation — such as single parents, *fictive kin* (either extended family who are as close to you as immediate family or non-blood relatives who you consider to be family members), and multigenerational families — are not seen as ideal or may even be pathologized as problematic.

>> **Societal:** At the societal level, employees face workplace discrimination because of their congregational affiliation (Islamophobia), women are denied health-care services by faith-based organizations, and same-sex couples face barriers when they try to adopt or foster kids. White hate groups that use Christianity as the basis for their beliefs attack other racial groups, sexual minorities, and other religious groups. There is a significant rise in hate crimes against Jewish people and communities. I could go on and on. . . .

Because of how serious and pervasive these issues are, it's essential that social workers have a working knowledge of religious oppression and understand how it presents in society today.

Seeing how religion and spirituality fit into social work practice

Religion, faith, and spirituality are important personal, social, and cultural components of a person's life. People turn to their faith and congregation for spiritual guidance, for education, for financial help, for community, and for emotional and psychological support. In addition to providing support, faith and religious doctrine play an important role in shaping family values and a code of conduct in and out of the home. Faith communities esteem elders and keep them active, connected, and healthy. Elders in the faith practice may have jobs that are vocational or domestic outside of the congregation. In the faith space, they may hold positions of leadership, mentorship, or as members of the board of leaders.

The faith community can be considered an extension of the home and an integral part of a person's social network. People derive joy, strength, and collective power from this aspect of their lives. Social workers can't ignore this significant aspect of diversity in the life of the people they serve. Part of social work value and principle is to provide culturally competent and responsive services. Religion is a dimension of diversity that falls under this purview.

Sometimes social workers are reluctant to address or inquire about spirituality or religion because they don't feel like they have the expertise to handle spiritual questions or crises. They may also feel that this subject falls under the care of the person's faith leader, as opposed to the social worker.

Another reason social workers may not address this dimension is because social workers and those in the helping profession tend to be less religious than the clients they service. Social workers identify more as spiritual than religious. Social workers may also believe that religious organizations have discriminated against and oppressed vulnerable populations, so they may not necessarily want to actively inquire about this dimension of a person's life.

At the same time, clients report that they fear there is a difference in levels of faith and religiosity between themselves and their care providers and they would prefer to go to their faith leaders for help before they go to social workers or other helpers like counselors or psychologist. Their reluctance can unfortunately be confirmed when they seek services or treatment and their faith is unaddressed or invalidated. This problem must be redressed.

How do you address spirituality or faith with clients? Do you have to share the same faith as them? Do you have to become a religious expert and a social worker? Should you enroll in a comparative religious studies program or divinity school? What if you're nonreligious. Isn't this impeding on your right to be free from religion in the workplace? Excellent questions!

Research shows that social workers who are intrinsically religiously motivated (see "Defining religion and spirituality," earlier in this chapter) find it much easier to approach issues of faith and religion because they have familiarity with it. This can be good *and* bad. They can feel too familiar and think they understand all aspects of the person's faith and miss things. Being totally unfamiliar is okay, too. You don't have to become a religious expert to incorporate or inquire about spirituality.

REMEMBER

People turn to their faith during times of illness, hospitalization, death, trauma, social unrest, and for coping. They use their spirituality and their faith community to feel better, to get support, and to make social changes. Keep this in mind. Religion is particularly important for older adults and marginalized populations. Sometimes, their faith traditions are the only spaces that provide support and validation to them.

TIP

You can address this dimension by, well, addressing it. You may be tempted to say, "I'll wait for someone to bring it up, and then I can address it." But that's not good practice. You need to query for it in your engagement and assessment of the client or system just as you would for another biopsychosocial domain. You can use formal assessment tools, or you can simply embed questions about it in your assessment tool. The important part is that you *ask*. Then use the information the client gives you to plan your treatment or intervention.

If the person is religious and their faith is important to them, ask which aspect of it is helpful and which is not. They may be questioning their faith. I get this quite a bit in my work with trauma survivors. Or their faith may be a source of support to them. These separate answers will lead to different treatment plans.

TIP

If people are having true religious questions or having spiritual crisis beyond what you're able to offer, you may need to consult or refer them to a faith leader. Be sure to vet the faith leader first and make sure that their advice, as well intended as it may be, won't cause more harm or distress to your client. This is where social work ethics also come into play — you need to refer your clients to people who value justice and dignity and the worth of the person. Don't send a client to someone who will try to erase parts of their identity or do conversion therapy. That's unethical.

If you're doing a community project or engaging in activism, see who the faith leaders are in the community and build relationships with them. Invite them to be part of coalitions, as stakeholders and legislative partners. They hold tremendous influence and power in the community, and you'd be missing a significant stakeholder by not inviting them to the table.

2

Exploring the Various Specialties in Social Work

Chapter **7**

Assisting with Mental Health and Wellness

P eople are *feeling* it these days. They're stressed, distressed, overwhelmed, and sometimes in deep crisis. These feelings come from stress associated with their jobs, relationships, finances, and how they feel about themselves in the world. The COVID-19 pandemic was a national and global crisis that pushed people and society to its limit.

At the same time some people are feeling stressed and maxed out, other people are living their healthiest best selves. They're paying attention to their mind, body, and relationships, and trying to make the world better. Some people thrived during the pandemic. They were able to rest and take a break and found the quarantine, the monthly financial federal support, and the ability to work from home transformative.

This is a pretty big pendulum. How can something that is so painful for one person be transformative and healthy for someone else? How do we define wellness or illness? Is it a subjective phenomenon where it's up to each person to decide if they're well or not?

In this chapter, I talk about the continuum of wellness. I also cover the social work approach to working in the mental health field and how social workers think about the cause of a person's pain and the best ways to help foster healing and thriving.

Understanding Mental Health and Well-Being

Mental health is a person's internal state of well-being. It's their ability to manage their thoughts, feelings, reactions, and general state of being. This state is determined by the way they think, their biology, and their social context. In other words, how their brain is wired, their perspective on life, and where they are in life — including their identity and their sociocultural contexts (such as the person's demographic characteristics, where they live, and their class status) — impact their internal state.

How you were raised, where you were raised, your genetic dispositions, your access to care, and your own outlook on life determine your state of mind. These things shape your reactions to what's happening to you. Having poor mental health means that a person is experiencing distressing symptoms and it's getting in their way of living their life. The clinical definition is that it's impairing their functioning.

Let me give you an example. When some people feel low or have the blues, they generally feel sad or tearful but are able to go on with their day and can be relatively productive. For people who suffer from depression, when they feel low, they can't get out of bed or can only do the absolute bare minimum. They miss a lot of work because they simply can't muster the strength to do the daily activities of life. Depression is more than the blues — it's debilitating. People with depression usually come to see me because chronic absenteeism is impacting their work or they can't find work and their loved ones have had it. If they're students, they aren't able to go to school.

REMEMBER

Well-being is measured by the following factors that make you feel good about life and give you the sense that you can thrive:

>> Your adaptability

>> Your ability to effect change or have power in your life

>> Your sense of optimism, satisfaction, and overall happiness

>> Your community and affiliation

>> Your sense of belonging

REMEMBER

Well-being isn't the *absence* of negative feelings or incidents — it's the *presence* of key factors, including feeling like you have some ability to impact your life and how you feel about your life. In other words, you aren't bound by your moods or environment — you can navigate it.

Personal, social, and societal factors impact a person's mental health and can tip the scales on the continuum of wellness:

>> **Personal:** On the personal level, your genetic makeup, your emotional regulation, and your use or misuse of addictive substances all impact your reactions. Some mental health issues like schizophrenia or bipolar disorder are organic or biological in their origins and can be passed down intergenerationally. In other cases, a person's emotional regulation or ability to manage their emotional reactions is determined by how they were raised. If they were raised in a stressful home with harsh parents who had big emotional reactions, they may grow up to be an adult who themselves has big reactions and little control of their emotions. Abusing substances (drugs, alcohol, tobacco) also impact your psychological and emotional well-being. Your day-to-day functioning is driven by your need to consume the additive substance. Exposure to violence, oppression, poverty, and environmental neglect are additional risk factors or vulnerabilities for developing a mental health condition. They add to what we call *adverse life experiences*. The more adverse life experiences you have, the higher your chances of developing or exacerbating a health condition.

Conversely, protective factors can help act as buffers against distressing events that lead to functional impairments. At the individual level, protective factors may include your temperament and your ability to tolerate and manage your feelings. Have you ever met folks who seem unflappable? Or do you know two people raised in the same household with not-so-great parents, and one of them is doing well and the other is definitely not? That's not because one of the siblings is good and the other is bad. It's because one was biologically blessed with an even-keel temperament. No matter where they were raised, they're able to thrive.

>> **Social:** On the social level, having supportive, loving relationships and community are significant protective factors. Even if you have a genetic predisposition to mental health issues, your social environment — like your parents and a supportive community — can help you thrive.

>> **Societal:** On the societal level, your income level, your access to health care, the levels of oppression you face, and the actual physical environment you live in all impact your well-being. If you have access to health care and can afford to go, you have a leg up. If your health-care provider is sensitive to your identity, you can easily get to them, and they're in your network, you've won the mental health jackpot.

Being a social worker who works in the mental health practice, I aways keep in mind risk factors and protective factors that impact someone's mental health.

TWO WAYS OF TREATING SYMPTOMS: THE TRADITIONAL MODEL VERSUS THE RECOVERY MODEL

There are two schools of thought on how people's symptoms are seen and treated:

- **Traditional:** The traditional or medical model, which is what most mental health clinicians are trained in, approaches mental health problems based on the person's symptoms and function, and makes a formal diagnosis using the *Diagnostic and Statistical Manual for Mental Disorders* (DSM). In this model, a person usually presents with a set of behaviors, thoughts, and emotions that are creating a disturbance or impairment in their life. There is dysfunction in their thinking, and this significantly and negatively impairs their ability to be in the world. With this approach, clinicians measure symptoms through screening and assessment tools and provide a diagnosis and a course of treatment, which may include therapy, medication, and psychosocial supports.

- **Recovery:** The next school of thought is the recovery model, which sees mental illness through the lens of recovery. It doesn't focus on symptoms. Instead, it focuses on giving people the tools they need to control or manage their *lives* instead of their symptoms. It focuses on living *with* their mental illness as opposed to *away* from it. The recovery model is strength based, self-directed, and peer-directed, and it works to help people find their full potential. It sees recovery as a lifelong journey, one that most people can attain despite or with their symptoms. The treatment process can include work with peer-led groups where a person elects to create their own recovery plan using principles of hope, personal responsibility, education, self-advocacy, and support.

How is the recovery model different from the traditional model? Let's say someone comes for help because they're hearing voices. With the traditional model, you would do an assessment and screening, make a diagnosis, and try to eliminate the symptoms and improve the person's quality of life. With the recovery model, you would meet the person, ask them if they think hearing voices is a problem, and give them options for treatment, including meeting with a peer who is also on a mental health journey. The person may decide that the voices aren't a problem, or that they even like the voices, and they just want some tools for tuning out the voices during sensitive times of their day. With the recovery model, they're totally in charge of their own care and don't necessarily need to consult with professionals to heal.

The recovery model is gaining momentum and there is strong evidence to support its approach. For now, though, the traditional model is what is most frequently used and recognized.

Acknowledging the Stigma of Mental Illness and Mental Health Treatment

Many people are suffering from emotional distress or psychological pain but are reluctant to get help because of the stigma associated with mental illness diagnosis and treatment. They avoid or delay getting treatment because they're afraid of the implications. They may be concerned that their friends or family, employer, and other people in society will have a negative perception of them and even avoid or punish them because of their mental health status.

This delay or avoidance in getting treatment causes real harm. People suffer and, in some cases, die prematurely because they aren't getting treatment. Stigma against people with mental illness is very real and is rooted in history. In the past, people who were suffering from mental health conditions were thought to be insane, witches, or hysterical, or they may have been seen as people with "weak constitutions." They were ignored, put in asylums or intuitions, jailed, murdered, or used as medical experimental subjects. It's really only since the late 1960s that the federal government has had policies and funding to support mental health care. The public awareness and support for mental health care waxes and wanes.

TIP

Stigma around a public health issue manifests in three core ways:

>> **Self-stigma:** Attitudes, beliefs, and thoughts that people have about their own status or condition. Self-stigma produces profound feelings of shame, disconnection, and disgust, and it leads people to not get help or to isolate.

>> **Public stigma:** Negative, hostile, prejudiced, avoidant, and discriminatory attitudes and behaviors others have about mental illness. This is depicted in TV shows and movies about "crazy" people, crime reports, written material, and an overall cultural message that mental illness is a terrible, ostracizing condition that happens to "other" people.

>> **Institutional stigma:** Structures or systems that provide mental health support or policies that are punitive, discriminatory, or limiting (unintentionally or intentionally). The institutions don't provide funding or full funding for mental health supports, or they create major legislative or policy hurdles for services. For example, it takes a lot of work for mental health-care providers to get Medicaid accreditation. Because it's so cumbersome, many providers choose not to get certified to provide care for people with Medicaid, which makes it difficult if not impossible for people who receive public assistance to find quality service and service providers. Because of institutional stigma, the *people* are seen as a problem, rather than the *system* being seen as the problem.

REMEMBER

Stigma is even more pronounced for people from underrepresented or marginalized groups, such as people who identity as LGBTQIA+ or members of racial and ethnic minority groups. People with these identities are less likely to seek help and less like to get quality help when they find it. LGBTQIA+-identifying people want to receive mental treatment but don't have access to people who specialize in the issues they face. Some racial and ethnic groups have *collectivist cultures*, where help is given from the community and not usually by outsiders. This is a strength of the community, but it can sometimes be a barrier to getting help if something in addition to community support is needed. There are also cultural messages to keep things like mental illness in a family or community secret. Some groups may believe that people who seek help are severely disturbed and will bring shame to the family or community. Other times, people are encouraged to rely on their faith or pray more when they share their struggles.

Folks of color are often refused for mental health services (they're incarcerated instead), are misdiagnosed or diagnosed with a more severe and more stigmatized diagnosis (for example, conduct disorder or schizophrenia), or have clinicians and service providers who are insensitive and cause more injury. Queer folks also face stress and stigma when they try to seek help for mental health issues. When they find help, they're over-diagnosed with personality disorders such as borderline personality disorder. For both groups, these harmful practices perpetuate racism, homophobia, and transphobia and are deeply painful. When someone finally shows up to get help and faces these kids of interactions, they internalize the shame.

Stigma isn't just a subjective experience where someone thinks a provider has a negative view of them. It's believing the provider has a negative view of them and treats them as less than, which leads the person to feel devalued. Because of this, they may isolate to cope with the stigma and end up having worse symptoms or doing harmful things to cope.

The effects of stigma with underrepresented groups has been repeatedly demonstrated by social science research. Reviews of patient's clinical notes reveal that folks of color, folks with substance use disorders, and folks who identify as queer were diagnosed with more severe labels and described using punitive and harsh language. This has real consequences because patients' clinical charts inform future and current providers about their behaviors and what treatment options they're presented with. Patients who had less stigmatized language in their charts were given wider options for treatment and had better outcomes.

Social workers are taught about diversity, equity, and anti-oppression in their education and in their clinical internships. One of the goals in their internship learning plan is that they must demonstrate how they'll engage in anti-racism, diversity, equity, and inclusion in their internship. The profession explicitly addresses the issue of stigma. Students and practitioners are taught to have self-awareness, to have historical knowledge of the population they serve, to practice with cultural humility, and to empower people. Organizations that provide mental health services are also charged with having a diverse workforce and training their workers in anti-racist and multicultural practice models. Social workers can't claim to be unaware of these issues — they're connected to a core value of the profession.

Identifying the Social Worker's Role in Mental Health

When someone is finally ready to get help or support for a mental health issue, finding a good provider or system of care (if they require more than one type of mental health support) can be a real challenge. Social workers provide help and support in a number of ways:

>> **They can help people navigate a complicated health care system and link them with providers as a case manager or social service resource person.** I always have a list of different types of providers and services no matter what job or role I have. Part of social work is being community engaged and connected to local resources.

>> **They can work as mental health providers in a variety of roles.** For example, they can be psychotherapists, group facilitators, educators on psychosocial and emotional needs, or specialized milieu providers.

>> **They can run agencies or programs that provide mental health services.**

>> **They can work on legislative policies that impact mental and behavioral health.** They advocate for or help write policies that help people get services. For instance, there was strong legislative push to provide more mental health care supports for schools after the COVID-19 pandemic. School social workers were instrumental in helping shape legislation that called for the addition of school-based social workers to provide mental health supports for school-aged children. This provided funding to schools for better public access to mental health care.

People can get mental health care or services from public and private providers. Additionally, folks who struggle with mental health and substance use can get services at places that specialize in mental health and addiction.

Public mental health

Public mental health is the notion that society at large is responsible for ensuring that people are set up to have happy, productive lives. The goal is to prevent addressable mental health issues and support mental well-being. The public health model starts with the universal approach of providing access to services that impact the protective factors for mental health wellness. Examples include teaching emotional regulation skills to students in schools; providing strong parenting support for caregivers; giving people access to high-quality health care; and creating communities that are free of violence, environmental degradation, and oppression. It uses public funds to support these efforts and makes the services available to all people.

In the social work profession, one of the grand challenges for leaders of the field is public mental health and building systems of care that allow people to thrive. These are large-scale initiatives and investments that are meant to be for all people and accessible to the public.

TIP

Here are some examples of public mental health services:

>> Early infant and childhood programs like Head Start

>> Therapeutic preschools that offer rich learning environments for children and families who need socio-emotional learning supports

>> School-based programs such as positive behavioral supports programs that offer emotional regulation skills to all students

>> Group homes

>> Medicaid insurance coverage for mental health care

>> Suicide hotlines and crisis response teams

>> Hospital-based services for mental health

>> Veteran or military services for mental health issues

>> Community-based mental health and rehabilitation centers

>> Victims services funded by county and federal resources

>> Violence prevention programs

>> Supportive programs that address isolation and loneliness for older adults

>> Mental health policy advocacy programs

>> Mental health research

Social workers work in all of these areas and across the life span. In fact, social work principles and values state that our work should be in service of the public. We provide help and relief to *all* people — especially to disenfranchised groups that suffer from stigma and oppression.

Private mental health

When people think of getting mental health support, they usually think about getting counseling services in a private practice office and paying out-of-pocket or through private insurance. This kind of support falls under the umbrella of private practice.

Licensed clinical social workers are the number-one providers of mental health services in the Unites States. This surprises most people who aren't in the social work profession. Clinical social workers or behavioral health social workers must have a master of social work (MSW) degree and be licensed. They can provide assessment, diagnosis, treatment, and evaluation for mental health concerns. People who can access private mental health services can get individual, couple, family, and group treatment.

Insurance companies usually cover the following issues related to mental health care:

>> Talk therapy in person or through virtual appointments

>> Emergency care or crisis intervention (for example, for suicide attempts or overdoses)

>> Substance use treatment

>> Inpatient hospitalization (staying in a mental health hospital for a period of time to get stabilization or continue treatment)

>> Intensive outpatient care (structured psychiatric treatments that last three to six hours a day, anywhere from three to seven days a week)

>> Medication (access to a psychiatrist or pharmaceutical interventions)

Social workers play a vital role in legislative and policy advocacy concerning mental health issues, operating through social work organizations and engaging in political action forums. They wield the power to impact legislation, shape mental health policies, and actively participate in the political sphere to raise awareness and advocacy surrounding mental health. In a world where stigma still surrounds mental health, these efforts are paramount in reducing prejudice and fostering greater access and equity in this critical realm. By addressing the legislative and policy dimensions of mental health, social workers contribute significantly to dismantling the barriers that prevent individuals from seeking the support they require while ensuring that everyone has access to the mental health care they deserve.

Dual diagnosis

Another area of mental health care focuses on mental health and substance use. This is called *dual diagnosis* or *co-occurring disorders.* When someone presents for treatment, a good practice protocol is to screen for mental health and substance use. This screening helps identify folks who may need treatment for both issues. Because so many people use substances to cope, social workers receive education on substance use and misuse in their educational setting.

Co-occurring disorders are treated in two ways:

>> **One provider treats the mental health issue, and another provider treats the substance use issue.** This is historically what has been done, but the problem is people get the runaround when they seek services. They'll be told, "We can't help you with your mental health issues until you get your addiction under control." But then when they present for substance use treatment, they're told, "Your mental health issues are preventing you from progressing in your substance use treatment, and we can't give you more services until you get mental health care." Other times, they get conflicting messages from their therapist and addiction specialist.

TIP

If this is the only option, the client should at least sign a release form allowing the two providers to talk and provide coordinated treatment.

>> **One clinician treats both the mental health issue and the substance use issue.** This best-case scenario is called *integrated treatment*. Integrated treatment improves outcomes for clients because it addresses the runaround issue and is less stigmatizing. You don't have to be a super clinician to provide integrated treatment — there are therapeutic and substance use models that are able to holistically address the client. Integrated treatment models should be universal models that all clinicians should be trained in.

Developing Your Assessment and Diagnostic Skills

When a person presents with mental health struggles or issues, you must tease out what's troubling them and determine the best course of treatment. A robust assessment process that is sensitive and culturally responsive will elicit the best information for intervention planning.

Assessments are usually done in the first couple of sessions through a structured interview process that attempts to understand the following:

>> The pressing issue or presenting problem (in other words, what brought the person to seek help)

>> Demographic and life status information about the client (age, race, ethnicity, gender, sexuality, employment history, military affiliation, family status)

>> The person's *biopsychosocial history* (which includes information about their personal background, their childhood, their health history, and their areas of support)

>> Any legal involvement (for example, child custody issues or criminal charges)

>> The person's developmental history

>> Any traumas or adverse life experiences the person has had

>> A risk assessment (to determine whether the person is at risk for hurting themselves or others)

>> Any community supports and areas of strength the person has

This information gives a contextualized picture of the client. It tells you who they are now, what's bothering them, how they were raised, and what you should focus on.

In some instances, you may need to give a formal diagnosis to treat the person and be compensated. People are usually given an initial or principal diagnosis. Over time, you may discover that they have more than one clinically relevant issue. Most people have more than one diagnosis — for example, it isn't unusual for someone to suffer from depression *and* anxiety. Other times, you don't need a formal diagnosis, and this information is just background information that helps you understand your client better.

Either way, you're getting very sensitive and personal information about a person. Because of this, social workers are taught to engage people in a competent, respectful, and sensitive manner. Social work graduates often express the highest confidence in their assessment skills immediately after graduation, citing it as the skill set they feel most competent in. This is very good news because conducting an assessment requires empathy and deep listening skills. You have to be attuned to what the client is saying, note their nonverbal cues, and pay attention to your own reactions.

The uses and limits of the Diagnostic and Statistical Manual of Mental Disorders

The *DSM* is one of the most universally used tools for diagnosing and understanding mental health disorders. It's the standard text for the mental health profession. The *DSM* was first developed in 1952 and has been updated over the years. The updates reflect emerging research and the latest understanding of how mental health issues present. The DSM impacts what is taught in clinical programs and what insurance companies recognize as clinical issues worth covering. The current iteration of the *DSM* is the *DSM-5-TR*, and it's 1,050 pages long.

The *DSM* classifies mental health disorders in three major sections.

>> **Section I:** Orientation and introduction to the manual, categorical and dimensional approaches to diagnosis, classification structure, cultural and structural consideration.

>> **Section II:** Diagnostic criteria and codes. This is the actual diagnosis and description of the condition.

>> **Section III:** Assessment measure, emerging measures, and conditions for further study — what's coming.

In its evolution, the *DSM* has become developmentally informed and more culturally sensitive. The American Psychiatric Association (APA), which publishes the *DSM*, has had to issue apologies for a number of issues related to the *DSM* and the mental health profession (for example, for codifying homosexuality as a mental illness and its contribution to prompting systemic inequity toward people of color and Indigenous people). These are egregious violations and have caused people tremendous pain (sometimes their own lives). Think about what it means to have a part of your sexual identity be classified as a mental disorder and to be treated a person with an illness.

The *DSM* can be considered a policy and political instrument because of the power and authority it has on deciding what counts as a mental illness and who is mentally ill. When a diagnosis is codified in the *DSM*, the mental health experts and clinicians have decided that the issue rises to the level of needing attention, research, and treatment (and reimbursement for the providers). And for some people it determines what considered is as "normal," "typical," or culturally appropriate or normative.

Whose pain and suffering gets to count? When something finally makes it into the *DSM*, people may celebrate it as a win and as a social and political recognition of their pain. This can be tricky because it means that someone's experience is finally acknowledged, but it's being acknowledged as an illness. For example, for a long time, post-traumatic stress disorder (PTSD) was not recognized as its own diagnosis. People who suffered the symptoms of PTSD were bounced around from provider to provider and given multiple diagnoses. PTSD has symptoms of depression, anxiety, and compulsive disorders, so sometimes people got all three diagnoses and were given disparate care and treatment.

The healing power of appropriate diagnosis and treatment

The *DSM* or a diagnosis codifies or makes real someone's condition. It finally puts into writing what someone has been experiencing and suffering through. Some people find diagnosis to be a labeling process that further stigmatizes the person who is experiencing the distress. People from marginalized backgrounds aren't given robust assessments and screening; as a result, they end up with very serious and harsh diagnoses without much evidence.

For example, little Black boys or Black youth are routinely labeled as having attention-deficit hyperactivity disorder (ADHD), bipolar disorder, or conduct disorder for behaviors that don't rise to those levels or are actually symptoms of trauma or PTSD. Poor diagnoses and assessments have terrible consequences that follow a person the rest of their lives.

However, an appropriate or accurate diagnosis can be positively life changing for someone. It gives a name to their experience and allows them to not internalize the shame or guilt they feel about their symptoms. When I see someone for therapy, when they do something that's consistent with their diagnosis and is baffling to them, I say, "Remember, this makes sense. You aren't crazy or bad. It's just part of the way your diagnosis or mental illness is showing up right now."

Screening tools

Diagnosing and assessing a client is a process that includes an interview. The interviewer can use an interview guide or a structured questionnaire. An interview guide can be one that the agency or clinician created or a supplementary interview form like the cultural formulation interview that specifically focuses on the client's cultural background. This interview form can be found in the back section of the *DSM*.

Clinicians also administer validated screening instruments that test for the presence of symptoms, the frequency of symptoms, and the severity of symptoms. They can then use this information to inform their diagnosis.

Because social workers are attuned to a client's whole system, they use multidimensional tools to understand the client. They usually use an *eco map* (a graphical representation of a person's social system). An eco map visually represents the person's family, kin, close friends, school, social clubs, place of worship, healthcare providers, and any other relevant information.

TIP

A holistic assessment process usually assesses and screens in the domains outlined in Table 7-1, which also includes examples of related screening tools.

TABLE 7-1   **Domains to Be Screened and Related Screening Tools**

Domain	Related Screening Tools
Depression	Beck Depression Inventory
Anxiety	Patient Health Questionnaire (PHQ), Generalized Anxiety Disorder-7 (GAD-7)
PTSD	PTSD Checklist, Clinician Administered PTSD Scale (CAPS)
Substance use disorders	Michigan Alcohol Screening Test (MAST), Drug Abuse Screening Test (DAST)
Suicide	Columbia Suicide Severity Risk Scale, Ask Suicide-Screening Questions
Childhood concerns	Child Behavior Checklist
Spirituality	Faith, Importance and Influence, Community, and Address (FICA) Spiritual History Tool
Genogram of the family	Culturagram

TIP

There isn't a standard scale for strengths, but you can use strengths-based questions to assess for areas of strength, resiliency, capacity, and hope (see Chapter 1).

Let me give you some examples of how screening and assessment tools are used. Let's say you're seeing someone who has general complaints and in the structured interview continues to give vague or unspecific descriptions of what they're experiencing. You can use one of the screening tools in Table 7-1 to ask very specific questions about the person's experience and quantify their symptoms. This is helpful for both you and your client because it gets them in the habit of thinking about exactly when and how the symptoms bother them.

Another example is a couple who comes in for treatment. You can talk to the individuals separately and the couple together. You may give them instruments that assess for conflict, cohesion, substance use, and trauma. After getting all this information, you'll have a holistic picture of what's distressing the couple and also be aware of any individual diagnoses they have.

REMEMBER

When an individual gets a diagnosis that is in line with what they're experiencing and is validating for them, it can be very healing for a number of reasons:

>> It groups their symptoms into a patterns they understand and can reference in the future.

>> It makes them feel seen and less alone.

>> It can create a community of people who share that diagnosis.

TIP

One of the things I sometimes do in counseling sessions is read the symptoms associated with a diagnosis and ask the person, "Does this match your experience?" They often tear up and say yes, it does. When they present for help, they often erroneously think there is something wrong with them or that they're too sensitive or weak. I reassure them and tell them that there is nothing wrong with them as a person or with the way they're wired — we just need to work with their diagnosis.

Sometimes their diagnosis can work in their favor, and other times it can be a barrier. For example, I had a client with an anxiety disorder who worked in risk management. Their attention to detail and ability to think about the worst outcomes made them an ideal risk officer. But when they turned that same energy or coping style to other parts of their life, like planning a vacation, they got stuck trying to manage and anticipate all the risks associated with a trip.

Having a mental health diagnosis is complex and is not necessarily just a negative experience. You can help explain the utility of a diagnosis and help your client understand the diagnosis in context.

REMEMBER

Although social workers can diagnose, assess, and treat clients, they can't do psychological testing such as personality tests, intelligence tests, neurological tests, academic achievement tests, and attention tests. Sometimes clients need these evaluations and assessment reports for various reasons (courts, schools, health-care providers). If so, you'll have to refer them to a psychologist or other appropriate professional. You can use the results of the tests to inform your work with them and add them to your diagnostic and assessment process.

The assessment process

There is an art to the assessment and screening process. You must pay attention to how you ask the questions, how you pace the questions, and your client's reactions to the questions, and you have to know when to stop the process if the client is becoming overwhelmed.

TIP

You aren't just getting information from your client — you're also modeling for them how you'll work with them. Research shows that in addition to the treatment modality, the clinician's empathic engagement determines successful outcomes. In other words, how you *are* with a client matters as much as what you're *doing* with the client.

REMEMBER

Make sure your assessment tools and process are developmentally informed and targeted to the right audience. If you work with children, your office will probably be bright, happy, and full of inviting toys, and you'll usually dress more casually and do a lot of floor work. Conversely, if your practice is geared toward adults, your office should have warm lighting and a range of comfortable seating and not be overly stimulating. You don't have to be casually dressed because you won't be expected to sit on the floor.

Assessment is a key part of the helping process, outlined in detail in Chapter 3.

Treating and Specializing

After getting a strong idea of the presenting problem, you'll determine a treatment plan with your client.

TIP

Notice I used the word *with* and not *for*. Treatment goals and interventions should always be a *joint* effort between the client and the mental health professional. Clients are the best expert on themselves, and they know their capacity much better than you do. This approach is called a *client-centered treatment plan*.

Treatment should also be focused on the presenting issue or the area that is most pressing for the client. Part of the social work professional code of ethics is that clinicians should practice within their scope and in their specialty. If something comes up that is beyond your current training, you have a few options:

>> You can seek supervision and consultation.

>> You can go to trainings on the topic.

>> You can refer the client to a group or a short-term treatment that addresses that issue.

If someone presents with a complex issue that is *significantly* beyond your scope or something you don't have the time to fully address, don't take on the client. Instead, refer the client to another trusted clinician. Don't experiment on people. Being enthusiastic is not a substitute for competence.

TIP

If you're a newly minted graduate just starting in your work, you aren't expected to be a specialist. You're usually given weekly supervision and guidance and growing in your scope of work.

REMEMBER

One reward that comes with working in the mental health area of social work is the opportunity to specialize. Over time, you'll find that as you work with an issue or population, you gain expertise. For example, you may specialize in grief and loss, substance use, or sexuality. Or you may specialize in working with a population like refugees, survivors, gender-diverse people, people of color, or children. Specializing increases job satisfaction and client engagement. Your area of specialty is exactly what they're looking for and exactly the people you want to work with. There is great professional and moral alignment.

Creating a robust client-centered plan

A successful treatment plan must be client centered. A client-centered plan considers information from the assessment and diagnostic process and thoughtfully integrates it into the next steps.

A successful treatment plan is also theory driven and uses concepts from the theory or model to shape the plan. You can't be too general or theoretically inconsistent with your plan. For example, it can't just say, "The client will get better coping skills"; something better might be, "The client will understand their core beliefs and use ABC model to work on changing their thought patterns."

Client-centered plans have the following dimensions:

>> **They include the voice of the client.** You should write in quotes exactly what the client wants. It can be as simple as "I want to get better" or something more directed like "I want to not miss so much work."

>> **It should be strengths-based and build on the client's interests and capacity.**

>> **It should reflect the client's preferences and choice.**

I had a client who was increasingly becoming more reclusive, experiencing panic attacks, and avoiding places that reminded them of their trauma. In this case, evidence-based treatment modalities for anxiety and PTSD recommend exposure-based techniques where we work on gradually or intensely having the client practice facing their fears. In this case, we would go from something that is low anxiety producing (like going out on their porch) to something high anxiety producing (like going to out to dinner at their favorite restaurant). After building rapport and doing an assessment, I told the client about exposure techniques that are ideal for working with their symptoms and asked if they would be open to creating a plan where we start with something low and move up.

I was so excited to approach them with this information because I was hot off a very expensive training with the leading expert in the field. Well, my client looked at me, smiled, and said no. They weren't open to any of this and wanted me to help them with an issue they were facing with their boyfriend. That was what was most pressing to them, not my silly scary interventions that are evidence supported. I put down my notebook and worksheets and shifted my goals to my *client's* desires. Even if I didn't think this was the best use of our time, it was critical that I engage them in the areas that *they* wanted to address. Eventually, we came back to the exposure techniques because they wanted to attend a concert and didn't want to miss out because of their anxiety. Because they trusted me to listen to them, we eventually got to work on the core issues that were causing them global problems.

Sometimes, clients are mandated into treatment and don't want to be there or have any goals besides ending the session. In these instances, you can still create client-centered goals that align with the agency's requirements for the client. You have to approach these situations using a theory that works with reluctant or mandated clients. When you use those approaches, you aren't participating in coercion or state-sponsored harm. You're being respectful of the client and their circumstances and inviting them to co-plan with you. This approach is almost the intervention itself.

Specializing in a treatment or population area

Social workers trained in mental health can specialize in a treatment modality, a population area, or both.

>> **Treatment modality:** The approach that people use to addresses the mental health issue or diagnosis. It usually requires advanced training, supervised clinical hours, and sometimes specialized tools or a manual. There are treatment approaches that are evidenced based that you will see mentioned in mental health providers bios.

>> **Population area:** The specific group you work with, like school-aged children, migrants, people who are incarcerated, or older adults.

For example, a social worker may specialize in co-occurring disorders with post-partum mothers. The population is mothers and the specialization is post-partum distress and substance use. The social worker has to have specialized knowledge on maternal health, mental health, and substance use.

TIP

For now these are some of the top treatment specializations or approaches that clinical social workers pursue, along with the population:

Treatment	Population
Cognitive behavioral therapy	Children and adults
Motivational interviewing	People with substance use disorders
Dialectical behavioral therapy	Mostly adults
Emotionally focused therapy	Couples
Multisystemic therapy	Families
Exposure therapy	Children and adults
Assertive community treatment	People who are unhoused (homeless)
Eye movement desensitization and reprocessing for trauma	Mostly adults

In addition to receiving specialized training and treatment, clinical mental health social workers develop expertise working with a particular population. This means they have depth and breadth of knowledge and practice working with a group and may exclusively work with that group because of their specialization.

What usually happens is that the social worker begins working with a group and finds their passion. They pursue specialized knowledge or evidence-based interventions that address the needs of the population. Population or subject area of specialty can span across the life span and in the community. Here are some examples:

>> Subject areas
- Addiction
- Anti-racism
- Community mental health
- Criminal justice reform
- Grief and loss
- Group practice
- Homelessness
- LGBTQIA+
- Maternity issues
- Multicultural practices
- Palliative care
- Parenting
- Refugees
- Trauma

>> Populations
- Adolescents
- Adults
- Child welfare
- Children
- Couples
- Families
- Older adults
- Survivors
- Young adults

Chapter **8**

Providing Trauma-Informed Care

I n the helping professions, including social work, trauma is a big subject. Both organizations and practitioners can focus on and be sensitive to trauma. An organization may describe itself as *trauma informed,* which means the organization is sensitive to people's past and current trauma and it will take that trauma into account when it provides service. For instance, an after-school program that provides tutoring services can say it is trauma informed because the teachers and staff have training that makes them sensitive to the backgrounds of the children they work with. (It can be hard to provide a calm environment for learning if a kid is exhibiting stress reactions that a typical math tutor doesn't know how to handle.) A *trauma specialist* works one-on-one with a child, family, or adult to address the traumatic incident and the impact it's having.

Believe it or not, most social workers *love* the topic of trauma. They want to understand it and help people heal. Laypeople look at us like we're nuts when we say we love working on this topic. But maybe this chapter will convince you to look more into this subject.

In this chapter, I explain what kinds of events count as bad enough to be considered traumatic. Then I explain how trauma impacts a person's brain, body, and relationships. Because I don't want to bum you out and leave you sad, I talk about the coolest aspect of trauma work, which is healing — it's incredible to see people come out the other side of their pain. Finally, trauma work can take a toll on the worker, so all trauma-informed work talks about self-care for the helper — as flight attendants tell you before every flight, you need to put on your own oxygen mask before helping others with theirs.

Seeing the Impacts of Trauma and Stress

Trauma has become part of the cultural lexicon. People use the term to describe their reaction to a range of events — everything from the cancellation of a favorite TV show, to the loss of a dear pet, to an interaction with a rude family member, to a pandemic. The problem is, if everyone and everything is traumatic, then nothing is traumatic. Calling everything traumatic dilutes the word and doesn't honor or acknowledge the magnitude of suffering that people who've experienced trauma face.

It's important to understand what events or experiences meet the trauma threshold so we have a common understanding of what we mean by a traumatic event or experience. A clear and full definition of a condition gives the treatment provider a good road map for the treatment process. It's also important to distinguish something that's uncomfortable or shocking for someone from something that is truly traumatic.

Understanding the difference between trauma and stress

So, what is big and bad enough to count as trauma? Is it how bad the person felt when they experienced an event? Is it how bad the event itself is? Who gets to decide if something is traumatic? Does it matter or is it all subjective? These are questions that philosophers, social scientists, and doctors have been debating for a very long time. The answers to these questions determine whose pain and suffering gets counted, who gets help, who is believed, and who is qualified to treat the injured person.

REMEMBER

How a person adapts to a situation depends on the person's stage of development, personality, life experiences, and life situation, as well as the intensity and duration of the stressor. You can think of people's experiences with hardship on a continuum that ranges from stress to trauma.

Defining stress

Currently, the discussion of trauma centers on the understanding of stress and how people cope, adapt, or succumb to it. *Stress* is defined an outside pressure or strain. Stress is an external or environmental demand and an indication of how capable the individual is to meet the outside demand. It's the relationship between the outside force and the person. For the most part, some measure of stress is necessary for humans to be challenged, adapt, and grow.

For example, let's say your New Year's resolution was to start a "couch to 5K" running plan and run a 5K. It wasn't easy, but you stuck to the plan and eventually ran the race. After the race, you realized, "Hey, I can do hard things! I'm going to sign up for a 10K race next time." This was *good* stress. It was a motivating factor, and when you overcame the challenge, you felt more confident about your future ability.

Stress has gotten a bad rap because when people talk about stress, they're really talking about toxic stress — the kind of stress that overwhelms you and exceeds your ability to cope. Graduate school and the new experiences that come with it can be stressful, but the stress is productive. Students are challenged, rise to those challenges, and grow. But for some students, the stress that accompanies the start of graduate school can become so overwhelming that it can lead to academic struggles, and in severe cases, it may even force them to discontinue their studies. When stress reaches a point where it significantly impairs or debilitates a person, it can be classified as a form of toxic stress. This kind of stress is overwhelming. It still doesn't meet the threshold for trauma, but it's an experience that overwhelms your attempts to adjust and adapt.

Defining trauma

Whereas stress can be positive (see the preceding section), trauma is always bad — there is no upside to trauma. *Trauma* is not merely experiencing a stressful event; it's experiencing an event that you perceive as life threatening and overwhelming. Trauma disrupts normal coping abilities, leaving the person feeling helpless and without control.

Trauma can be caused by "acts of God" — for example, natural disasters like hurricanes, tornados, floods, or wildfires. Trauma can also be caused by "acts of man" — for example, interpersonal trauma or harm or violence done by individuals.

There are two general types of trauma:

>> **Type I trauma:** A single event of catastrophic proportions, such as a natural disaster, a violent act, a death, or a loss or threatened loss of family, friends, and community.

>> **Type II trauma:** Chronic and repetitive abuses experienced predominantly in childhood.

Not all traumas fall into these two broad categories, though. Here are some other examples of trauma:

>> **Complex trauma or cumulative trauma:** Traumas caused by multiple factors, including interpersonal violence, neglect, or abuse.

>> **Collective trauma:** A psychological reaction to a traumatic event that affects an entire society (for example, a pandemic or a terrorist attack).

>> **Historical trauma:** Complex and collective trauma experienced over time and across generations by a group of people who share an identity or circumstance. This term is usually used to describe colonization and historic oppression of Indigenous peoples.

>> **Vicarious or secondary trauma:** The negative inner transformation of helpers who work with trauma survivors.

Trauma isn't just about how a person reacts to a difficult or uncomfortable situation. Both the event *and* the reaction to the event must be grand, and, for the most part, they must be directly experienced.

PTSD: A FORMAL DIAGNOSIS OF TRAUMA

When a person has experienced trauma and is having symptoms and reactions that are impairing their ability to function in their life, they're diagnosed with post-traumatic stress disorder (PTSD).

In order for someone to be diagnosed with PTSD, the traumatic event must involve one of the following:

- Direct exposure to actual or threatened death, serious injury, or sexual violence

- Indirect exposure for people who work in frontline work (such as rescue workers, emergency personnel, journalists, and mental-health and trauma clinicians)

People react to the traumatic incident by having symptoms that include flashbacks, avoiding people or places that remind them of the event, having a negative worldview, and being highly reactive (jumpy, easily startled, or hypervigilant).

Not all people who experience traumatic experiences go on to develop PTSD. In fact, most people can weather the event and overcome the situation with supportive friends and family. But given the magnitude of the traumatic event, it would make sense if someone developed PTSD in response to a traumatic event.

Sometimes when people with PTSD see other people who experienced the same traumatic event as they did *not* struggling the same way they're struggling, they blame themselves. They may think something is personally wrong with them or that they're weak. As a social worker, it's important to understand trauma and trauma reactions in order to help people not blame themselves or experience shame because of their PTSD.

Recognizing the impact of stress on the brain and body

One of the fundamental things you have to know if you're interested in trauma is the *stress reaction*, or what's commonly known as the *fight-or-flight response*. The way a person instinctively reacts to stress and how their brain makes sense of the stress play a huge role in how traumatic the event ends up being for them.

In the daily course of life, our brains are constantly assessing outside information and determining if we're safe or unsafe. They're assessing for stress and threat all the time. Even as you're reading these words, your body is humming along and thinking about whether you're safe or unsafe. If you're safe, your brain tells your body it's okay to proceed with your plans — keep reading. If you're unsafe, your brain alerts your body to react to the perceived threat. For example, suddenly someone or something dangerous enters the room — your brain alerts your body and tells it, "Hey, you aren't safe. You should do something." This process of digesting external information (the threat) and preparing for rest or action is a regulatory function of our bodies.

When your body faces a dangerous situation there are four automatic reactions that can get activated:

>> **Fight:** The instinct to attack the threat. For example, if you're hiking in the woods, and you come across a small bear, your first reaction may be to fight the bear. It's a small bear, and maybe you can overtake it and live to tell the tale. I wouldn't recommend this approach, but as I said, it's automatic and reflexive. Fighters fight.

>> **Flight:** The instinct to run away from the threat. On that same hike, when you encounter the bear, your first reaction may be to run! Technically, this isn't the best approach either — the bear is likely faster than you are, and when you run, it'll likely chase.

>> **Freeze:** The instinct to become immobile or play dead. This reaction is an evolutionary mammalian reaction. When a predator animal perceives the prey as dead, it may stop attacking the prey and release it from its grip, giving the prey the opportunity to escape. In the same manner, humans sometimes freeze to survive a dangerous encounter and appear to be less of a threat to the attacker. On the hike, your instinct may be to freeze and hope the bear walks right by you in search of a pot of honey.

>> **Appease:** The instinct to placate the attacker in some way. With the bear, your instinct may be to give it snacks or pet it or do something to indicate you're not a threat. Similar to freezing, your goal is to survive the encounter. People who are kidnapped or in prolonged hostage situations must appease their abductors or abusers to survive. This leaves profound psychological wounds and takes work for the person to have self-compassion and not feel shame.

REMEMBER

People and society have judgments about a person's reaction to a traumatic encounter. We romanticize fighters — we hail them as heroes and read news stories on their extraordinary abilities. We don't usually see news stories about people who flee, freeze, or, even worse, appease. We make judgments about why they didn't do something sooner or faster, or why they stayed in terrible situations. The reality is, people's reactions are what they are, and there is no right or wrong way to react. The first part of working with trauma survivors is to explain these reactions and normalize the individual responses.

REMEMBER

A person's reaction to stress is automatic and reflexive. You can't help your automatic reactions — by definition, they're automatic. Survivors may feel guilty that they weren't fighters or that they froze in reaction to an attack. But no one should judge automatic reactions. What's important is surviving the event and giving your body a break to rest and process the encounter — a process called *rest and digest*. Resting gives your body the opportunity to record the event in your brain and move the information to the higher-processing part of the brain. For example, after surviving an encounter with a bear, you might do something different next time, like taking a different route, bringing bear spray with you to stay safe, or becoming a bear tracker so you're never the prey.

In the case of a traumatic encounter, the person is overwhelmed by the traumatic reaction, and the stress reaction is highjacked. The information isn't fully processed. In many ways, it haunts the survivor. The memory comes back in the form of flashbacks or dreams. The person may constantly be "on" or have a fight-or-flight reaction to events that aren't stressful. It's as though they think they're constantly under threat. They don't think of the traumatic event as something in the past — they think of it as something that just occurred. This often impacts people's ability to sleep, and disrupted sleep can lead to irritable behavior. Some folks need a break from these symptoms and may do self-harming but temporarily self-soothing behaviors like drinking excessively or misusing drugs. Trauma also impacts the way a person sees themselves, their relationships with other people, and the world in general.

Looking at how trauma affects relationships

When someone experiences a traumatic event, it challenges the way they see the world and others. It impacts the meaning that a person attributes to what happened, a process aptly called the *meaning-making process*. Trauma shatters a person's sense of a predictable world, one that's relatively safe and in which the people in their lives are safe. Big existential questions arise: Why me? Why now? Where was God? Is there a God? Why do bad things happen to good people? Is there a point to any of this, or is it all meaningless?

The source of the injury is an important factor in how people process the traumatic event. Here are the three main sources of trauma:

>> **Acts of God:** If the source is an "act of God" (meaning, a natural disaster or a disease), a person may feel singled out or personally and unjustly targeted to suffer. It may cause them to question their fundamental beliefs about their faith. What was once a source of personal solace is no longer comforting, and this impacts how they cope.

>> **Acts of man:** Another source of injury could be an "act of man," or something between people. When a person is attacked or injured, it's usually (but not always) by someone they know or someone in close proximity to them. If the victim is a child, they often mistakenly blame themselves for the harm and suffer a great deal of shame. If the victim is an adult, they can also self-blame, but often they feel betrayed and perplexed by the encounter or injury. They question their judgment and ability to make sound decisions and wonder if they know anything at all.

>> **The environment a person is exposed to:** For example, a person can live in an under-resourced area with lots of gun violence, or in a political condition where there are acts of terror and statelessness, or in a climate where there is pervasive oppression and prejudice. In these situations, an individual may feel safe in their own home or when they're with their family and friends — they may not describe their lives as full of trauma. But even if they don't describe their lives as full of trauma, they live in dangerous conditions that keep their nervous system on constant alert. Their bodies are on constant alert, even if their brains are not. This has a wear-and-tear effect on the person long-term and can lead to early death or accelerate the aging process.

You can't outthink or outtrick the body. That's why even the toughest people have to seek treatment eventually — they can't outwit or outrun their trauma.

REMEMBER

Whatever the source of the injury, these encounters with the stressors can make a person feel hopeless and helpless and flood them with negative feelings that can sometimes turn into a negative worldview. This is called a *depressive state*, and it usually follows this pattern: This stinks, I stink, the world stinks, and it's all going to keep on stinking. And because everything stinks and isn't going to get any better, I'm going to act like a stinker and do not-so-good things to myself and to the people I see and love.

A person who is feeling this badly may act out this depressed and anxious state by:

>> **Having unstable moods:** When someone feels everything, feels nothing, or can't modulate or control their emotional reactions. People describe it like being on a roller coaster.

>> **Engaging in addictive and compulsive behaviors:** When people self-medicate or self-soothe by abusing substances like alcohol or drugs. People can also do self-destructive behaviors like cutting or harming their bodies.

>> **Communicating poorly:** When someone blows up or is silent when they should speak up.

>> **Feeling hopeless and helpless:** When someone feels like things will never get better and that there is nothing they can do about their life circumstances or emotions.

>> **Being hostile or violent toward themselves and others:** When someone tries to harm themselves or others.

>> **Impaired parenting:** When someone's parenting is compromised because their trauma symptoms are getting in the way. For example, they may lose their temper often or they may not be able to emotionally connect with their child.

Initially, friends and loved ones may be understanding and patient with someone as they cycle through these reactions and behaviors. However, if the unpredictable and negative behaviors persist or become entrenched in a person's character or personality, they'll start losing key relationships and roles. They may elect to come into treatment at this point; they may be ordered into treatment by their employer; or their partner may give them an ultimatum. Trained trauma providers will do an assessment or screening and help the person understand how the trauma has impacted their life and what steps they can take to heal from it.

Assessing and Treating Trauma

When a person comes for treatment of trauma, an assessment or screening is done to determine the severity of the symptoms. Then a treatment plan is devised to address the condition. The situation, the environment, the person's age, their stress response, and their support structure are all critical components of the assessment. A trained clinician has to understand the origin of the trauma and be able to give a thoughtful and targeted intervention. That means they should have a working knowledge of how much the adverse experiences have impacted the person over time. It's also important for clinicians to know the difference between a child's response to trauma and an adult's response to trauma.

Understanding how adverse childhood experiences impact people

In the stress and trauma literature, you'll come across a very significant study called the Adverse Childhood Experiences (ACE) Study, which demonstrated the relationship between stress, trauma, development, and health. The ACE Study was one of the largest studies of its kind. It asked adults questions about their health and their exposure to adverse childhood experiences. In this section, I briefly describe the study because it was a *huge* deal in the trauma world and codified the types of things we should consider in the screening and assessment process.

For the study, the researchers defined *adverse childhood experiences* as "psychological, physical, or sexual abuse; violence against mother; or living with household members who were substance abusers, mentally ill or suicidal, or ever imprisoned." The respondents were asked questions about their health and medical history. The analysis of the results revealed that people with more incidents of adverse childhood experiences were at greater risk of chronic diseases and mental health problems like depression, anxiety, PTSD, and risky behaviors. The greater the number of adverse childhood experiences, the higher the probability of having complex health and mental problems across their lives.

Even more significantly, people who experienced more adverse childhood experiences were more likely to need the services of multiple public services like special education, child protective services, mental health services, and criminal justice services. So, what and how much happens to you really matters.

REMEMBER

The ACE Study is considered a landmark study because it clearly demonstrated that traumatic experiences don't exclusively impact a person's psychological state — they impact a person's entire life and even their mortality rate. The younger you are when traumatic things happen to you, the worse off you may be if you don't have good support.

What the study also showed is that if people who've experienced trauma (especially children) receive good treatment, it can prevent a whole host of health and social problems down the road. Because of the ACE Study, many researchers and clinicians were able to get research and treatment inventions started by significant funders like the Veterans Administration (VA), the Centers for Disease Control and Prevention (CDC), and the National Institutes of Health (NIH).

To learn more about the ACE Study, head to www.ajpmonline.org/article/S0749-3797(98)00017-8/fulltext.

Assessing trauma in children

Children and adults manifest their trauma symptoms differently. Kids aren't just "little adults." How a child reacts to things varies depending on their age. This is called *developmental distinction* — there is a difference between how a 1-year-old and a 3-year-old reacts, and there is a difference between how a 3-year-old and a 6-year-old reacts.

When children are exposed to trauma, they may be too young to express their trauma in words. Depending on their age, they'll express their distress through age-related behaviors. In most cases, they'll demonstrate their trauma through behaviors such as play activities or the lack of play, how they relate to their peers, and how they relate to their caregivers. Because children may lack the ability to verbally describe what they're worried about, they may have recurrent, involuntary, and intrusive recollections of the event. It may show up in their play or in their dreams.

For example, they may have nightmares related to the event and have difficulty falling asleep because falling asleep is too scary. Their play may be centered exclusively on the event, such as drawing the event, acting out the event, or bringing up aspects of the event to the people they come into contact with over and over. They may tell the grocery store clerk, another child at the park, or someone at temple about the traumatic event. They indiscriminately share information because it preoccupies most of their thinking. A parent may feel embarrassed or baffled by this oversharing, but this is normal until the child has the tools to deal with the trauma.

Here's how trauma reactions are manifested from very young children to older kids:

>> **Preschool:** They may show signs of traumatic stress by having separation anxiety, crying outbursts unrelated to an event, poor eating patterns, and nightmares.

>> **Elementary school:** As they progress through school kids may have a hard time concentrating or paying attention, they may refuse to go to school (because they're afraid of separating from their parent), and continue to have a hard time sleeping.

>> **Middle school and high school:** They may develop depressive or anxious symptoms, began using or abusing drugs or alcohol, and become involved in risky or self-harming behaviors.

Across the developmental spectrum, these behaviors can be off-putting to peers and socially isolating. It may push them to spend time with other kids who engage in risky or nonhelpful behaviors — that may be the space where they feel understood.

With this knowledge in mind, when assessing for trauma, clinicians usually ask about the history of the exposure to trauma (what kinds of difficult things the child experienced) and the symptoms related to the exposure (how they reacted to the event). Trauma studies have proliferated, so many instruments have been developed to measure the incident and impact of trauma. They're categorized by age range, type of trauma, and reactions to the trauma.

REMEMBER

You wouldn't use the same tool for a 3-year-old as you would for a 15-year-old. What's important is that the assessment tools help capture what's happening in the life of the person and help create a treatment plan that responds to what you discovered through the assessment.

For children, involving caregivers and family members in the treatment process is critical. It starts by doing psychoeducation for parents and caregivers on how trauma impacts the child's life.

Helping parents understand the impact of trauma in their children's lives

The usual parenting guides and tips on addressing problematic behaviors may not work for kids who have experienced trauma. That's because a child having a trauma reaction to something is different from a child who's just pushing the limits.

Kids' reactions to trauma can be perplexing and troubling to parents or caregivers. For instance, when children are adopted or saved from abusive situations and are placed in calm settings, they don't instantly calm down. Their nervous systems take a while — months or even years, depending on how severe their abuse was — to calm down. Parents may be too lenient or too punitive because they feel like they have to protect the child from themselves or feel guilty that the child experienced a trauma. Or the parents may have experienced the trauma at the same time as the child or been a survivor of another traumatic event, and they may have poor coping or parenting capacities and injure or neglect the child.

TIP

Giving a parent basic and critical information about how trauma impacts a child's sense of safety and their behavior will help demystify the child's erratic or big emotional or behavioral outbursts. This usually leads a parent to be more patient and mindful of their own reactions to their child's behavior. A parent can help their child by understanding what's triggering or activating the child.

For example, if a child experienced a terrible car accident, they may be triggered by sirens or may take a long time to get into a car. As the social worker gleans more information about the traumatic event, they can help decode what may be triggering to the child and give a heads-up to the parent. Parents can plan around the trigger and help the child eventually face the trigger with the help of a trained social worker. The goal is for the child to be able to be happy and not haunted by the incident and have fewer reactions to things that remind them of the incident.

The parent's emotional attunement to the child's inner world is critical. The parent needs to be emotionally and physically available to the child in a consistent and predictable manner, no matter how the child behaves. This is essential. Even when the child is throwing fits or withdrawing, the parent needs to find ways to comfort and connect with the child. It's normal for a child to push and pull and be all over the place after going through something tough. A parent can create a predicable environment that has regular routines for meals, playtime, and bedtime, and they can make sure to announce any changes to that routine. This will help create a rhythm in the house that says, "Even if you feel distressed and dysregulated, we have a baseline structure that can help you be soothed and grounded."

An emotionally available and responsive parent gives the grieving child the opportunity to feel all their feelings without judgment, but a parent doesn't have to be a perfect saint who never gets tired or feels frustrated by all these reactions. In fact, one of the things the social worker should share with parents is that they *will* feel tired and drained. The parent should have planned breaks and supports for themselves.

REMEMBER

After the parent and the child understand their triggers, reactions, and feelings, the parent can help the child gain positive experiences and healthy coping skills for the future. They can give the child opportunities to experience joy with activities that the child is interested in and likes. This allows the child to experience happiness and feel some control over their life. It also gives them a chance to master something and feel good in their body. Trauma can have a deep impact on the child's well-being, but it doesn't have to be deterministic. Many kids overcome trauma symptoms with the support of family, friends, and social workers who are trained in the treatment of trauma.

Treating trauma

There are many evidence-based treatments for trauma symptoms for kids and adults. They range from short-term symptom relief interventions to long-term interventions that really dive into the trauma narrative. Regardless of the length of the treatment models, the essential components of trauma treatment include the following steps:

1. **Perform trauma screening and assessment.**

   Treatment starts with screening and assessment. That answers the basic question, "What happened?" You have to ask people what happened to them and really listen and believe them when they tell you. Trauma work means believing victims.

2. **Educate the person on the impact of trauma on the body and brain.**

   After you hear what happened to the person, you help the person understand how this stress and trauma impacted their nervous system and how they think about the world. Many of the people I work with are constantly on edge, even when there is no stress or threat because their response to neutral stuff is extraordinary. In other words, they always feel and act as though there is a bear in the room ready to eat them up. They drive themselves and the people around them nuts because they seem like they're just "too much." Part of trauma work is explaining and normalizing these or other types of reactions that clinicians see in trauma survivors.

3. **Help the person build skills and use techniques to regulate their emotions.**

   In this step, you get into part of the work where you help people deal with their reactions. We call this skill building and emotional regulation. You give them skills to calm or soothe their own bodies. You teach them how to not freak out and how to not be freaked out by their reactions.

   For some people this could be the end of treatment — they understand their condition and they have tools to manage their symptoms. Other people want to process the traumatic event and not just tolerate the symptoms — they want to work through the trauma story and not be haunted by it. In that case, you proceed to the next step.

4. **Help the person tell their own trauma narrative.**

   The trauma specialist uses evidence-based or scientifically supported approaches to help the person process the trauma narrative. This has to be thoughtfully done by a trained expert. Otherwise, you end up opening very painful wounds and making the person worse than they were before.

For trauma survivors, memories are like live electric wires. Their memories are very real to them, and talking about their past means reliving it. So, working through the trauma narrative requires skill, training, and care.

When the person is able to work through the trauma narrative, they're able to heal from the incident. They're no longer organizing their reactions and life around the trauma. They don't live their lives as though there is a bear in the room all time. Imagine the relief that must be and what else you could be doing if you felt like the whole world wasn't out to devour you!

5. Give the person problem-solving skills.

Trauma survivors may require assistance in developing problem-solving skills, especially during times of stress. Problem solving is a multifaceted process, and when someone is dealing with trauma or experiencing trauma-related symptoms, they can become trapped in the overwhelming emotions tied to their traumatic experiences. Clinical professionals play a crucial role in helping individuals process these emotions, equipping them with coping strategies for when symptoms resurface, and guiding them in logically working through solutions that are tailored to their needs.

Trauma causes tremendous injury and can leave people feeling low and hopeless, but don't give up. People have tremendous capacity to grow and heal, and that's what makes trauma work so profoundly satisfying! Plus, the area of trauma work has gained tremendous popularity and research in the past 30 years. That means people understand the symptoms of trauma much better and are coming up with better and more targeted interventions. People don't have to live in pain forever. There are great treatments — in fact, you could go broke getting all the certifications available.

Some of the most researched and popular treatment modalities include the following:

>> **Trauma-focused cognitive behavioral therapy (CBT) for adults and children:** A structured therapy that helps individuals reframe negative thought patterns and develop healthier coping mechanisms after experiencing trauma.

>> **Narrative therapy:** A therapeutic approach that encourages individuals to explore and rewrite their life stories, providing a fresh perspective on past traumatic events.

>> **Exposure therapy:** Gradual and controlled exposure to traumatic memories or triggers to reduce emotional distress and desensitize individuals to their trauma-related fears.

>> **Dialectical behavioral therapy:** A therapy combining cognitive and mindfulness techniques to help individuals manage intense emotions and develop healthier emotional regulation strategies after trauma.

>> **Eye movement and desensitization therapy:** A technique that involves guided eye movements to help individuals process traumatic memories and alleviate associated distress.

>> **Medication-assisted therapy:** Treatment that combines therapy with medications to alleviate trauma-related symptoms, particularly when substance use disorders are involved.

>> **Internal family systems therapy:** A therapeutic approach that explores the different aspects of an individual's personality to heal and integrate fragmented parts affected by trauma.

>> **Group therapy:** A supportive environment where individuals share experiences, coping strategies, and support, fostering healing and resilience through shared connections.

>> **Integrated therapies:** A comprehensive approach that combines substance use disorder treatment with trauma therapy to address the interplay between these issues and promote recovery.

All these treatment models mean that there is really good help for people in pain. They don't have to suffer, and there *is* a path to healing. In order to get certification in these modalities, you would need to get your master of social work (MSW) degree, and then go through monthslong training and supervision to qualify for the certification.

In each of these treatment modalities, healing usually occurs in stages, where a person first shares their story from beginning to middle to end. They then process the grief and loss associated with the trauma. After that, they begin to integrate what happened to them as something that occurred in the past and not as something that is haunting or controlling their current life. They begin to have fewer symptoms, experience positive emotions, reconnect with people and activities they loved, and maybe even have a greater appreciation for life.

Taking Care of Yourself When You're Treating People with Trauma

When working with trauma survivors or in frontline social work, workers need to be mindful about their own mental and physical health and find ways to mitigate the stress involved in this type of work. If you have good supports in place, the work can be extremely gratifying and make you feel like you're responding to a calling or doing work that has inherent value. On the other hand, if you don't have healthy supports or coping skills, repeated exposure to distressing clients and information can create personal vulnerabilities called *secondary trauma, vicarious trauma,* or *compassion fatigue.*

Vicarious or secondary trauma occurs when the worker has symptoms that mirror the trauma survivor's symptoms. They feel jumpy, have intrusive thoughts about the things they're hearing, or start feeling numb or disassociated. They start losing their ability to empathically connect with the survivor. They find themselves feeling disconnected from the work and find the work is disrupting their own worldview. Vicarious or secondary trauma doesn't always happen, but it can be an occupational hazard.

Additionally, some folks who enter the helping profession may have experienced trauma of their own or overcome very difficult experiences. (This may be what motivated them to enter the profession in the first place.) The shared experiences they have with the clients they serve may trigger them when they're actively working with survivors and may impair their ability to provide the best service. The worker can have a reaction that may be temporary exhaustion or something much more intense like psychological burnout.

WARNING

Burnout is characterized by long-term exhaustion, disconnection, and a deep sense of hopelessness. Instead of ushering in healing and change, the helper becomes disconnected, may be punitive or harsh with clients, and may end up leaving the job or profession because they can't bear to do the work. Very good and talented people who have the potential to have lasting impact may leave the work and profession prematurely. And they spend a good deal of time getting training to do this type of work in the first place.

The good news is that there are factors that can protect workers who do this work and evidence-based strategies that can buffer stress related to trauma work. Two of the most important things that can help workers — especially young or new workers — are training and supervision:

>> **Training:** Quality training gives workers the knowledge, skills, and tools to be effective in their helping role. It increases their expertise and sense of ability to enact change. It also allows them to not be overwhelmed by intense or complex cases because they have the skills to address the symptoms they're seeing. It's also fun to continue to grow in your passion area — you get the chance to meet people who are also passionate about this work and create a supportive culture of peer professionals.

>> **Supervision:** Quality supervision gives folks moral and practical support. Good supervisors check on the well-being of their workers and offer insights and solutions. They need to do both things to be effective. A nice but not so bright supervisor won't ultimately help a vulnerable worker. They end up commiserating with the worker and making them feel like there really is no remedy for their problem. On the other hand, a supervisor who understands the tasks affiliated with the job but is emotionally unresponsive or unsupportive can contribute to a worker's feelings of emotional exhaustion.

Given the intense nature of working with trauma and stress, workers need to feel like the place they work at cares about them and wants what is best for them. This type of work is not transactional. It's emotionally, psychologically, and spiritually challenging, and having the moral support of the workplace and supervisor goes a long way toward helping workers stay and do the good but hard work.

Recognizing the importance of self-care for maintaining your job satisfaction

Similar to the popularity of trauma-informed work, self-care has gotten a lot of attention in popular culture lately. This is a good thing. People are living harried lives and are breathless and worn out. Self-care or well-being activities keep a person grounded and connected to the things that personally nourish them.

WARNING

As with all things popular, self-care has been commodified and monetized. People have come to think of self-care activities as pampering yourself and spending money on luxurious things. These activities are fun and indulgent, but they won't have sustaining power. For some people, they may even financially compromise them or make them think the only way they can take care of themselves is by spending money they don't really have.

TIP

The self-care component of those expensive or luxurious activities may actually be the social time or the alone time spent doing those things. And those things you can do without spending money or only when you're feeling low or prickly.

Some very good research has been done on well-being practices that help increase job satisfaction and overall happiness. The research indicates that devising a personal self-care plan that is personally meaningful and mitigates stress is best.

Creating a robust self-care plan

The most important component of a self-care plan is having some self-knowledge. You must take an inventory of your life and think about what you personally find meaningful and nourishing. Sometimes people confuse self-care planning with self-help or self-improvement planning. They think of it like writing New Year's resolutions. Then they create a plan that ends up making them feel guilty for not doing the planned activity or, worse yet, derive no joy from the activity.

For instance, most people know that healthy eating habits and physical activity are good for them. So, typical self-improvement plans include eating less and moving more. Unfortunately, these tend to be deprivation- and guilt-based models. People buy big fancy exercise equipment or create meal plans that are low in calories or just end up eating cabbage soup all day. Then the equipment ends up collecting dust, and the meal plans get left behind. This is because the plan was centered on doing something positive but ultimately wasn't connected to what's personally meaningful. And let's face it: How much cabbage soup can one person eat?

This is why the self-inventory is important. Think about what makes you feel calm, brings you joy, or makes you feel connected to yourself. The following domains can guide your thinking about what is personally meaningful to you:

>> Biological

- Getting enough sleep

- Having adequate nutrition and meals

- Exercising or engaging in physical activity

>> Psychological

- Finding a work-play balance

- Getting effective relaxation

- Connecting with nature

- Managing your time effectively

>> Interpersonal

- Getting social support

- Getting peer support

- Getting supervision and consultation

- Getting supervision

>> Spiritual

- Engaging in self-reflection

- Meditating

- Finding spiritual connection to a community

- Cultivating hope and optimism

From these domains, pick an area that you know is important to you or necessary for you to function at your best. Are you a person who *must* get a full night's rest, eat breakfast, spend time with the people you love, get continuous learning, have things written out and planned so you aren't overwhelmed or anxious, have contact with nature, or spend time doing meditation or self-reflection? Think about what's a *must* in order for you to be a functioning, happy person.

Most people think they should put exercise or good diet as their self-care plan when those things might not actually be as important for them personally. Sure, working out and eating well are good, but they may not be the things that make you feel connected and grounded. The activity you need may be getting a good night's sleep or eating breakfast.

When you know which area means the most to you, create a plan for implementing the activity in your life on a consistent and manageable basis using the following steps:

1. **Review your past attempts to meet a goal and analyze what was helpful and what was a stumbling block.**

   - What went well in the past that helped you do this activity?

   - What prevented you or got in the way of your doing the activity?

   - What resources do you need to do the activity?

   - How long do you need to do the activity to have good outcomes?

2. **Determine how you'll implement your goal this time around.**

   Detail exactly how you'll do the activity. Think about what got in the way or helped you do the activity in the past. Include the lessons learned from Step 1 into your implementation. For example, if your goal is to connect with nature, your plan may look like something like this:

   I will go for a walk during my lunch break for 15 minutes on Monday, Wednesday, and Friday. I will look at the weather forecast those days and bring appropriate shoes and outwear to do this.

   Maybe you stopped doing the activity in the past because you thought connecting with nature as taking long hikes on the weekend. But then you remembered that you felt good when you spent time in the park across the street from your office.

   If you walk for 15 minutes, it gives you time to eat your lunch, stretch your legs, and get some fresh air. You can still do long hikes on the weekend if you have time. But this small, consistent weekly activity will help sustain your daily life.

Being very modest with your goals is best because you need quick wins in the beginning in order to build momentum.

Here are some other examples of implementing goals:

- If you want to exercise, don't plan on exercising for an hour five days a week unless you're already doing that. Think about maybe getting some kind of physical activity two or three days a week.

- If you like meditation or self-reflection, think about doing an activity for 10 minutes or so a few days a week or even once a week and gradually do it more often.

3. Share the plan.

Sharing a plan makes it real. Research shows that people who write down their plan and share it are more likely to stick to it.

REMEMBER

Be thoughtful about who you share your plan with. Share it with someone who will champion your plan and encourage you. Don't share it with someone who is a naysayer or punitive. You want someone who is in your corner and will celebrate with you or say, "Let's try again" when you veer off plan.

4. Monitor the plan.

Monitoring means you keep an eye on your activity and have a way of keeping track of it. It usually means putting the activity on your daily planner or calendar and carving out time in your schedule for it like it's a job — the job of taking care of yourself.

5. Notice and appreciate changes.

After creating, implementing, and sticking to a plan, take a moment to reflect on the process and appreciate this connection. This is a beautiful thing, and it's good to pause and notice.

Identifying the signs and symptoms of exhaustion and burnout

Sometimes, a self-care plan isn't enough. The intensity of workplace stress or the magnitude of the trauma you're exposed to may be too much. The signs and symptoms that you may need professional help and support include the following:

» Feeling emotionally numb

» Reliving the trauma your clients experience

» Having trouble sleeping

>> When you do sleep, having disturbing dreams

>> Having little interest or taking little joy in the work you used to love

>> Feeling irritable

>> Not being able to focus or having a foggy brain

>> Wanting to avoid work

>> Feeling discouraged about the future

WARNING

These are major symptoms of secondary trauma and mean that you need to pause and take a break from work, if you can, and get some mental health support. Just as the clients you serve need a place to talk through and process what happened to them, you need a place to unpack some of what you've been carrying. Reevaluate what aspects of the job you need to address so you can go back to what you love to do. In some cases, you may need to pivot and do different types of work or realize you need more training and support. What's important is that you address the issue and put on your oxygen mask so you can help others.

Chapter **9**

Helping People Overcome Substance Use and Addiction

Whether you're interested in helping people with addiction, or you think it's for other people to work on, this chapter is for you. Addiction is essential knowledge for *anyone* who wants to be in a helping profession because we often come across people who use and misuse substances, whether they're coming to us to address these issues or not. In fact, we often work with people who struggle with mental health issues *and* substance use issues.

Many social workers may initially perceive substance use and addiction as unrelated or unimportant to their field. However, this social issue is often intricately linked to various aspects of social work practice. Plus, knowing about substance use and addiction can significantly enhance your effectiveness as a social worker.

In 2021, according to the National Center for Drug Abuse Statistics (NCDAS), 41 percent of all Americans drank alcohol and, of those people, 20 percent have alcohol use disorder. Similarly, 50 percent of people report having used illicit drugs in their lifetime, but 25 percent of people who use illicit drugs end up developing dependency and addiction. Beyond illicit or illegal drugs, of the total people who have drug use problems, 25 percent have opioid disorder, which includes painkillers and heroin. And with the use of drugs comes drug-related deaths, mostly in the form of overdose: In 2022, more than 106,000 people died from drug-involved overdose.

These numbers and rates indicate that substance use is an area that needs attention. The opioid epidemic in the United States is destroying entire communities and generations of families.

Soon after becoming a social worker, I realized that I had to have strong knowledge in this area. In this chapter, I share some of my knowledge with you. I start by clarifying terms and definitions. I cover the current thinking on why addiction occurs. I also discuss how people developing severe use or addiction and the major classes of drugs. Then I end on a high note (no pun intended) by discussing treatment for substance use.

Addiction, Substance Abuse, Substance Use: Why Language Matters

The language we use to describe a condition or group of people matters. It can box people in or make people feel seen. It can give insight into a condition or *pathologize* (view as abnormal) or further *problematize* (treat as a problem) the condition. Words not only have the power to hurt, but also can create and define reality.

Understanding the language used to describe the world of addiction is important, because there is a lot of *stigma* (negative attitudes and stereotypes about a group) affiliated with substance use and people who use substances. These negative attitudes and stereotypes turn into negative interactions. And these negative interactions make a huge difference in the life of someone seeking help. If they're treated inhumanely or with bias, they're likely to refrain from seeking more help and only get sicker.

For society, stigma impacts who we think is deserving and (not deserving) of help. When we think someone is worthy of help, we channel funds to the cause and deem it a moral imperative. When we don't think someone is deserving of help, we punish them, usually in the form of incarceration or refusing them help and blaming them for their failings.

In this section, I walk you through the language of addiction, as it stands today, so you're sure not to do any harm with the words you use.

Language is constantly evolving. What's sensitive and appropriate as I write this book may not be sensitive and appropriate down the road. If you're not sure about the language surrounding addiction (or any other issue, for that matter), talk with your peers and supervisors in the social work profession.

Tracking the evolution of language

People who are struggling with overusing and/or depending on substances have been called *weak, indulgent, sick, addicts*, and *nuisances*. These harsh labels are a way of keeping them at arm's length and making it obvious they're not like *us* — after all, *we* would never be caught in such a condition. (Never mind that we probably have addictions of our own that may be socially sanctioned — I'm talking to all you caffeine drinkers out there.) People who struggle with substance use disorder are keenly aware of how other people see them, and it makes them reluctant to get help.

Beyond being unpleasant, negative language creates stigma, and stigma has enduring psychological and social costs. Research shows that when treatment providers used the term *substance abuser* versus *someone who has a substance use disorder*, they were less likely to offer options and were more punitive in their approaches toward the person.

What's the difference between the two terms? It's the difference between using person-first or identity-first language and using characterological language. *Person-first language* separates the condition from the character of the person. It avoids using adjectives to define someone. It describes the person as *having* a condition rather *being* the condition. For instance, a person uses or misuses substances — they are not an abuser or an addict. It also denotes a relationship with the substance and the person as opposed to something being characterological or endemic to the person. Saying someone *has* a condition instead of *being* the condition sets a neutral tone and distinguishes the person from their diagnosis.

In 2013, the *Diagnostic and Statistical Manual of Mental Disorders* (DSM), the handbook used by health-care professionals for the diagnosis of mental health conditions, which includes substance use, did away with the terms *abuse* and *dependence* and adopted the term *use*. For example, someone has *alcohol use disorder* or *opiate use disorder*. It also conceptualized addiction as being on a spectrum, with severity ranging from mild to moderate to severe. In other words, use occurs on a continuum.

The term *substances* refers to things like alcohol and drugs, whether they're legal or illegal. *Substance use* refers to the ingestion of substances.

Substance use can occur once or repeatedly over a lifetime. How much a person is using can have very little impact or a significant impact on their life. You can use or try something once, occasionally, recreationally, or chronically. Simply using something does not denote a disorder, even if the substance you're using is illegal.

A few years ago, we used the term *abuse* — we said someone had a *substance abuse problem. Abuse* meant that the person was using drugs and alcohol with regularity and it was having negative consequences in their life. The shift to *substance use disorder* along with a description of the frequency of use avoids the negative association of *abuse*.

TECHNICAL STUFF

This shift from *abuse* to *use* was due to research that showed that when people used the term *abuse* or *abuser* to describe the level of use, they ended up having negative and hostile views of the patient. The very words they were using to describe the condition impacted how they felt and saw the client.

Prior to the word *abuse*, the term *chemical dependency* or *addiction* was used to describe substance use disorder. Dependency meant that someone was using substances daily and the use was resulting in a physical and psychological need for the substance as a matter of survival. The addicted person was fully absorbed by the need to use drugs.

TIP

You may still use the term *addiction* to describe the field, but you shouldn't use the term *addicts* to refer to the people who are using substances. In other words, people *use substances* or have *substance use disorder*, and health professionals can do *addiction research.*

In addition to substances, there are non-substance-related but behaviorally addictive disorders that are categorized as *process addictions*. These are conditions that focus on the behaviors, which are characterized as compulsive and often impulsive — people engage in the behaviors despite the consequences. The behaviors (for example, shopping or gambling) are similar to using a substance in that the person exposes themselves to the behavior, and that interaction alters their mood. They feel pleasure or "normal" when they do the behavior, even when they know it's causing significant harm to them.

A process addiction that the DSM formally recognizes is *gambling disorder*. Scientific research supports the idea that gambling disorder uses the same reward pattern in the brain that is seen with substance use disorders. Other process addictions that you'll hear folks discuss are around the following areas: exercise, food, gaming, sex, shopping, and internet use. In the near future, these behaviors will most likely be codified and formalized into a category of sorts in the DSM.

If you're looking for a quick guide to language surrounding addiction, here you go:

Instead of this . . .	Say this . . .
A drug abuser, alcoholic, addict, or drunk	A person with substance use disorder
Failed a drug test	Tested positive for THC
Habit	Substance use disorder
Abuses	Uses
Former addict	A person in recovery, a person who is no longer drinking or using drugs
A baby born to parents who used drugs	Addicted baby

Considering who we think deserves help

Now that you understand the basic terms, let's turn to the people who are using substances and talk about how to help them. The stance or approach to help is motivated by our understanding of why the problem occurs. Does it occur because of a character flaw, poor coping skills, bad behavior, traumas, biology, genetics, or social problems? Where is the problem located, and what do we do with folks who need help? The answer to these questions colors our view on who we think deserves help.

Four major approaches or models try to explain addiction and what we should do to solve the problem:

» **Moral model:** The oldest and, in my opinion, the most problematic model is the moral model. This model asserts that addiction stems from poor and immoral personal decision making. In other words, there is a flaw or character weakness that leads to intentionally poor behavior and decision making. Given the intentional aspect of the problematic behavior, it makes sense to punish the person exhibiting this behavior. The moral model also lends itself to derogatory and stereotypical social labels, such as *drunk, dope fiend, junkie,* and *crackhead.* There are significant demographic (gender, race, class, sexuality) associations with these horrible labels — just think about what "junkies" or "crackheads" look like on TV.

The moral model is the pervasive cultural model and leads to poor policies and programming. Legislators promote or implement programs that try to scare or shame people into getting sober and have huge consequences when people relapse. Relapse is seen as a further indicator of moral failing. Messages around morality also get internalized by folks who need help, so they try to hide their use, are reluctant to ask for help, and in some cases, die from not getting help.

>> **Spiritual model:** Another model that's pretty popular is the spiritual model. This model doesn't really care what *caused* the addiction, but it offers a spiritual solution to the problem. You're probably familiar with 12-step programs, such as Alcoholics Anonymous, which promote community, surrendering to a higher power, and abstinence as the mode for healing — these programs fall under the spiritual model. Many people find this model helpful because of the community and relational nature of the intervention. On the upside, there is radical acceptance of the person who shows up — everyone is welcome and worthy of help — and relapse is normalized. On the downside, the person has to admit they're not in control of themselves and they need all the help they can get, which is tied to morality.

>> **Medical, biological, and disease model:** In this model, which is the most prominent and widely used model today, addiction is seen as a treatable chronic disease. There is no cure for it, but there is a range of medical and behavioral interventions to treat the illness. Significant attention is being paid to neuroscience and work on understanding the biology of addiction. This model explains what's going on in the brain when someone ingests a substance that causes them to experience highs, intoxication, withdrawal, and dependence.

This model is significantly less shaming and pathologizing than the moral model. It explains why people behave in ways that are counter to their values and in self-destructive ways. When you understand what's happening to someone's brain in the throes of addiction, it softens your approach toward the person and, more important, brings better programming options. It offers help rather than punishment. This is where we see diversion and rehabilita-tive programs instead of prison or jail programs.

This model also leads to better behavior treatment plans. As a clinician, if I know you're in the early stages of treatment and you're still dealing with the physiological effects of tapering down your use, I'm going to create a plan that matches it. I won't do an all-out abstinence plan and try to convince you to white-knuckle it and then blame you and offer you fewer options in the future because you "blew it." What I will do instead is build into the plan what we'll do if or when you relapse. I plan for situations rather than blame the person.

>> **Sociocultural model:** This model talks about environmental and cultural factors of addiction, which usually means how much access a person has to drugs and alcohol and what people in the community think about it.

- **Access:** How available are substances in the community and what kinds of substances are available? Research shows that early exposure to substances impacts rates of use and misuse. The younger a person is when they try drugs and alcohol, the more likely they are to have a problem. This is especially true with illegal drugs. When people grow up around drugs being used and sold in the neighborhood, it indicates there is neighborhood disorder and an informal system for getting money. So maybe the person has substance use disorder because of the neighborhood they grew up in and what they saw growing up.

- **Social norms:** Why people use substances also has a lot to do with societal attitudes about substance use and what's being modeled for the children. Some cultures are very specific about what's okay to consume and how much of it is okay to consume. They may approve of alcohol with meals or with family but disapprove of drunkenness. Maybe alcohol can be used for ceremonies or rituals but not for coping. Social and cultural models may overly normalize problematic use, meaning it may be culturally acceptable to be intoxicated frequently, or they may have very strict rules on what's acceptable and ostracize people who use or misuse substances.

Recognizing the stigma affiliated with substance abuse disorders

People have very strong feelings, attitudes, and perceptions about folks who use substances — and the feelings are usually negative. These negative attitudes and perceptions make the substance use disorder a stigmatized condition. People may think moral and character deficits are the reason for the addiction, so they punish, discriminate, or refuse to help the person, which, as you can image, creates terrible health outcomes — especially if the health-care provider is the one with the negative feelings.

The stigma surrounding substance use disorder has major consequences:

>> People don't want to be related to, work with, or see people with substance use disorders in public.

>> People believe we should deny housing, employment, social services, and health care to people with substance use disorders.

>> Health-care and social-service providers feel resentful toward clients with substance use disorders.

>> Health-care and social-service providers don't offer the full range of services to folks with substance use disorders because they have low expectations of them.

>> People with substance use disorders who expect stigma understandably don't seek or access services.

>> People with substance use disorders who experience stigma drop out of care and have worse outcomes, compounding the stigma.

REMEMBER

Stigma creates lasting consequences. Paying attention to language is not just an exercise in being polite or kind — it saves lives.

The Brain and Addiction

How does someone develop a problematic relationship with a substance or become addicted? It all starts with pleasure and pain. People ingest or use substances because doing so brings pleasure or because they want to avoid pain — or often both.

TECHNICAL STUFF

The benefit of using the substance doesn't have to be direct — it can be a benefit from the activity *associated* with the substance. For example, if you're hooked on coffee (that's me!), maybe you like the smell of it, the process of getting just the right cup, adding just the right amount sugar and milk, and mixing it all together. All of this happens before you even take a sip. Similarly, for people who use drugs and alcohol, procuring them is the first part of the process.

Substance use became problematic when engaging with the substance turns from pleasure into a coping mechanism and then, surprisingly, into consuming the substance to avoid getting sick from withdrawal. Using the substance shifts from pleasure to dependence — you need the substance to function like a normal human being. This addiction becomes a problem when you're consuming the substance despite the negative impact it's having on your health and/or relationships.

The physiology of addiction

Understanding the impact that drugs and alcohol have on the body and brain is foundational to understanding how addiction manifests in a person's life. The first thing to understand is how the substance enters the body, which can occur in four major ways:

>> **Ingestion:** A person drinks, chews, swallows, or lets something dissolve on their tongue. This is the most common way that substances are consumed.

>> **Inhalation:** A person breathes the substance in through their mouth into the lungs. Smoking and vaping fall into this category.

>> **Insufflation:** A person draws the substance up through their nose, or *intranasally*. The nasal cavity is lined with a mucous membrane with a strong supply of blood vessels, so the substance quickly makes it from the nasal cavity into the bloodstream.

>> **Injection:** A person uses needles to inject the substance into their veins. Injection is the most direct way of getting drugs into the bloodstream and to the brain. Because of this, injection is the most dangerous route.

After the substance is in the body, it gets to the bloodstream, where it's circulated throughout the body in about a minute. After the substance reaches the brain, it interacts with certain chemicals in the brain to produce the substance's effect. Drugs can mimic the effects of brain chemicals and activate and amplify a reaction in a much more intense way. This is why people see or feel things much more intensely under the influence of drugs — there is artificial intensification or a "high." Different substances impact this intensification or pleasure at different rates. Drug use affects the brain much more than natural rewards, such as food or interactions with people with like. Sure, chocolate and friends are good, but they're no match for something as intense as heroin.

The body adapts to this new or artificial activation — it becomes the new normal. This condition is called *tolerance*. The dosage that *used* to give someone an extraordinary experience is now basic. They need the substance to be at baseline. The body becomes accustomed to this new normal and develops physiological dependence. As the brain as a whole adapts to the presence of drugs, the various regions of the brain also are impacted. Over time, the brain areas responsible for judgment, decision making, memory, and learning physically change and create specific pathways into the brain circuit. This is why substance use disorder can't be blamed on character or personality flaws — there are literal brain changes from consuming substances.

What's also problematic about these cellular adjustments to the brain is that drugs make the brain less responsive to these same substances over time. A person has to consume more and more of the drug just to feel stable and even more to feel high. When the substance is withdrawn, the person experiences physical pain and discomfort that may be unbearable. Now they're no longer trying to get high — they're just trying to feel normal. This is why it's important to medically supervise or help people taper off their use of substances instead of encouraging them to quit cold turkey. The body and brain need time to physiologically adjust.

Chronic use of substances can lead to damages to a person's physical health, such as heart disease, liver disease, lung cancer, and damage to other organs.

The psychology of addiction

Physical dependence on a substance is accompanied by psychological dependence on the substance. The person needs the substance to cope with their daily life. The substance becomes more and more central to the person's life. They become pre-occupied with procuring and using the substance at the personal and social cost to their personhood. They spend tremendous time, energy, and effort getting, using, and recovering from using the substance. The person defines their sense of self in relation to the substance and organizes their life around it.

People who have substance use disorders use substances to cope with feelings and situations. They don't use it for pleasure or to escape. In fact, this is the hallmark for developing a disorder. This type of relationship with the substance becomes evident when the person isn't able to easily give up the substance despite knowing what it might cost them.

For example, one of my clients who has become dependent on marijuana will tell me they need it to cope and deal with their anxiety. They've had a series of jobs that screen for drug use and are drug-free workplaces. My client will go to great lengths to conceal their marijuana consumption, including purchasing urine from the internet. I offered to refer them to a psychiatrist to treat their anxiety so they don't need to risk their job by using marijuana, but they still insist on using marijuana. This is what using to cope means — it's psychologically necessary for them to get through their daily life, and there is an irrational justification for using.

When there is physical and psychological dependence, the behaviors that are the hallmarks of addiction follow (see the next section).

The behavior of addiction

When people think of substance use disorder, they're often thinking of the behavior impairment, such as intoxication, being high, or being unable to control impulses and behaviors. These impairments do happen, but they're driven by the physiology of addiction and maintained by the psychological craving and dependence.

People build a tolerance to the substances and engage in a range of risky and problematic behaviors to procure and use the substances in order to manage the physiological dependence and avoid withdrawal. Depending on the substance, the person may compulsively drink, use drugs all day, seek multiple partners for sexual encounters, or spend all their money and time on the substance. And they do this at the expense of work, family, and friends.

The situation is exacerbated by the fact that the person's tolerance for risk increases over time and their boundaries shift. For example, a person can go from binge drinking on weekends to drinking after work to drinking *at* work. The line for what's acceptable just keeps moving, and the consequences keep increasing. What's worrisome and devastating to friends and family is the compulsive nature of the behavior and the continued use despite significant negative consequences, including loss of friends and family. People deep in the throes of substance use may get arrested, have their marriages crumble, lose jobs, contract diseases, and/or lose or gain a tremendous amount of weight.

This behavior is baffling for the folks around them. A person who was once responsible and loving has turned into someone who lies, steals, and constantly puts their life at risk. The severe and chronic condition of substance use means that loved ones are in a constant state of fear of the worst — their loved one dying because of the substance use.

These behaviors are also what has led the condition to be stigmatized and caused a tremendous amount of shame for the individual. But, of course, these behaviors make sense when you understand the physiology and psychology of substance use. The behaviors are not separate from the physiology and psychology, and that's why treatment and rehabilitation are critical for recovery. People cannot be expected to "behave" themselves out of these problems — they need medical and behavioral help.

Alcohol and Major Classes of Drugs

For people in the helping field and for folks who want to specialize in addiction, knowing the major classes of substances, what aspects of use make them pleasurable, and what aspects of use are harmful is important.

The categories of substances fall into these areas:

>> Alcohol

>> Stimulants

>> Sedatives

>> Opiates

>> Cannabis

DISPARITIES IN JUSTICE

There are significant social consequences and issues of justice related to the type of substance and the demographics of the user. When marginalized communities use a substance, it's sanctioned and criminalized much more harshly than when dominant groups use the substance.

The most overt form of this disparity is the difference in sentencing between an infraction related to cocaine and one related to crack cocaine. The distribution of just 5 grams of crack carries a minimum five-year federal prison sentence, whereas for powder cocaine, distribution of 500 grams — 100 times the amount of crack cocaine — carries the same sentence.

Both drugs have the same base, cocaine — the difference is the user. Black people are disproportionately arrested and sentenced for crack-related drug charges, with 80 percent of people *sentenced* for crack being Black, whereas 60 percent of crack *users* are white or Hispanic.

In the following sections, I provide a general description of the substance and the highs and lows of using the substance.

REMEMBER

With all drugs and alcohol, the younger the person is when they come into contact with or consume the substance, the more likely they are to develop substance use disorder in the future.

Alcohol

The chemical name of drinking alcohol is ethyl alcohol or ethanol (EtOH). Alcoholic beverages are made by fermenting different types of grains, fruits, and vegetables; the fermentation creates ethanol, which is an ingestible form of alcohol. Alcohol can come in the form of beer, wine, liquors (gin, vodka, whiskey, tequila, rum, brandy), or sake. Alcohol concentration varies by liquor content — beer has the lowest level of alcohol content and hard liquor has the highest.

Alcohol is legal and one of the most ingested substances in the world. People consume alcohol on a spectrum from mild to moderate to severe. The risk for developing a drinking problem depends on how much, how often, and how quickly someone ingests alcohol. As someone develops more of a dependence or tolerance, they need more alcohol to feel normal.

One of the symptoms that may alert me to someone potentially having alcohol use disorder is when I ask them how much they drink, and they ask me if beer counts. That answer always makes me chuckle. Yes, beer counts.

TECHNICAL STUFF

One standard drink is 12 ounces of beer, 8 to 9 ounces of malt liquor, 5 ounces of wine, and 1.5 ounces of hard liquor or distilled spirits.

TIP

How much drinking is okay? Really not much. The U.S. Department of Health and Human Services (HHS) has this nice advice, "Drinking less is better than drinking more." Here's how the Centers for Disease Control and Prevention (CDC) defines light, moderate, and severe drinking for men and women:

	Men	Women
Light drinking	12 drinks in the past year but 3 drinks or fewer per week	12 drinks in the past year but 3 drinks or fewer per week
Moderate drinking	3 to 14 drinks a week	3 to 7 drinks a week
Severe drinking	More than 14 drinks a week	More than 7 drinks per week

Binge drinking is drinking four to six drinks in the span of two hours. Think college students on Friday nights.

TECHNICAL STUFF

There are sex differences in the alcohol consumption recommendation not because of discrimination or patriarchy. Women are more vulnerable to the adverse consequence of alcohol because they metabolize alcohol differently than men do. Women have less body water than men. When alcohol hits a woman's bloodstream, it builds up in concentration much faster than it does in men. So, the same amount of alcohol has a greater systemic influence on women.

This is lots of data and is helpful when educating clients and patients about safe and moderate kinds of drinking and for pointing out problem drinking.

REMEMBER

Drinking is a cultural norm and often romanticized — think of a person who is pouring a glass of wine while making dinner, having a glass with dinner, and then having another glass with dessert. If they're doing that daily, that's a problem drinking pattern.

The highs of drinking include the following:

» The enjoyment of the drink itself

» When consumed in low or moderate levels, increased expression, happiness, euphoria, and care-free feelings (because of lowered inhibition)

>> Social acceptance

>> The involvement of alcohol in ceremonies and rituals

>> Relief of stress and tension

>> When consumed in moderation, potentially good for your heart, memory, and movement

The lows of drinking include the following:

>> Poor judgment and low inhibition

>> Impaired driving and safety

>> Poor health outcomes (such as liver disease, digestive problems, high blood pressure, and increased risk of heart failure), as well as the complication of other chronic conditions

>> Sexual dysfunction

>> Birth defects in babies exposed in utero

>> Neurological complications due to the impact on the nervous system

>> Increased risk of cancer

>> Medication interaction (increasing the toxic effects of medications)

Stimulants

Stimulants are prescription drugs (such as amphetamines [Adderall, Ritalin] and diet drugs) and illegal drugs (like methamphetamine, cocaine, or bath salts). They come in the form of pills, powders, rocks, and injectable liquids. Addiction develops with patterns of binge use — people with a severe form of stimulant use disorder may inject themselves every few hours until they deplete their supply.

Simulants are considered power drugs because they can make a person feel more awake and alert. They produce feelings of superhuman powers or grandiosity.

Stimulants cause the brain to release the feel-good brain chemical called *dopamine*. Dopamine is a chemical neurotransmitter in the brain that's involved in the pleasure circuit that regulates mood, thinking, and movement. All these things are tied to pleasure and speed up functioning. A person thinks faster, moves faster, and talks faster when dopamine is released in their brain.

Higher doses and repeated use of stimulants can make a person develop paranoia and hallucination. Because of the highs or pleasure these stimulants produce, when a person stops using them, there is a crash, which can lead the person to develop cravings, tolerance, and dependence. A person who regularly consumes stimulants may develop mood dysregulation and physical problems. (The body wasn't meant to be in a perpetual state of induced wakefulness and high speed — it needs balance and rest.) As alluring as stimulant-induced euphoria and grandiosity seem, they come at a high cost.

The highs of stimulants include the following:

>> A sense of euphoria and exhilaration

>> Increased activity and energy

>> Improved mental and cognitive performance

>> Reduced appetite

>> Periods of wakefulness

The lows of stimulants include the following:

>> Low energy and irritability

>> Anxiety

>> Depression

>> Fatigue

>> Drowsiness

>> With heavy use, agitation, panic aggression, and suicidal and homicidal tendencies

Sedatives

Sedatives are the opposite of stimulants — they make people feel relaxed. They slow down or depress the activity in the brain and spinal cord so people feel relaxed and can sleep. The purpose of sedatives is to help a person feel less anxious and have decreased agitation. In the health-care setting, a person may go in for surgery or a medical procedure and be given sedation. Dentists use sedation to help patients feel less anxious. People with anxiety disorders or insomnia may be prescribed sedatives to help them cope with their symptoms.

Prescription drugs such as barbiturates, benzodiazepines (including Ativan, Klonopin, Valium, and Xanax), and sleep medications (including Ambien and Lunesta) are all sedatives. They can be ingested or snorted. Sedatives are considered controlled substances because of their potential for misuse and abuse.

In addition to reducing anxiety and inducing sleep, sedatives such as benzodiazepines can cause euphoria, which is what makes them addictive. But the brain adapts to the drug, and the person ends up needing higher doses to have the same impact and will feel bad when they don't have the sedative. As with other drugs, it goes from pleasure to dependence.

The highs of sedatives include the following:

>> Sedation

>> Sleep

>> Tranquilization

>> A dream-like intoxication that dampens memory and causes loss of inhibition

>> Making an unpleasant world go away

The lows of sedatives include the following:

>> Drowsiness

>> Highly addictive

>> Slowed breathing and central nervous system activity, which can lead to coma and even death

>> Reduced attention

>> Impaired judgment and coordination

>> Poor memory

>> Agitation and unpleasant awareness after coming out of intoxication

Opiates

Opiates reduce the perception of pain and mimic *endorphins* (neuropeptides that relieve pain and induce feelings of pleasure and well-being) in the body. They can occur in natural forms (such as heroin, which is derived from the poppy seed) or in synthetic forms (such as prescription opioids and fentanyl). Opiates can be ingested in pills, liquids, and candies.

Technically, *opiates* are derived from the poppy plant, whereas *opioids* are made in a lab. Opioids are made to mimic opiates and are developed to be stronger and more potent than opiates are.

Opiate use disorder and deaths related to opiate overdose have been getting lots of attention from researchers, academics, and legislators. This attention is very much needed because deaths related to opiate overdose have doubled in the last decade.

Physicians can prescribe pain relivers in the form of opioids to help patients manage pain after medical procedures or for chronic conditions. The most widely known prescription pain relievers are OxyContin and Vicodin. Currently, synthetic opioids (such as fentanyl) are causing the most opiate-related overdose deaths.

Fentanyl is a powerful opioid that is similar to morphine but is much more potent. It is typically used by physicians to treat chronic pain for things like cancer or after surgeries and other procedures. Fentanyl can be administered as a shot, given as patch, or taken in the form of cough drops and lollipops.

There is an epidemic of fentanyl-related deaths for a number of reasons:

>> **The biggest reason for the rate of deaths is that there is just tons of fentanyl in the marketplace.** Fentanyl costs less to make, is easier to distribute with the emergence of the *dark web* (a hidden part of the internet that requires specialized software to access, often associated with illegal activities, anonymity, and the sale of illicit goods and services), and can be a hundred times more potent than heroin. It costs much less to manufacture fentanyl than it does to grow fields of poppy plants for heroin.

>> **Another significant contributor to fentanyl deaths is that most people don't know they're taking fentanyl.** It's being added to other drugs to increase the potency of the drugs in a process known as *lacing* or *cutting*. Given fentanyl's high potency, even a tiny amount (the size of a grain of rice) can be deadly to the user. Unsuspecting people who are buying another drug may not be aware that they're ingesting fentanyl.

>> **Because of fentanyl's potency, the propensity for addiction and overdose are very high.** This is why we have an epidemic.

One measure to help combat the fentanyl epidemic is the administration of a nasal spray called naloxone (brand name: Narcan). Naloxone reverses overdoses and saves lives.

The highs of opiates include the following:

>> Pain relief and mental relaxation

>> Extreme euphoria and intense high, especially when injected

The low of opiates include the following:

>> Highly addictive

>> Suppressed breathing

>> Can cause death

>> Death if withdrawal occurs without medical supervision

Cannabis

Marijuana comes from the cannabis plant, which has more than 100 compounds. Two of these are tetrahydrocannabinol (THC) and cannabidiol (CBD). THC is mind altering and produces a high, whereas CBD is not impairing. Marijuana can be smoked, vaped (in electronic vaporizing devices), or mixed or infused in foods and beverages.

TECHNICAL
STUFF

People use the words *cannabis* and *marijuana* interchangeably, but technically, *cannabis* refers to all products that are extracted from the *Cannabis sativa* plant, whereas *marijuana* refers to products from the plant that contain large amounts of THC.

Considerable private and public investment is being made in medical, recreational, and psychedelic research into marijuana. Across the United States, more and more states are legalizing marijuana for medical and/or recreational use. People are discussing the benefits of marijuana, which include pain relief for patients, decreased rates of racialized arrests, and increased revenue for states and businesses.

The cannabis plant as a whole has not been approved by the U.S. Food and Drug Administration (FDA) for medical use. Instead, some drugs that contain CBD *have* been approved to treat epilepsy, nausea, and vomiting in patients receiving chemotherapy and loss of appetite and weight in people who have HIV/AIDS. Cannabis is being researched to treat chronic pain, anxiety, post-traumatic stress disorder (PTSD), multiple sclerosis, and irritable bowel syndrome (IBS).

Despite these benefits, is marijuana bad for you? This conversation is as complicated as the one we have about alcohol. Marijuana is increasingly legal and socially acceptable, yet there are health and legal concerns for people who misuse or develop a disordered relationship with it.

For addiction researchers and clinicians who work with people who have substance use disorder, there is a growing concern about the increasing availability of marijuana, especially for young people. This is because people *can* become addicted to marijuana and develop cannabis use disorder. Unfortunately, we can't predict who will have this response. Some people may try marijuana and use it recreationally; others will become addicted. This is why the increased access to marijuana is alarming for clinicians and researchers.

WARNING

People who start using marijuana during adolescence are at risk for using marijuana to cope and for *cross-sensitization*, in which they have a heighted behavioral response when they're introduced to other drugs like opiates. So, marijuana can be a gateway drug for people who are genetically predisposed to really like and respond to it and other drugs.

Marijuana has a significant impact on the developing teen brain and can alter gene expression for young people who have a genetic predisposition to develop opioid use disorder. Most folks who work in the field take a morally neutral stance on legalization of marijuana. They just want to make sure that there are public health supports in place to mitigate the unfettered access people will have to marijuana.

Here are the highs of marijuana:

» A pleasant high

» Can treat chronic pain, mitigating the side effects of chemotherapy, epilepsy, and other promising areas of research including mental health treatment for anxiety and PTSD

» Socially accepted

The lows of marijuana include the following:

» Development of marijuana use disorder

» Impairment of memory, learning, and attention

» Cross-sensitization to other drugs

PSYCHEDELICS: WHAT A TRIP

Psychedelics differ from other drugs because people don't experience dependence, tolerance, or withdrawal with them. People have been using psychedelic plants and drugs for mind-altering experiences and for rituals and religious and healing purposes for centuries. Individuals who want to experience loss of control or a dreamlike state with sensory and perceptual distortions can consume psychedelics and have experiences or "trips" that people describe as spiritual. For some people, these experiences or trips can be very unpleasant and produce anxiety. Other people have no recollection of their experience with the drug.

Psychedelics come in natural and synthetic forms. They can be derived from plants, mushrooms, or peyote cactus, or made in labs in the form of pills. The strength, potency, and impact of the drug are unpredictable.

Apart from using psychedelics recreationally, there is considerable research on the use of psychedelics to treat severe PTSD. Approved programs using this approach are using very small doses of psychedelics in a controlled, monitored, and supported context. These programs are also using microdosing to treat anxiety and other mental health symptoms. For people who have severe childhood experiences or high exposure to trauma, being in a protected trance-like state to work on tough memories may be one of the only ways to directly address the trauma. This is still early research, so by the time you read this, it may have been refuted as dangerous, or it could be revolutionizing the field. This area is something to keep an eye on.

Treatment for Substance Use

A public health approach to substances tries to prevent problematic use by providing accurate, non-sensational, and developmentally appropriate news.

TIP

I offer all these caveats because giving too much information too soon to kids makes them curious and want to try things — the opposite effect of what we want.

In addition to prevention measures, treatment should be given holistically and offer as much choice as possible. One size does not fit all. People need to be given a range of options and be supported in their choices. That way, they're more likely to stick with the treatment and recover without relapse.

In this section, I talk about what works and what doesn't, where people can get help, and the importance of family and community supports.

Understanding what works and what doesn't

Early in my career as a social worker, I was intimidated by the field of addiction and thought of it as highly specialized field that required even more training and extra letters after your title. I got this idea because that's exactly what was being taught at the time. Substance use disorders were thought of as a separate and super-bad problem for "those" kinds of people. When people showed up needing treatment for mental health and substance use, we made them choose which condition they wanted to address first or, in most cases, made them have multiple providers who were treating different conditions. These poor folks would spend their entire week going from appointment to appointment.

I'm here to tell you: That approach does not work. All direct-practice workers need to have a working knowledge of addiction as a chronic health condition and be trained in holistic treatment modalities that address substance use as a component of the treatment. It can be done pretty seamlessly if there is sound treatment planning.

Here's what *doesn't* work:

>> Morality approaches that try to shame the person into getting better

>> Prejudiced and negative views of clients who use substances

>> Abstinence-only models (quitting cold turkey)

>> Isolating the person and not giving them social supports

>> Poor access to treatment

>> Difficult admissions criteria and policies

>> Punishment and incarceration

Any problematic approach to substance use disorder is rooted in a moralistic view that sees addiction as a problem with the individual and one that the individual could control if they were better behaved. We know this point of view is wrong on many levels. It's the kind of policy and stance that creates harmful zero-tolerance policies and produces terrible health outcomes, including early and preventable drug-related deaths. (If you can't tell, this point of view gets me good and mad!)

Now, let's get to what works. Is it super-magical advanced training? Not really. A holistic, strengths-based approach works. Here are the elements of a strengths-based treatment approach:

>> Viewing the problem as having a biological, behavioral, and social component

>> Using prevention strategies

>> Thinking of addiction as another medically chronic disease that warrants public attention and support (with primary care providers and emergency room doctors addressing substance use disorder as part of their overall treatment of patients)

>> No matter the circumstance, having hope that people have the capacity to heal with supports

>> Offering a person treatment options (for example, 12-step programs, motivational approaches, or medication-assisted treatment), even when they relapse (*Note:* This is the most important element of what works!)

>> Not forcing people into treatment

>> Using harm reduction and self-determination strategies to motivate people

>> Using medical support when available and possible

>> Incorporating family and community supports as much as possible

>> Decreasing barriers to accessing treatment as much as possible

These approaches destigmatize substance use and leave the possibility for recovery open for the person. Thinking of a person as human instead of as a problem matters. Plus, these approaches are humanistic and backed by science.

Knowing where people can get help

When a person says they're ready to get treatment for a substance use disorder, where can they get help? Should they just find the first Alcoholics Anonymous (AA) or Narcotics Anonymous (NA) group and go to meetings? Maybe.

Providers who treat substance use disorder will determine the best place for the person based on several variables, including the type of substance used, the associated medical and mental health problems, what the client is willing to accept, and what kind of insurance the person has.

REMEMBER

Even if someone is ready to go to Alaska to recover and find their inner child, like they do in the TV show *Intervention*, their insurance may not cover it. That makes the most well-planned treatment moot.

TIP

Clinicians typically recommend the least restrictive care as the first option. People refuse to enter or drop out of treatment facilities if the facility is too restrictive or if they aren't able to meet the requirements of the program (like dropping everything for six months and going to Alaska).

REMEMBER

Here are the levels of care where people can get treatment, starting with the least restrictive:

>> **Outpatient:** Up to three hours of individual counseling and group therapy a week

>> **Intensive outpatient:** Up to ten hours of individual counseling and group therapy a week (usually, three hours of group and one hour of individual, therapy three to five days a week)

>> **Partial hospitalization:** Ten hours a day in a hospital setting five to seven days a week

>> **Halfway houses or community-based residential programs:** A home-like environment where the person lives and gets treatment for three to six months

>> **Residential facility or rehab facility:** A live-in setting where individuals receive comprehensive care, typically for an extended duration, focusing on recovery in a supportive environment

>> **Inpatient hospital with detoxification services:** Hospital-based care that specializes in safely managing withdrawal symptoms, usually for a short duration

>> **Inpatient hospital with a residential component:** Hospital-based care that combines detoxification services with a longer-term residential program

What usually happens for someone with severe use and insurance is what you see on TV: They go to a treatment facility that allows them to be medically supervised while they taper off the substance. If the facility has a residential component, they can stay there for a period of time. They're discharged from the facility and usually do intensive outpatient treatment for a month or so, and eventually they land in outpatient treatment. It's helpful for people to work their way down to being more independent. Depending on how long someone has been using and the severity of their use, they have to tend to treatment like it's a job. Their brain pathways take a while to recover from tolerance and dependence. And the person has to build a whole new life and social circle.

If the person doesn't have insurance, the social worker will look for places that take folks without insurance or see if they can qualify for Medicaid or government-sponsored insurance and, if so, find a facility that takes Medicaid and has an opening. The limited availability of facilities that accept Medicaid is a huge barrier to treatment. People who are ready for immersive treatment have to get by until they can get into a place where they can get care.

Understanding how people get better and what treatment involves

People don't have to hit rock bottom in order to get treatment. We can use evidence-supported approaches to motivate them to move toward change. These approaches assess where the person is in their understanding of their condition and how much they want to change. They may feel perfectly fine and not see their substance use as problem. If so, giving people a referral for an intensive outpatient facility is a waste of a referral and a bed. They'll most likely not come back to see you. Even if you're correct in your assessment of the situation, your mismatched intervention doesn't make sense.

REMEMBER

All treatment process starts with evaluating your own biases, prejudices, beliefs, or need for power in relation to people with substance use disorders. You have to do some self-reflection and think about why you may or may not have strong reactions to this population.

After self-reflection, you do an assessment and screening. Assessment is an ongoing process that looks at the person's life in all its dimensions, including discussing the role of substance use in the client's life. There are usually formal screening tools that ask whether someone uses drugs or alcohol and screens for the severity of their use to see if it's problematic. Assessment and screening should be standard and routine for most social service providers, whether they specialize in addiction treatment or not.

TECHNICAL STUFF

There are classic screening tools for substance use. For alcohol use, CAGE-AID, TWEAK, and Michigan Alcohol Screening Test (MAST) are administered. For drug use, the screening tools Drug Abuse Screening Test (DAST) and National Institute on Drug Abuse–Modified Alcohol, Smoking, and Substance Involvement Screening Test (NM ASSIST) are used. These screening tools alert the clinician that there may or may not be problem use. Other instruments assess the severity of use. (You don't need to get into the nitty-gritty of how much someone is using something unless it's flagged as a problem.)

After you get a sense of what kind of substances someone is using and the severity of their use, you can assess for other dimensions:

>> The extent to which the problem has caused consequences in their lives

>> How much tolerance they've built up

>> How much they depend on using the substance to function

>> How much time they spend obtaining, using, and recovering from the use

>> How much cognitive impairment (memory loss, poor attention and learning) the substance has caused

>> How much the substance has physically harmed them

The combination of the assessment process and screening questionnaires create a picture of the role of the substance in the person's life. From there, you need to ask the person how important it is to them to make a change. You may think they'll die if they don't make changes, but they may not be there yet. So, what should you do? Give up? No, not at all. Think of it as a process. Now that you know where the person is, you use evidence-supported approaches to provide treatment that matches their level of readiness.

In my work with trauma survivors, people come in to work on their trauma symptoms. I often note substance use issues in my assessment, but they may not be able or ready to tackle it, so I weave it into treatment. They may be using the substances to cope or to avoid. After I do some skill building and build a rapport, I start using harm-reduction approaches to decrease their use and taper them off the substance. At some point, if there is severe use, we focus on the substance use as the primary issue and spend lots of time working on addressing the physiological, psychological, and behavioral components to using, tying it to their trauma. I also like working closely with a psychiatrist and referring the client for medical care. Finally, I incorporate family members and community supports to help build informal supports. If I sense that the client actually needs to check into a residential facility for a higher level of care, we work on it together. It's always about incorporating choice and options and not being upset if there is relapse. In fact, we plan on relapse as a normal part of the process. This multipronged approach gives the person the best shot at recovering.

REMEMBER

As a social worker, I'd be remiss if I didn't mention that there must be structural supports to care. People should have access to high-quality care in their communities. If they're ready for help but what's offered to them is jail, we're creating harm for communities and generations.

IN THIS CHAPTER

» **Understanding why people get sick**

» **Navigating complex health systems**

» **Creating thoughtful care plans**

Chapter **10**

Adding Support in Health-Care Settings

When most people think of health care, they think about physical health — how a person feels in their body and what they can do if they feel bad or have a health scare. What they may *not* think about is the context of health and health-care access — in other words, where and how a person is getting their health-care needs met.

Two groups of people *do* think about these issues:

» **People who don't have access to health-care providers:** They think about the context of health care not because they're budding public health experts or social workers but because their lives depend on the care they can't access.

» **People who work in health care:** People in public health and social services are thinking constantly about how they can meet the needs of patients given the demands and limits of the health-care system. They care about the well-being of people, so health-care access is important to them.

Social workers who work in health-care settings bridge these two groups. They help clients get connected to health-care providers and systems. They also work *in* the systems and help patients navigate complicated health-care settings and get connected to community resources to continue healing. The work doesn't end with the discharge papers — social workers follow people in their communities and make sure they have the resources to stay healthy. Continuity of care makes a significant difference in the recovery process and quality of life.

Prevention is another area of focus for social workers who work in health care. Health-care social workers are dedicated to both alleviating and preventing health-related issues. They operate at all levels of practice to reduce instances of poor health and collaborate with health-care systems to relieve suffering. They work on preventing future health-care challenges for vulnerable communities, working at the macro and community levels. They focus on early prevention, especially for infants, and for individuals at risk of hospitalization, including those with disabilities, older adults, individuals with low socioeconomic status, or those in rural regions with limited transportation access.

In this chapter, I explain how health issues impact a person's chances at life and the roles social workers play in this process. I walk you through where health concerns arise, help you understand some of the core health issues people face, and show you how social workers can create client-centered plans of care.

Seeing Where Social Workers Fit into Integrated Health Care

In the past 20 years, health-care systems and providers have recognized the role that biopsychosocial factors play in patients' health outcomes. In response, new models of health-care delivery are emerging. These care models use *integrated health care* (a team approach to provide health care).

If you're a patient with multiple conditions and needs, in the past you would usually have had to coordinate all your care on your own and talk to each of your providers separately. In an integrated health-care model, the health-care providers all speak to each other, share records, and coordinate your care in an organized, systemic way. The care team is made up of social workers, nurses, physicians, and other allied health professionals.

Integrated health care can occur at the highest level, where providers share facilities, collaborate on treatment planning, and share or integrate their medical records. Or it can just come in the form of a care plan that tries to coordinate communication and create collaborative treatment plans. The important aspect is that there is coordination among providers and it isn't solely left to the patient.

WHY ACCESS TO HEALTH CARE MATTERS

People's overall happiness and satisfaction in life are deeply impacted by their wealth and health. When you have financial stability, you have less stress and more control of your life. You have options, which decreases stress. Less stress and more options equals more happiness. By the same token, how much control you have over your health and where you go for help significantly impacts your coping and happiness.

Think about how a simple cold or flu can hijack your life. Now imagine if a little cold turns into bronchitis, which turns into pneumonia because it's left untreated for a long time. That small cold has the potential to derail your life. If you have good insurance and paid time off at your job, the cold that morphs into bronchitis is an inconvenience, but you can deal with it — you can go to your primary-care doctor, get a prescription for antibiotics, and take a few days off work to convalesce. If you don't have insurance or paid time off, that minor illness may be the stressor that lands you in a homeless shelter.

This is why access to health care is so important. It can prevent minor issues from snowballing into major issues — and wiping out a person's whole life.

REMEMBER

Patients who receive services using the integrated health-care model have better health outcomes. When health-care providers talk to each other and create a comprehensive plan, patients aren't getting duplicate services, the runaround, or mixed messages. Not only is this better for the patient, but it's better for the bottom line. When people who frequently use emergency care as their primary care are given integrated health care, they have fewer hospital admissions and emergency calls, stronger adherence to medication and care plans, healthier habits, and more connections in the community.

Social workers play a significant role in coordinating integrated health care. They can help develop the plan, implement the plan, or be the service provider. They're the critical ingredient in this process. In the following sections, I walk you through where social workers fit into integrated health care and what they do.

Where they work

Here are common health-care settings where social workers can be found working:

>> **Outpatient care facilities:** In this setting, treatment doesn't require an overnight stay. This could include visits with a primary-care doctor or health clinic.

>> **Acute-care settings:** In this setting, short-term services are provided for emergency or trauma care, usually in a hospital.

>> **Rehabilitation facilities:** In this setting, patients receive skilled nursing and other medical care for recovery (usually from a hospitalization) until they're well enough to return home.

>> **Behavior health facilities:** In this setting, people receive services for substance use, mental health, and physical health.

>> **Palliative care facilities:** In this setting, people with serious medical conditions receive care that focuses on providing relief from symptoms.

>> **Hospice care facilities:** In this setting, people who have terminal illnesses receive end-of-life care.

What they do

Social workers are involved in four key areas in integrated health-care delivery:

>> **Behavior health:** Social workers link patients to services or themselves provide substance use and mental health services in community health centers, in primary-care doctor offices, in hospitals, and in schools. Their job titles may be *behavior health clinician, peer counselor,* or *behavior health consultant.*

>> **Care coordination:** Social workers coordinate holistic care support for people who have chronic and/or multiple health conditions. They communicate with an interprofessional team so patients have connected services in hospital, community, and home settings. They work closely with Medicaid- or Medicare-eligible patients. Their job titles may be *care coordinator, care manager,* or *case manager.*

>> **Community practice:** Social workers operate in various settings, such as community clinics and home-based services, where they provide essential care. Additionally, they play a crucial role in training peer providers to meet the health-care needs of the community. The social workers are in the community as opposed to the patients coming to them. Their job titles may be *patient navigator, community organizer,* or *community health worker.*

>> **Management and leadership:** Social workers work as team, program, or supervisory leaders for interdisciplinary teams. They may serve as the primary leader for an organization or system that focus on health-care provision. They may create or implement health policies at the federal, state, or county level. Their job titles may be *program director, supervisor, chief executive officer,* or *team lead.*

These dynamic roles help improve the lives of people, holistically address why people need health care in the first place, and ultimately reduce the overall cost of health care.

Understanding the Social Determinants of Health and Health Disparities

Health is not the result of a single variable — it's influenced by a number of things, some personal and others structural. The variables contributing to health aren't necessarily medical either. Social factors such as income, education, and neighborhoods impact health outcomes. Researchers have demonstrated that factors like low education, low social support, and segregation contribute to mortality in a similar manner to the way physical ailments like chronic diseases or heart failure do.

REMEMBER

People who have more resources and opportunities have better health outcomes. These findings created a nationally and globally known framework called *social determinants of health* (SDOH). SDOH is the prevailing model for public health interventions and public health policy right now. The most commonly cited determinants or factors that impact health are:

>> **Individual behaviors:** Lifestyle choices that people make or engage in that impacts their health (for example, diet, activity level, smoking, and alcohol consumption)

>> **Genetics:** Inherited physiological conditions and susceptibility to illness

>> **Social environment:** Income, employment, education, social support, and family network

>> **Physical environment:** Neighborhoods, green spaces, clean water, access to nutritious foods, and clean air

Historically, the approach to understanding health problems was confined to addressing behaviors and physical conditions. Now it has expanded to include the other critical domains: social and physical environment.

These factors interconnect and influence a person's health. They're also shaped by political factors and illuminate why we see huge health disparities among groups.

Social workers have always operated with this framework. It's nice to see that other disciplines are wholeheartedly adapting our ecological approaches into their care models.

Social workers can work with the micro or downstream determinants (such as individual behaviors) by creating care plans that are client centered and holistic. Social workers can also do macro or upstream care where they work on neighborhood development, community assets, transportation, and education as public health issues; these efforts can also target marginalized groups such as people in poverty or underrepresented groups.

Recognizing disparities in health outcomes

When it comes to health and health care, different groups of people are offered different types of care and experience different outcomes. Cultural and personal biases seep into every aspect of society, and health care is no different. People who are poor, people of color, and women experience bias in the health-care system, and that bias leads to a lower level of care and, consequently, poorer health outcomes than middle-class or wealthy people, white people, and men experience.

Disparities in health care — in other words, the differences between the quality of care different groups of people receive and the resulting outcomes — have to do with a few factors, covered in the following sections.

Access to care

Access to health care is about a person's ability to get timely health-care service for optimal health. In the United States, people do not have equal access to care, and definitely not in a timely manner. There are significant lags in care for people without health insurance and people of color. People who have government-sponsored insurance (Medicare or Medicaid) have trouble finding health-care providers who will see them.

Quality of care

Quality of care is measured by six domains — safety, timeliness, effectiveness, efficiency, equity, and patient-centered care. People shouldn't have to wait a long time for care. When they do get care, it should be done in the safest manner, using the best scientific knowledge, in a respectful, nonbiased manner. A person's personal characteristics (such as their age, gender, race, ethnicity, or sexuality) should not lead them to have poor health-care experiences.

In the United States, data reveals that there is great disparity in quality of care based on social status and racial and ethnic identity. What's particularly alarming is that people may experience negative health outcomes when one part of their identity is stigmatized but they otherwise have great resources. For example, Black American mothers have the worst outcomes when it comes to health, no matter their income level.

Note: I'm specifically saying "Black American" because these same statistics are not seen with foreign-born Black mothers living in the United States, which means it's not the personal physical health characteristics of Black American mothers that's the problem — it's because their health-care providers don't refer them to services they need or recognize when they're at risk. Even when they do have responsive health-care providers, the stress of living in a racist society creates internal stress, and their babies are born underweight, which is one of the biggest risk factors for infant mortality. So, the mothers and their babies are at increased risk simply because they are Black.

Equity or discrimination in health-care provision

There are three main areas in which discrimination occurs in health-care provision — poverty, racism, and sexism.

REMEMBER

These disparate health outcomes reflect structural inequality. People with less economic means, racial minorities, and women don't care about their health any less than wealthy white men do. They just face tremendous challenges in receiving and maintaining high-quality health care.

POVERTY

Poverty is directly correlated with poor health outcomes and access. People in poverty have more chronic diseases, higher mortality rates, and lower life expectancy than people who are economically stable do. A person who is in the top percent of income earners can live 10 to 15 years longer than a person who is in the bottom percent of income earners.

REMEMBER

Children make up the largest group of poor people, and they grow up to be poor adults with chronic health issues.

Poverty tends to be concentrated in neighborhoods or communities and lasts for generations. Poor communities have aggregated risk factors. They have reduced access to health resources and the resources they can access are strained. Because poverty is concentrated, communities that have less resources have more people with chronic needs. Often, these communities become stigmatized and further marginalized.

RACISM

For people of color in the United States, health disparities are a glaring social problem. Folks of color have higher rates of chronic diseases such as heart disease, cancer, and high blood pressure. With the exception of Latino people, folks of color have premature deaths compared to their white counterparts.

TECHNICAL STUFF

Latino people in the United States have a mortality advantage: Although their socioeconomic indictors are similar to the Black population, they have mortality rates similar to white Americans. This has been referred to as the *Hispanic paradox*. When researchers investigated this more, they discovered that Latinos who are foreign born — specifically, Mexican immigrants — had the best health outcomes. U.S.-born Latino people had outcomes similar to other disadvantaged groups. Being low income, born in the United States, and leaving their ethnic communities increased their health risk factors.

Infant mortality rates are shockingly high for children of color, with the highest rates for Black infants, followed by American Indian infants. Black mothers, regardless of income or social status, have higher death rates than mothers from other racial groups. When Black mothers have access to health care, they experience biased and discriminatory care. Their safety is compromised because they aren't given appropriate screenings and are often sent home instead of being given care when they show up in the emergency room. This leads to tragic outcomes. Black women are three times more likely to die from pregnancy complications than white women are.

Black women have more *fibroids* (benign tumors in the uterus that can cause postpartum bleeding) than white women do. Additionally, Black women display signs of preeclampsia earlier in their pregnancies than white women do. Given these facts, Black women should be followed closely and given a targeted level of care. Instead, the data shows that Black-serving hospitals have high rates of maternal complications and poorer birth outcomes.

Black women also have less access to insurance and less access to contraception care and counseling, which leads them to not have prenatal care or receive prenatal care very late into their pregnancies. Receiving pregnancy-related care late in the pregnancy increases pregnancy complications such as premature births and underweight babies.

SEXISM

Gender inequities impact health outcomes and access to care. In the United States, women live longer than men but have higher incidences of chronic conditions, depression, and disability than men do. Women have more chronic diseases and at higher rates. When it comes to access to health care, women struggle to have continuous insurance coverage. Although more women are being educated and entering the workforce, there is still a wage gap and a disparity in the types of jobs available to men and women. Women also often have to leave the workforce when they have children.

Identifying barriers to accessing health care

Unequal and poor health outcomes show up in severity of illness and the type of care available and given to patients. Really sick people or people with multiple ailments can't afford to see doctors. By the time they finally get in to see someone, the care is done in an emergency setting and the follow-up care may be too costly or too cumbersome to follow through.

Health disparities impact how people access and engage with health-care systems. Here are the core factors impacting people's access to care:

>> **Lack of insurance coverage:** People can't afford to pay for health insurance or have insurance copays or bills that are cost-prohibitive. Because of this, they delay getting care or go without needed care.

>> **Shortage of health-care providers:** There aren't enough health-care providers who take government insurance (Medicare and Medicaid). Not enough providers specialize in care for underrepresented groups such as people who identify as LGBTQIA+. There are also not enough providers and hospitals in rural areas.

>> **Stigma, racism, and bias:** Providers may have negative views and beliefs regarding patients with certain behaviors and backgrounds and create unwelcoming or harmful care.

>> **Transportation:** People can't find transportation to and from medical appointments.

>> **Language and citizenship status:** People who have limited English speaking skills have poorer health-care experiences and delay getting care. Immigrants face discrimination, stigma, and fear of being deported when they disclose their health-care needs.

>> **Lack of health literacy:** People have a hard time understanding clinical information and are not able to follow directives from their health-care providers.

All these factors play a significant role in why people don't have access to care or why they don't access care when it's available to them. It's not because they're lazy people who don't care about their health or follow doctors' orders. Very serious and real barriers are preventing them from getting lifesaving care.

Addressing social problems as part of health care

More and more primary-care offices and acute-care settings are addressing social problems as a part of their medical care. They screen for social risk factors and health-related *social needs* (food, housing, transportation, utilities, and interpersonal safety). Research shows that people who frequently turn to emergency rooms or hospitals for care tend to need help in these areas. They're overusing emergency services and not accessing primary-care settings.

In an effort to bridge this gap and alleviate the financial burden on health-care systems, insurance companies are offering incentives to doctors and health clinics that embrace SDOH models. They do so by providing bonuses or allowing health-care providers to retain a larger portion of their billings when they excel in terms of quality-of-care measures.

The measurements of quality are:

>> **Patient experiences:** Patient report that they're receiving quality care.

>> **Patient outcomes:** There are fewer readmissions to the hospital, and patients experience better health outcomes (for example, lower blood pressure).

>> **Processes:** Providers adhere to best-practice processes and stick to protocols for a particular illness. They aren't skipping parts of the process because they don't have time or don't feel like it.

>> **Utilization:** Patients are using the appropriate services — they're not turning to emergency rooms for routine care.

By incentivizing or rewarding efforts that address these quality measures, the entities that control the financing structure create a new culture for how services are provided.

REMEMBER

What can clinical settings do to impact the health-related social risk factors like housing or interpersonal violence? Public health folks like to use the metaphor of a stream when discussing health interventions. Upstream are macro-level interventions, midstream are mezzo-level interventions, and downstream are micro-level interventions (see Chapter 3 for more on macro, mezzo, and micro):

>> **Upstream:** Upstream strategies look at improving community conditions and use policies and regulations to create healthy community support for all people — for example, developing green spaces or providing access to reliable transportation, secure housing, and good food. All these areas target

the social health risk factors but at a much higher level than the midstream intervention. You might not think that a good bus line would be tied to someone's health, but if a patient needs to use the bus line to get to their doctor, you can see how these two factors are connected.

>> **Midstream:** The midstream level addresses social needs. This is where there is universal screening that assesses for the health-related risk factors. Social workers and integrated health teams can provide care and supportive services to meet patients' social and medical needs.

>> **Downstream:** The downstream level involves the most direct interventions, the ones we think of when we think about health care — one-on-one interaction with a provider done in a clinical setting and where direct physical care is given.

Providing Patient-Centered Care

Patient-centered care has become the standard of care planning over the last 20 years. In the past, when patients presented for services, they were examined, diagnosed, and given a prescription and instructions. Care was one-directional — the doctor told the patient what to do, and it ended when the patient left the office. What the patient did with the instructions or the prescription wasn't considered part of the health-care team's domain — that was up to the patient. Today, this view is seen as dated; even more important, soon it won't be funded by insurance companies. Care is measured by patient outcomes and their experience with the provider. So, having a good bedside manner or a thoughtful approach will be a core part of health work (if it isn't already); if you don't have it, insurance companies may not reimburse you.

Usually social workers who work in integrated health-care settings work at the midstream level, where they coordinate and deliver complex care. In that role they do complex goal setting and create a robust coordinated care plan through a patient-centered care approach. The patient-centered approach creates a humanistic plan from a strengths-based perspective. It doesn't view a person through their illness or through noncompliant or compliant behavior.

This is important because folks with chronic health conditions need empathetic and sustained support. Their conditions aren't going away overnight or with one pill. Besides, this approach produces good results. People who are given person-centered plans are more likely to have better self-management skills, self-care activities, medication adherence, and reduced psychological symptoms. Insurance providers are also mandating these approaches. Quality is measured by cost-effectiveness and culturally sensitive care.

In the patient-centered model of health care, clinicians and patients make decisions together. This approach is the most effective and most holistic. We're shifting from the idea that the doctor knows best. This top-down approach is paternalistic and infantilizing. The doctor knows *medical information* best, but the patient is the best expert on *themselves.* Good care adapts medical care to the person and creates a workable plan. This style of decision making is called *relational decision making*, and it's the best approach for chronic diseases. It empowers people to make decisions that make sense for them, and there is buy-in to the care plan. That leads to successful outcomes for both parties.

Because this care approach facilitates a strong connection between patients and their care team, there is a decrease in no-shows for appointments. People stop thinking of their care team as bill collectors and as people they have to dodge.

Creating a patient-centered plan

So, how do we create a patient-centered plan? It starts with remembering the values of the planning process. The patient-centered care approach values holistic care, respect, choice, and dignity. It views the process as collaborative, not prescriptive.

REMEMBER

You must give people the opportunity to have preferences and choices when possible and you must use that information in the actual plan. There is nothing more disaffirming than someone asking you for your thoughts and then disregarding your thoughts when it comes to the implementation phase.

TIP

Now that your heart and spirit are in the right place, these are the steps you can take to create a patient-centered plan:

1. **Do some self-reflection.**

   Answer the following questions for yourself:

   - Am I seeing the person in front me as a whole person?
   - Do I believe that this person is an expert on their own life?
   - What unhidden and hidden biases do I have about this person's background?
   - How will I make sure that my biases don't interfere in my work with them?

2. **For the initial assessment, develop a set of reflective open-ended questions.**

   Be sure to ask the person the following:

   - What is most important to you?
   - What is bothering you the most?

- What have you used in the past to help yourself get through things?
- Who helps you?
- Who do you help?
- What part of your culture or identity is important to my understanding you?

3. **Build a plan that centers on what's important to them and is strengths based.**

Be sure that the patient knows the full scope of the problem and the range of options for treating it.

4. **Incorporate important people in their lives as part of the plan.**

5. **Monitor and evaluate the plan so it continues to be current and effective.**

In addition to making the plan patient-centered, care should be provided in a calm, welcoming space that accommodates the patient and their family. Don't try to have critical conversations in hallways or in passing.

The appointment-making process shouldn't be cumbersome — it should be coordinated, consistent, and efficient.

You should support the patient before, during, and after the visit. Your engagement style should be empathetic and flexible, and you should be open to negotiate on what the patient needs.

In addition to supporting what the patient needs, you should use the best evidence-supported plans to help foster change and provide self-management tools. It's outdated to think that people make changes only if they want to make changes. Social workers help people move along in the continuum of change because we have the training to do that.

For example, let's say a patient comes in for diabetes management and they smoke. The patient knows they should stop smoking. But that isn't what's bothering them the most or what's most important to them. They want to be more independent and be able to drive again. The care team should devise a plan around increasing independence and then *eventually* address the smoking behavior. Smoking cessation requires a thoughtful approach that's a combination of nicotine replacement or medication assistance and talk therapy — you can't shame or pressure people into it. In this case, the patient doesn't even want to quit, so you wouldn't want to set quitting smoking as a goal initially.

Engaging family members in care

Families play a significant role in the care of their loved ones. They may be the main source of support or, as in most cases, they may be a source of support and a source of stress. Social workers in health-care settings spend a good deal of time working with families and managing these complete family dynamics. They provide critical information to families so they can help with the decision-making process or understand what's happening to their loved one. They help answer questions about what they can expect, what they should be alarmed by, and what they should do if there is crisis.

Early engagement and building a strong rapport with families is excellent practice and can help prevent future problems. If families feel like you're working with them and you're on the same team, they'll feel less defensive. A health-care crisis is one of the hardest experience a family can have. Good care can be a lifesaver for the patient and tremendously healing for the family.

How can a social worker provide good care for families?

>> **Focus on communication.** Ideally, you'll provide regular and structured communication with family members. This kind of communication helps families feel less anxious and decreases their fight-or-flight responses.

>> **Create a family-centric plan.** Your plan should promote well-being for the whole family or have family health as the goal. That can help motivate the whole system to rally behind the patient. It also addresses the SDOH. For example, you may encourage a father to take paternity leave if his work allows it, or you may have the whole family adopt more nutritious meals or engage in more physical activity. This builds in positive health habits on the whole and makes the whole family unit better.

>> **Increase community connections.** Engage extended family, *fictive kin* (non-blood-related people who count as family), and community supports in the care plan. Health-care providers offer formal help, but most of the day-to-day help and support happens through family, friends, and faith communities. It's critical for social workers to strengthen connections to family and community members. This fosters a sense of belonging and reciprocity among members. When people look out for one another, they feel better and, in turn, they can expect care when they need it. Building community support also address health-care needs upstream — more people benefit from the intervention. Social workers who use thoughtful teamwork and involve family members in the health-care process contribute to achieving the best possible outcomes.

Chapter **11**

Working with Kids in Schools

When I was in grad school studying to become a social worker, I vowed to only work with adults. Children were charming and fun, but I didn't want to work with them or their complicated families. When I finally graduated, my first job was a home-based position where I drove to half a dozen different people's homes every day to provide individual counseling. A month into this position, I told my boss, "I need a job where the clients come to me." I had gotten lost on the road too many times (this was pre-GPS). My boss said, "Well, the only position I have is school-based, and you adamantly told me that you did not want to work with children." I put on a big fake smile and said, "Oh, no, I was just joking — I can work with anyone. Besides, I'm great babysitter and I nannied all through college." I really needed a job and my student loan payments weren't going to pay for themselves. So, I transferred my cases and started working in a middle school as a school-based social worker.

To my delight, I *loved* working with students and their parents in the school setting. I went on to specialize in this area for many years. I've worked in elementary, middle, and high school settings in urban, suburban, and rural areas. I learned that each school was its own entity, as was each classroom. I've seen some of the roughest and toughest students turn into sweet teddy bears who loved to learn in one classroom and got kicked out or severely punished in the next, where the teacher was frustrated and ill equipped. This showed me that the *students* weren't the problem — it was their environment. And guess who is in charge of the environment? Grownups. We have the power to shape the lives and experiences of young people every day in this setting. We need to make sure we do right by kids and intervene when there are barriers and problems.

This is where school-based social work comes in. School-based social workers work with the school system to help kids and their families thrive academically, socially, and emotionally.

In this chapter, I talk more about why schools are great places for social interventions, the roles of school-based social workers, the common issues and challenges in school-based work, and how social workers can intervene in a meaningful way.

Not all schools or school districts have school-based social workers. However, that's changing more and more — the COVID-19 pandemic demonstrated that the social and emotional well-being of kids and their families is as important as their academic endeavors. The Every Student Succeeds Act of 2015 represented a pivotal moment in education because it underscored the significance of addressing the social and emotional dimensions of learning. In the realm of school-based social work, it's imperative to take into account broader policy factors at the macro level, recognizing the considerable impact that politics and policies wield over the education system, especially in the current political landscape. This chapter gives you a sense of what school-based social work entails and the kinds of situations and interventions school-based social workers use to make a difference.

Seeing Schools as Places for Social Support and Interventions

When I travel overseas and talk about the American education system, people in other developed countries are shocked that higher education costs so much here. In developing countries, where there isn't free public education, they say how lucky we are to have the kind of education system we have and that education is a blessing. Both statements are true. Free public education as a right is critical in order for a society to function and is, indeed, a blessing. The quality of the education determines the future opportunities afforded to the child. This is where there is work to be done, and it's where the social work profession enters.

It's worth emphasizing that, although we often associate student advocacy with direct practice in social work, a significant amount of advocacy work occurs daily behind the scenes within the political and economic sectors of society. A multitude of factors affect the educational landscape, including family, community, and political systems. Research — particularly focusing on adverse childhood experiences (ACEs), numerous developmental studies, and the growing influence of social media — has shed light on the education system as a setting where effective interventions can positively alter the life trajectories of many students. These studies hold even greater relevance for students facing a higher risk of poor educational and life outcomes, a demographic we're familiar with. COVID-19 brought these disparities into sharp focus, but it's important to recognize that they existed long before the pandemic.

REMEMBER

Education is inherently tied to life outcomes. It sets the path for future earning potential and the ability to have material and social capital. How well you do in school and the networks you build in your educational pathways open or close job opportunities for you. Jobs and income shape what kind of life you're able to lead and what you're able to pass on to the next generation. Because of poverty, oppression, and generations of trauma, there is deep inequality in who has access to quality education. Social workers work in school settings to address these issues and to give kids and their families a better shot at getting the good life.

Social workers who are passionate about improving student educational and life outcomes are frequently involved in macro-level work. This work includes policy initiatives, grant writing, and program development aimed at preventing and alleviating barriers for students in school settings. It also involves collaborating with legislators and educational stakeholders to identify educational disparities and solutions to increase educational budgets and important social resources like mental and physical health programming.

Education as a public right and schools as public institutions

Schools are the most democratically accessed social institutions in the United States. They offer the promise and hope that each child has an equal chance of getting a high-quality education no matter where they live. In the United States, the concept of school as a public good and a fundamental right came into being during the Progressive Era (the early 1900s) because social workers and educators advocated for laws banning child labor and establishing compulsory public school. Each state is given the authority to carry out this charge with support from the federal government.

While this was happening, views of child development and the developmental distinction between children and adults was also changing. Children were no longer seen as little people who would become adults at adolescence (or even by the age of 10, as per the Elizabethan laws that early settlers followed). Instead, childhood was seen as a protected time in life — one that needed to be nurtured — and education was a part of that new perspective.

According to this new way of thinking, in a democratic society:

>> **Schools should serve as the place to train children so they turn into productive adults.** Education is the vehicle for this public good, designed to help prepare little humans to grow into responsible and virtuous big humans.

>> **Education is perceived as a public good, strategically crafted to prepare kids for social efficiency.** Education enables them to contribute effectively to society by equipping them with essential life skills, fostering cooperation, and promoting civic engagement. This, in turn, ensures that the future workforce is composed of skilled and qualified workers, enhancing the overall well-being and harmony of the community.

>> **Education should allow individuals the ability to have social mobility or to move up the social and economic ladder and make a better life for themselves.**

All these ideals about the purpose and end goal of education ended up being more of a hope then reality. Children show up in kindergarten with very different levels of preparation, and they need unique services to succeed. This is because schools are neighborhood-based, and neighborhoods are physical and social spaces that are impacted by income, politics, and oppression and privilege. Schools are an extension of these dynamics. Poor neighborhoods have a lower tax base to fund the schools and, as a result, have less resources.

Plus, some (though not all) poor neighborhoods have characteristics of disorganization like high crime rates and illegal drug activity that shows up in the school system. The hope is that the school is a safe haven from those factors. Unfortunately, that isn't the case. The schools may mirror the neighborhood struggles. So, in addition to providing education, schools become a place where social needs have to be addressed. Students can't learn if they're hungry, tired, scared, or worried about their safety.

Beyond reading, writing, and arithmetic

Schools offer a place for education and academic mobility. Schools are also the sites for socialization and emotional learning. Kids spend a significant portion of their formative years in school. Schools serve as de facto parents and homes for kids. While adults are out working and being productive citizens, they send their kids to schools to get educated and to learn how to become good citizens. Grownups go to work, and children go to school.

REMEMBER

In addition to being a place for education, schools serve as the places for socialization, child care, and meals. In some instances, school may be the only safe and supportive space a child has access to. This fact was highlighted immensely during the COVID-19 pandemic, when many kids lost access to safe and supportive spaces, not to mention access to food and shelter. Kids learn how make and keep friends, how to interact with peers and adults, and the basics of what it means to be good citizens. In school, students learn about their rights and responsibilities as citizens, how to respect others, and the importance of community involvement. They also discover the value of being informed, making ethical choices, and working together with others to solve problems and contribute to a better society. Depending on the school, schools can be wondrous places where students delight in the discovery of new knowledge and experiences. However, in some cases, they run the risk of becoming mere warehouses for children, focused on rote education, and stifling creativity, resulting in uninspiring learning environments.

REMEMBER

Schools aren't always magical islands of learning. They're mirrors of the communities they're located in, and they reflect the resources given to them. Although the United States endorses its commitment to public education, it isn't a constitutional right. The allocation of resources for education is left to state and local authorities, and therein lies the issue of equity.

Research shows that there are huge disparities in educational outcomes depending on race and income. Children who come from under-resourced backgrounds and minoritized identities score lower on national standardized tests; repeat more classes; are in more special education courses; get lower scores on AP, SAT, and ACT tests; and go to schools where there are more altercations and the school environment is unsafe. These kinds of disparate outcomes require system-level interventions.

TECHNICAL STUFF

Because of these inequities and disparities, schools and community leaders have increasingly adopted the perspective that schools are educational and community centers, serving not only as places for learning but also as hubs for social intervention. Three distinct models have emerged to emphasize the multifaceted roles schools can play:

>> **The service model:** This model places schools at the heart of addressing the needs of both the child and their family and offers comprehensive support. This model ensures that students and their families have access to essential support, such as health care, counseling, and after-school programs that address both educational and well-being needs.

>> **The developmental model:** In this approach, schools receive sponsorship and support from their local communities, enabling them to tailor their programs to suit the specific needs and challenges unique to their area. This

model promotes flexibility and creativity, acknowledging that a one-size-fits-all approach may not be effective in diverse communities. It offers community-level supports such as adult education classes, community meetings, and recreational programs, catering to the specific needs and interests of the community. It promotes a sense of ownership and encourages community engagement.

>> **The organizing model:** This model takes a broader perspective, viewing schools as catalysts for systemic change. Instead of addressing educational issues school by school, this model recognizes that challenges often stem from broader issues of power and equity. Schools in this model become centers for organizing efforts aimed at reshaping education policies and practices on a larger scale, advocating for systemic improvements that address equity and justice in education as a community-wide concern. For example, an urban district facing educational disparities, several schools come together to form a coalition that advocates for policy changes at the district level. By pooling their resources and efforts, they influence decisions that address systemic issues, such as equitable funding and curriculum development. This organizing model shifts the focus from individual schools to systemic improvements, prioritizing equity and justice across the district.

These examples illustrate how schools, under different models, can serve as dynamic community centers that adapt to the unique needs and challenges of their communities, ultimately fostering overall growth and positive social change. Social workers are key professional partners in school settings. They're able to help with academics, with school environment issues, and with community-level interventions.

School social worker roles

Social workers are the ideal professionals to interface with school systems to help students and their families thrive academically and socially. Schools are made up of many systems that must work together to achieve successful outcomes. The subsystems of schools includes the classrooms, students, teachers, other professional staff, and administration. These subsystems are nested in local districts that answer to parents, the school board, and the state and federal governments. That's a lot of players and variables!

Social workers are trained to utilize a person-in-environment (PIE) framework for understanding and addressing social problems. That means they recognize that a person's life is shaped by factors in their environment and that the person, as an actor, also shapes their environment. This approach ensures that interventions are tailored to address both individual needs and the broader social, cultural, and environmental factors that influence a person's well-being. The PIE framework guides social workers in providing more effective and empathetic support, accounting for the complexities of individuals' lives. Because of this training, social workers appreciate the complexity of school environments and are excited to work in a vibrant, influential system.

So, what exactly do social workers do in schools? Lots of exciting things! They provide services to students, their families, the school, school personnel, and the larger community. Social workers are guests in the school settings. They're invited into the space by the school, which serves as the ultimate host. This is called *interprofessional work*. Social workers are one of the professionals in the space, and in this case, they aren't the primary service or profession. Teachers are the primary providers; social workers, school counselors, school psychologists, librarians, and nurses are the other professions that collaborate and work in school settings. Some schools have social workers as members of that specific school's full-time staff, while others have social workers for the entire school district who are deployed to different schools as needed. School-based social workers can also be contracted to work with the school and may be hired by a nonprofit agency or a human services agency.

TIP

From my experience, the best arrangement is the one where the school-based social worker is an employee of the school and hired to work only in one school, preferably with multiple social workers. (One social worker to 300 to 500 students is too much, but it's better than being a social worker for the entire school district.) When you're a full-time employee of the school, you're part of the school's system and not just a visitor. Plus, you have access to school-level benefits and protections. You aren't subject to the tenuous setup of *soft funding* (funding that isn't a permanent budget line item) or grants that *sundown* (expire).

Here are some of the roles school social workers can do at the micro (individual), mezzo (family and group), and macro (community) levels:

>> **Micro level**

- **Counseling:** Provide one-on-one counseling to students facing emotional, behavioral, or personal challenges.

- **Assessment:** Conduct assessments to identify the specific needs and strengths of students and their families.

- **Crisis intervention:** Assist students and families during crises, such as emergencies, mental health crises, or family issues.

- **Case management:** Coordinate services and resources for individual students and families, ensuring they receive the necessary support.

- **Advocacy:** Advocate for the rights and well-being of individual students within the school system and community.

>> **Mezzo level:**

- **Group counseling:** Facilitate group counseling sessions on topics such as emotional management, social skills, or bullying prevention.

- **Parent education:** Conduct workshops and programs to educate parents on various topics, including child development and parenting skills.

- **Schoolwide programs:** Develop and implement schoolwide programs to address issues like bullying prevention, conflict resolution, comprehensive sex education, or substance abuse awareness.

- **Teacher consultation:** Collaborate with teachers to address classroom behavior issues and develop strategies to support students.

- **Interdisciplinary teams:** Participate in interdisciplinary teams within the school to address complex student needs and develop individualized education plans (IEPs).

>> **Macro level:**

- **Community resource coordination:** Collaborate with community agencies to connect students and families with external resources like mental health services, housing assistance, or food programs.

- **Policy advocacy:** Advocate for policies and practices that benefit students' well-being and education at the district or state level.

- **Research and evaluation:** Conduct research to assess the effectiveness of school programs and interventions and make recommendations for improvement.

- **Program development:** Contribute to the development of school-wide policies and programs that enhance the overall educational experience.

- **Community outreach:** Establish partnerships between the school and community organizations to support students and families.

REMEMBER

Although there are lots of roles and levels of intervention, all school-based social work is systems work. Even if a child is being referred to you for one-on-one work, you have to involve the family and update the school on their progress — it's never isolated.

A good example would be what I call the "stinky kid referral." If you do school-based social work, you'll invariably get a referral for a kid who has an odor — a big-time smell that nobody wants to talk to the kid or family about. The smell may be there because the child's house doesn't have running water, the child has a medical issue, there is some level of neglect, the child refuses personal hygiene for a number of reasons, the child is from a different culture or country, or the child and their family just don't care about the smell. Each of these explanations requires work with family, referral for resources, or an intervention on hygiene. But it's never just a quick talk about hygiene and it's over. The smell is an indicator that there is more to investigate, and you have to do some work to get to the root cause of the issue.

WARNING

Although school-based social workers can do many things, it's also important to discuss what they *can't* do. School-based social workers have professional boundaries, even if the school district or the principal want them to do things that aren't part of their role. School social workers should push back or set clear boundaries about their scope of their work and what they can and cannot ethically do. Here are some things that school-based social workers are *not*:

>> **Enforcement officers:** School-based social workers do not engage in disciplinary actions against students, and they do not act as law enforcement officers. They don't police or surveil students' activities, and they aren't gatekeepers or agents of social control. Sometimes school districts or county agencies ask social workers to play these enforcement roles by making them truancy officers or deans of discipline. Social workers should actively resist these types of roles. They reinforce negative stereotypes of social workers as probation officers and people who engage in policing work.

>> **School counselors:** School social workers and counselors share some responsibilities, but the roles are distinct. School counselors primarily focus on academic and career guidance, while school social workers emphasize the social and emotional well-being of students. School social workers should not be involved in creating academic schedules or monitoring schedules for students.

>> **Child welfare workers:** School social workers are not child welfare workers or caseworkers from child protective services. They do not conduct child abuse investigations or make decisions regarding child custody. Their role is to assist students and families in accessing appropriate services when needed. If school personnel suspect child abuse or neglect, they must report it to the appropriate child protective service office and not just to the school social worker.

>> **Actual parents:** School social workers are not the legal parents or guardians of the children they work with. They provide support and advocacy, but they don't have parental rights or responsibilities. Some social workers lose sight of this and began to think of themselves as parents or better parents than the families of the children. Be mindful of this savior trap. The students love their parents and families. The social worker's job is to strengthen that bond and support, not replace it.

Identifying the Educational Policies School-Based Social Workers Need to Know

Early in my career, when I got a job to be a district-level social worker, my supervisor explained to me and another newly hired social worker that the school district had created these brand-new positions out of their IDEA legislation and that we would be working with students who had IEPs. We nodded our heads, said, "Of course," and left the office with our new charge. I turned to my new colleague and said, "Hey, do you know what IDEA or IEP is?" and she said, "No, but let's find out." I chuckle at this, because IDEA is a critical piece of educational legislation and IEPs are a very important part of social work in a school-based settings. You shouldn't enter a school building without this baseline information.

In this section, I explain the laws and policies that govern special education and the role of social workers in special education. I also discuss the law that protects homeless children and their families and how social workers help.

Laws

Two key pieces of legislation have directly tied into the work of school-based social workers:

>> **Individuals with Disabilities Education Act (IDEA):** According to IDEA, children with disabilities ages 3 to 21 must have free and appropriate education in the least restrictive environment. They have the right to special education and services to meet their needs. It gives the federal government funding to help states and local schools provide education for children with disabilities.

A child can qualify as having a disability if they have any of the following conditions:

- Intellectual disability
- Hearing or visual impairment
- Serious emotional disturbance
- Orthopedic impairments
- Autism
- Traumatic brain injury
- Specific learning disability
- Other health impairments
- Developmental delays

According to IDEA, these conditions allow them to seek accommodations and access to specialized educational supports through IEPs.

>> **McKinney–Vento Homeless Assistance Act:** This law protects children who are experiencing homelessness. It has a wide definition of homelessness and includes those sharing housing due to loss of housing, living in inadequate accommodations, staying in emergency shelters, or being abandoned in hospitals. It also covers those without a regular sleeping place (like those living in cars, parks, or abandoned buildings) and migratory children who've moved for temporary agricultural work. Unaccompanied homeless youth, including runaways and those separated from parents, are considered homeless and protected under the law, too. McKinney's definition is comprehensive, ensuring support and educational access for these vulnerable populations.

Kids who are homeless have the right to public education and the right to go to their original school. The law states that schools must identify children who are homeless and designate a liaison for these kids. This liaison should help protect the students' rights, provide support and services to the families, and help coordinate services with the school, social services, and other appropriate professionals.

SOCIAL WORK ROLES WITH IDEA

Under IDEA, students with disabilities have the right to a robust assessment process, to learn in the least restrictive environment, and to access the best educational resources regardless of their status. A social worker can get involved in almost all aspects of the special education process. Usually, a referral for special education services occurs when a teacher, parent, or other professional school personnel identifies a need or an accommodation.

For example, a teacher may notice that a child is unable to remain in their seat, impulsively interacts with other children, has lots of emotional outbursts that they can't seem to manage, and can't follow directions most of the day. They may reach out to the parent, the teacher, the school counselor, and the social worker and say that the child needs to be evaluated for services and accommodations. The teacher may need an aide in the class, and the child may need socioemotional supports in addition to academic supports.

Before a child can formally fall under special education services, they must first go through research-based interventions to see if those things help address the behavior. Maybe the issue is time and situational bound and doesn't require long-term intervention. During this phase, the social worker, school counselor, and school psychologist

(continued)

(continued)

may assess the child, family, and teacher; come up with interventions that are specific to the child; and monitor the child's progress. The goal is to see if these interventions improve the child's behavior so the child can be allowed to stay in the classroom with tweaks, or determine that the child does, indeed, need formalized supports and even periods of time where they're in a more secluded environment.

Social workers can help come up with the interventions, be a support to the teacher, and liaise with the family member. In some cases, the teacher may feel like the family or the child are not fully participating and may get frustrated and punitive. Other times, family members may not feel like the teacher is putting in enough effort or care about the process or their child. Social workers help with these dynamics and help keep everyone on track. If there isn't improvement or the improvements are occurring because of intensive supports and the child would regress if the supports were removed, the child will formally qualify for an IEP and services from a special education instructor.

The following laws are also critical education legislation that you should be aware of:

>> **Civil Rights Act of 1964:** This law applies to all levels of education, from K–12 schools to higher-education institutions. It prohibits discrimination in educational programs and activities based on race, color, religion, sex, or national origin at all levels of education.

>> **Americans with Disabilities Act (ADA):** The ADA applies to all public and private educational institutions, including K–12 schools and higher-education institutions. It ensures that students with disabilities have equal access to educational opportunities and services.

>> **Family Educational Rights and Privacy Act (FERPA):** FERPA applies to all educational institutions that receive federal funding, which includes most K–12 schools and higher-education institutions. It governs the privacy and confidentiality of student records. It outlines what's private educational information, who is allowed to know it, and under what condition.

>> **Title IX of the Education Amendments Act of 1972:** Title IX applies to all educational institutions that receive federal funding, including K–12 schools and higher-education institutions. It prohibits sex-based discrimination in educational programs and activities.

>> **Jacob K. Javits Gifted and Talented Students Education Program:** The Javits Program is a specialized program for gifted students within a school district or educational institution; it would typically apply to K–12 education and not higher education. Gifted education programs are often implemented in K–12 schools to meet the needs of intellectually gifted students.

ROLES FOR SOCIAL WORKERS UNDER THE MCKINNEY–VENTO HOMELESS ASSISTANCE ACT

In the late 1980s, the visible demographics of homelessness underwent a transformation, shifting from primarily single men on the streets to homeless mothers and their children. This shift prompted Congress to take action and enact laws to ensure that children experiencing homelessness had access to free and public education. Schools were tasked with two crucial responsibilities: (1) to identify students within their schools who were experiencing homelessness, and (2) to eliminate any barriers to the education of these children.

Today, schools that apply for and receive McKinney funds have the flexibility to use these funds for various purposes, such as providing before-school and after-school programs, tutoring initiatives, referrals for medical and mental health services, preschool programs, parent education, counseling services, social work support, transportation services, and other essential services that may not have otherwise been available through the public school program. In alignment with this policy, Congress has significantly increased appropriations to address these important educational needs. Social workers are usually the people responsible for keeping schools compliant with this law.

The biggest barriers for kids who are homeless is access to their school of origin. Whenever they're in a shelter setting, the shelter isn't usually located in the same neighborhood as their school. McKinney–Vento allows them to attend their original school and mandates that the school district provide free transportation to the original school. Depending on the school, this costly request is met with understanding or reluctant compliance. Social workers help act as resources, buffers, and resource supports for the kids and their families. They can work collaboratively with other service providers and make sure that the kids have the appropriate health care and access to enriching school activities and counseling supports to help them through these difficult situations.

Individualized education plans

Social workers can participate in IEPs in two primary ways:

>> **As general social workers, they contribute by sharing their observations of the child and highlighting the child's strengths.** These insights help shape comprehensive IEPs that not only address academic needs but also consider the child's social and emotional well-being.

>> **Social workers can be formally written into the IEPs as service providers.** In this capacity, they have a defined role within the plan, offering specific services tailored to the child's requirements. These services may include counseling, social skills training, or other forms of support.

Whether providing general insights or specialized services, social workers play a crucial role in ensuring that IEPs are well-rounded and designed to meet the unique needs of each student, ultimately promoting their growth and success in the educational setting.

WARNING

Social workers should be cautious about how many plans they're formally written into. IEPs serve as legal documents and binding agreements. If a social worker is written into 100 student plans, they won't be physically able to provide those services, and the school and parents would have grounds to seek redress with the school board or legal system. In other words, you could be sued for not providing support promised to a vulnerable child.

TIP

When developing goals in an IEP, the following should be included and considered:

>> **Student name:** Including the student's name conveys that the goal is individualized for the student.

>> **Setting:** This is the specific location where the service will take place, such as a social work office or during unstructured activities.

>> **Time frame:** This specifies the time frame within which the goal should be completed, usually within a 12-month period.

>> **Required condition:** This includes a clear description of the assessment materials or conditions under which the behavior will occur. Examples could involve observations, behavior charts, rubrics, or peer group settings.

>> **Behavior:** This information clearly identifies the performance being monitored and reflects an observable action, such as raising a hand, identifying coping strategies, seating arrangements, or scripted guidance.

>> **Criterion:** This defines the degree of accuracy, frequency, or evaluation schedule, indicating how the teacher will assess student performance.

>> **Accommodation:** This includes any assistance provided during the assessment, such as teacher prompts, seating arrangements, or scripted guidance.

TIP

When analyzing goals, be sure to consider the student's strengths, compliance with required areas of identified disability, areas for improvement, potential rewording of the goal or benchmarks, and any other relevant comments. This structured approach ensures that IEP goals for social workers are clear, measurable, and aligned with the student's needs and objectives. Even though these goals are very discrete and concrete, it's important to be cognizant of environmental factors that impact how a behavior manifests.

Make sure parents have input in their child's IEP. They know their kid the best and can give information on what triggers, motivates, or strengthens their child.

Behavioral, therapeutic, and emotional supports

Back in the day, we used to say that social workers helped with anger management skills. Now we know that anger is one of the ways kids express themselves. The goal is not to control or coerce children, but to give them the tools they need — through behavioral, therapeutic, and emotional supports — to recognize the range of their emotions, including what triggers them and what soothes them. When students are able to make the connections between their emotions and their reactions, they can channel their frustrations or pent-up emotions in a more productive way and be able to learn.

In the school setting, social workers are called in to help kids who have externalizing and internalizing behaviors:

>> **Externalizing:** Externalizing behaviors are when students do things that others can observe that are not productive or healthy — things like fighting, yelling, running away, pushing, abusing substances, or destroying property.

>> **Internalizing:** Internalizing behaviors are behaviors for the quietly distressed kids — kids who are anxious, depressed, disconnected, or hypervigilant. Their emotions are just as big as the externalizing kids, but they present differently. They may not come to school, they may sleep through class, and they may not engage with other students. They may also do self-harming behaviors and be referred to a social worker for those things.

In both of these cases, school-based social workers can provide therapeutic, mental health, or counseling services for students. They don't have to necessarily diagnose the students they see, but they should use evidence-supported and developmental interventions with them. With elementary-aged students, counseling should be play based and should always involve family. With middle school or high school students, recreational therapy (like using sports or art) has been shown to be effective. Groups are an effective intervention for all age groups — they help connect students to peers who are experiencing similar problems, give them a safe space to learn and share, and give them a chance to grow in their interpersonal skills.

Helping Students with Bullying and Harassment

Bullying is a prevalent issue in schools, and many schools respond to concerns about school violence by implementing anti-bullying programs. Children who are targets of bullying often suffer from depression, engage in suicidal behavior, experience low self-esteem, and face negative health outcomes such as sleep disturbances, tobacco use, truancy, and poorer academic performance. They feel lonely, struggle to make friends, and experience significant distress. Students with disabilities or those identifying as LGBTQIA+ are especially vulnerable to frequent victimization. School bullying can have long-term negative impacts, including drug use and engagement in delinquent and violent behaviors into adulthood.

REMEMBER

Bullying is not a normal part of childhood. It's harmful, and it needs to be addressed head on.

What kinds of bullying happen in schools and what works? In a school-based setting, the various forms of bullying include the following:

>> **Gender-based bullying:** This form of bullying targets individuals based on their gender identity and gender stereotypes. Girls are often bullied due to perceived sexual behavior (such as seeming promiscuous), while boys may face bullying for not conforming to traditional masculine stereotypes. This is one of the oldest and worst forms of bullying. Kids who are *gender nonconforming* (not strictly identifying as male or female) are often targets of this type of bulling.

>> **Cyberbullying:** Cyberbullying involves using digital platforms to harass or intimidate others. This is newest form of bullying, and it's particularly harmful because the bullying isn't confined to school hours. It can happen after school and on the weekends — there's no escaping it. Intervening is also tough when the bullying goes viral.

>> **Physical bullying:** This type of bullying involves physical acts of aggression, such as hitting, pushing, or other forms of physical harm. This type of victimization leads to chronic absenteeism. It makes the targets of the bullying not come to school and fall behind academically.

>> **Verbal bullying:** Verbal bullying includes name calling, teasing, or using hurtful language to belittle or harm someone emotionally. It's particularly painful for kids because they're developing, and peer perception deeply impacts their sense of self and esteem.

>> **Relational bullying:** Relational bullying centers around manipulating social relationships, often involving excluding kids from friend groups, spreading rumors, or sabotaging friendships. This is undercover bullying where the bully can be passive or a third party to the process — meaning they aren't the ones directly targeting the person, but they play a role in creating a harmful or hostile environment.

>> **Identity-based bullying:** Kids may be targeted due to aspects of their identity, such as their race, religion, gender, sexual orientation, disability, or immigration status. This kind of bullying leads to discriminatory experiences and makes them victims of hate.

What kinds of interventions are available to address bullying and what works? Here's the range of approaches that schools have taken to address bullying:

>> **Whole-school approach:** This approach involves monitoring and addressing bullying throughout the entire school environment, identifying the major places where bullying may occur, and ensuring a safe atmosphere. This is usually in spaces with low adult supervision.

>> **Classroom-level interventions:** Teachers play a crucial role by promptly addressing specific bullying incidents within the classroom. They enforce anti-bullying policies and take proactive steps to prevent bullying. They need to be trained on how to notice and address incidents.

>> **Parental involvement:** In this approach, schools provide parents with information about bullying and organize training sessions where parents learn strategies to address bullying at home and within the school community.

>> **Peer involvement:** In this approach, students are empowered to combat bullying through bystander training, which equips them with the knowledge and skills to intervene when they witness bullying, creating a culture of empathy and support.

>> **Anti-bullying curricula:** Some programs focus on teaching social and emotional skills and may incorporate disciplinary or restorative justice measures to effectively address bullying incidents.

Which intervention works best? A comprehensive approach that fosters a safe and inclusive environment is the answer — in other words, a combination of all of the above. These strategies may include creating education and awareness programs, enforcing clear anti-bullying policies, providing counseling and support services, and encouraging students to report incidents. Fostering empathy, respect, and open dialogue among students can contribute to a more inclusive and respectful school community.

Social workers are tasked with the intricate job of working with all parties involved in bullying situation:

>> **The target of bullying:** Coming forward when you're subjected to daily torment can be exceptionally challenging, especially if seeking help is perceived as a sign of weakness. Because of these complexities, whenever a child disclosed that they were being victimized and provided examples, regardless of the details, I validated their experience and worked with them to help regain a sense of safety within their body and school environment. I also discussed strategies they could implement when they returned home.

>> **The bully:** Many bullies exhibit a pattern of being both bullies and victims themselves. They may target others in response to perceived injustices or as a reaction to their own victimization. In such instances, as an interventionist, I had to hold them accountable, assist them in gaining insight into their actions, and engage them in a restorative process. A restorative approach focuses on repairing the harm caused by bullying and fostering accountability. Instead of punitive measures, it encourages dialogue between the bully, victim, and other affected parties. The aim is to promote empathy, understanding, and personal growth for the bully, while also helping the victim heal. Through this process, it seeks to prevent future bullying incidents and create a more inclusive and respectful school environment.

REMEMBER

All these efforts require training and the use of evidence-supported approaches. It goes beyond mere mediation or a passive approach, hoping for the best outcome. These experiences have deep and lasting effects on everyone involved.

Addressing Truancy and Empty Seats

Absenteeism is one of the most visible outcomes that schools are required to report on, because chronically absent children are at a greater risk of eventually dropping out of school and, thus, warrant targeted interventions.

Schools typically have two approaches to addressing this issue:

>> **Punitive:** In the punitive approach, the school may resort to penalizing the student and their family, sometimes involving legal charges and court appearances in an attempt to motivate them.

>> **Restorative:** Alternatively, schools can opt for a restorative approach, where they actively engage the student and collaborate with the family to understand and address the underlying causes of absenteeism.

From a social worker's perspective, the restorative approach, which avoids involving the legal system, is often seen as the most effective one. Absenteeism doesn't happen in isolation — it's a symptom of deeper issues. By addressing the root causes of absenteeism, better outcomes can be achieved for all parties involved.

Punitive measures not only tend to be ineffective but also can create additional hardships for the child and family. Plus, they may discourage the family from viewing the school as a source of help and support.

In this section, I delve into the costs of absenteeism for everyone involved, elucidate some of the factors that underlie absenteeism, and discuss which approaches have proven effective and which have not.

Identifying the cost of chronic absenteeism

REMEMBER

In most states, attending school is compulsory for children between the ages of 5 and 17. The legal age at which a student can drop out is typically 16. By law, school-age children are required to participate in some form of schooling until they approach adulthood.

Students may be absent from school for various reasons, and schools typically have policies in place to categorize and manage absences. These policies often specify how many absences can be excused, what types of absences qualify as excused or unexcused, which chronic excused absences are permissible (often tied to medical conditions), and which chronically unexcused absences constitute truancy.

TECHNICAL STUFF

The federal government defines *chronic absenteeism* as missing 15 or more days of school in a single year. However, states may have more varied definitions, often spanning from missing 3 to 18 days of school. To simplify matters, policymakers have advocated for defining absenteeism as missing 10 percent or more of schooldays. This can become even more nuanced when schools differentiate between missing half a day or a full day of school in the application of this definition.

Truancy is a form of absenteeism that is unexcused and unlawful. Truancy is linked to a disconnection from school, and this disconnect can set off a chain reaction. It often starts with detachment from peers and the learning environment, which, in turn, contributes to even more negative outcomes. These can include a higher likelihood of dropping out of school and engaging in risky behaviors. The legal system gets involved and helps enforce school attendance laws. Historically, law enforcement got involved to combat child labor and protect children. Now states and officers impose fines, including misdemeanor charges, and jail time for the parents of the truant child. It goes from being a school problem to a legal problem.

Why on earth would a school be okay with placing a child's parent in jail? Because truancy has huge economic implications for schools. School budgets are tied to the number of students who attend the school. More absences literally mean less dollars for a school. In schools where chronic absenteeism is prevalent, the budgets often fluctuate, and these schools are typically under significant stress. Poor schools are often tied to poor parents. Society stigmatizes poor parents and blames them for their problems. It's not good, fair, or helpful.

REMEMBER

Criminalizing absenteeism heightens stress and distress within the family unit, perpetuates inequities (with significant racial disparities in punitive discipline referrals), and can lead children and families into the justice system, which is exceedingly difficult to exit. What's difficult about the use of interventions by truancy officers is that the intervention initially decreases absences and makes it *seem* like the tough approach works. However, research shows that it's only effective in the short term. Students often return to being truant and go before the officers again, actually missing even more days. Sadly, when this happens over and over again, officers and school officials start blaming the child. But that never works. Contact with the jail system doesn't lead to rehabilitation. It leads to more contact with jails and creates more harm in the long run.

Understanding the root causes of absenteeism

REMEMBER

Absenteeism doesn't happen in a vacuum. For the most part, children and families start off having a positive experience with schools. It's in the first through third grades that we start seeing disconnection and problems. That's because schools start testing kids at this age and school starts becoming more rote and less play based. For students from disadvantaged backgrounds, this is where we may start seeing frustration, disconnection, and school refusal. Parents who are stressed and overworked may only have the capacity to survive and hope the problem works itself out. Unfortunately, unless this problem is addressed, it will snowball and may eventually land the child and parent in the carceral system.

Here are some reasons for chronic absenteeism:

>> Academic difficulty

>> Bullying

>> Lack of friends

>> Lack of parental engagement and oversight

>> Medical condition

>> Mental illness

>> Moderate skipping of classes

>> Poor relationship with teachers

>> Substance use

>> Transportation issues

>> Unwelcoming school environment

As you can see, the root causes of missing school are *not* because parents and children don't value school or care about education. The issues that lead to absenteeism are real barriers and require thoughtful engagement and intervention.

Engaging families and increasing school connection

What should schools do when kids are missing school; the family is unresponsive to calls from the teacher, principal, and counselor; and the school's funding is dependent on the child being enrolled? The best approaches involve many or all of the following:

>> **Sports activities:** Being involved in teams and sports provides physical activity and gives kids an opportunity to build a community.

>> **Interesting and engaging school curriculum:** Students who are engaging in enriching activities want to come to school and enjoy what they're learning.

>> **Positive school climate:** Students need to feel safe and connected at school. A positive school climate fosters a sense of belonging.

>> **Positive relationship with teachers and school personnel:** When students feel connected to their teachers and staff at the school, they grow and learn.

>> **Connection with peers and classmates who are doing positive activities, especially with peers from previous classrooms:** Having positive peer interactions and consistent friendships creates community in the school setting.

>> **School-based monitoring and mentoring program:** Students do well in school when they know someone is looking for them or will know if they aren't there. They also thrive when enriching mentoring programs are in place that have programming specific to their needs.

>> **Parental involvement:** Parental involvement increases student and family connection to the school. School environments need to actively engage parents as part of the overall success plan of the school. Parents will see the school as a partner and resource rather than an intrusive or punitive institution.

>> **Community-based truancy programs:** These programs must be safe, have incentives for parents and students who participate, and advocate for parents.

>> **Faith-based alternative education programs:** These programs give individualized attention in safer environments.

>> **Increasing student belief in self and belief in others:** When students have a sense that they can learn and achieve, it builds their confidence in their academic skills. Students also do better when they have a trusted person or community they can count on to be there for them.

>> **Referrals to transitional programs or alternative schools:** Sometimes students need to start in a separate program or school setting and transition back into traditional schools or programs. Reentry programs aid students coming back to school after extended absences, such as those who have been homeschooled, incarcerated, or hospitalized. Alternative education centers cater to students who've faced difficulties in traditional schools, offering smaller classes and personalized support to help them catch up academically. Transition schools for young children help kids transition from preschool to elementary education, easing their adjustment to a structured learning environment.

REMEMBER

Severe truancy policies or suspensions do not decrease absenteeism. In fact, they increase overrepresentation of non-white students in jails.

TIP

Students who feel safe, are academically interested and enriched, and are connected to their peers and teachers come to school. Social workers' first and most useful intervention is creating the first contact, doing a thorough assessment of the situation to get an understanding of the root cause of the problem, and then deploying an intervention that works for the child, family, and school. We know what works, so it's a matter of thoughtfully incorporating interventions.

For some kids, small-scale interventions like checking in and out with an adult they like in the morning helps them come to school. They know someone is looking for them and they feel connected to that person, so they look forward to going to school. This model is called *check and connect*, and it's particularly good for elementary-school children. Other times, it takes a multiprong approach, especially with teens who are physically bigger and simply refuse to get out of bed.

This is when we try to find something of value to the student and motivate the student by incentivizing them with something they like (for example, concert tickets): "If you get out of bed and go to school this number of days, you'll earn a ticket to see your favorite performer."

When students get to school, we work with them to address the barriers and increase their connection to school and community. Maybe they've fallen behind and they need help catching up with class; if so, we devise an alternative plan with them and their teachers and monitor their coursework until they catch up. Let's say we discover they like to play sports or music. We help them sign up for activities at school or in the community. When a parent starts seeing that the child likes school and is getting positive phone calls from the school instead of calls alerting them that their child did something wrong (again), they're more likely to respond to school personnel and show up for their kid's game or after-school performance.

REMEMBER

Parents love and care about their children. When schools show warmth and interest in the child and family, they show up. Social workers help foster this kind of connection.

Chapter **12**

Community Organizing, Development, and Activism

W elcome to the exciting world of macro social work, where the focus is on the big picture. In this chapter, I break down the essential concepts of macro social work, focusing on the importance of targeting change at the systems level.

So, why macro? Because individual or incremental change doesn't solve social problems. Micro-level interventions help alleviate pain and suffering for individuals, but they don't radically change the underlying *causes* of the problems. In contrast, macro-level social work isn't content with helping individuals cope with their problems — it seeks to transform things so the problems don't exist in the first place. Macro-level work is for dreamers, people with big ideas and big hearts.

REMEMBER

Systems can be groups, neighborhoods, communities, governments, and even entire continents. In this chapter, I focus on communities as the system. A *community* isn't just a group of people living in the same area — it's a complex network of individuals, groups, and organizations, all interconnected and interdependent.

Community work — specifically, community organizing —is a significant and beloved form of social work practice. Through advocacy, social workers amplify the voices of those who've been marginalized or silenced, advocating for policies and practices that promote social justice and equity.

This chapter outlines the steps to organizing and advocacy work. After reading this chapter, you'll be ready to make a difference at the community level, armed with the knowledge of power, tactics, and the art of macro practice.

Social Change: Where Should It Happen?

In the science of helping, one of the first questions we ask is: What is the best place to start making changes when we see a social problem — at the individual level, the family level, or the social level?

When the field of social work first formed, this question was debated for quite some time. The debate was framed as *case versus cause* — in other words, the individual case of the person or the root cause of the affliction? If you give the person immediate assistance but you don't change address the larger problem, it'll just impact the person again down the road.

Today we talk about providing help at the *micro* (individual) level or the *macro* (communities and systems) level. Macro social work unequivocally says that you address the cause because the problem will continue to persist if you only address the individual case. The macro level is where you find social workers who are community organizers and activists. They work on making systemic and institutional changes that can't be addressed at the micro level. They make changes by engaging citizens; advocating for policy changes; and advocating for the reallocation of resources, benefits, and opportunities for those on the margins.

They challenge the notions that social ills or problems are normal and inevitable and something that we'll always have to wrestle with. For example, they assert that conditions such as poverty or violence occur because society is indifferent or hostile to the interests or conditions of people who are impacted by these problems.

REMEMBER

Macro social workers ask the following questions:

>> Who gets to decide the what the social problem is?

>> How is the help given to address this problem?

>> Who allocates resources to this problem?

>> Who initiates and controls the helping process?

>> How are the people affected by the problem and change involved?

>> How is success defined, and who gets to define it?

These questions ask about the process and the mechanisms of change. They're system-level inquiries. They aren't focused on the individual experiencing the social problem — instead, they're focused on the conditions that brought on the problem and the mechanism for solving the problem.

What does this look like in real life? Let me use the example of domestic violence or what is now called *intimate partner violence*.

Micro social workers usually work with victims of violence and help them recover from abuse through counseling and/or legal advocacy. Macro social workers organize efforts to bring awareness to the issue and highlight that existing systems are based on the patriarchy, which condones or turns a blind eye to intimate partner violence. Intimate partner violence is not seen as a private family matter; instead, it's a pervasive social problem. Macro interventions create social movements around this issue and make collective efforts to change the way this problem is seen and defined. This movement is led by feminists and survivors, and the interventions include federal laws that criminalize battering, fund programs for the creation of housing and safe havens, and create policies for victim compensation and protection.

Macro practice is a collective and collaborative form of social work, and it seeks change on a large scale. This large-scale intervention can happen in policy practice, in organizational management, and in community practice. This kind of change may progress at a slower pace and requires a long-term perspective. Social workers must exhibit persistence and remain committed, with grit and determination being essential personal attributes. This chapter focuses on community practice.

Defining community

In the helping profession, people talk about working "in the community," working "for the community," being a "community organizer," or being a "member of the community." What does *community* mean in these contexts, and what does it mean to work in the community?

There are three major ways to think about community:

>> A physical place

>> A social identity

>> A political unit

Community can be a neighborhood, a place of worship, a professional affiliation, a membership in an identity group, or connect to a shared experience like migration.

TIP

What's important to note about communities is that they're targets or mechanisms for social change. Big social movements like labor movements and civil rights movements have activated and mobilized communities as levers for social change.

REMEMBER

How you define *community* determines how you work. In most instances, communities work in multidimensional ways and are not strictly limited to a place, social identity, or political unit — it's a combination of all three.

A physical place

Community can be defined as a physical space and place where people live, interact, and get their physical and social needs met. The focus of the physical community as an area of interest for social scientists and helpers came about because of two major social changes in the early 1900s: industrialization and urbanization. Modernization meant that fewer people lived on farms and in agrarian cultures. They moved into dense industrial cities, children worked or were left unattended for long periods of time, and people worked without labor protections.

The physical boundaries of the community or the geographic space for the community is determined by the people who live in it and by larger social entities such as county and governmental municipalities.

The boundaries of the physical community or how people think of their space is determined by the people who use the physical space. Do they use it for housing, schooling, recreation, entertainment, health care, or worship? How people come to identify with their neighbors depends on how much of the physical space and infrastructure they use and rely on to meet their needs.

People with more resources tend to have neighborhoods that have lots of institutional supports dispersed across the city. They can go to lots of different places in their physical space and have their needs met. There are libraries, access to the arts, and multiple sites for social interactions.

In less resourced spaces, people tend to be more engaged within their own neighborhoods. There are fewer resources, so they tend to get their needs met in a more concentrated space, like a religious space or one community center that meets multiple needs.

Social workers who intervene in neighborhoods as a physical place think about giving community members more power and voice in what happens in their neighborhoods. They mobilize people to become significant stakeholders that politicians and developers must consider before they make decisions about the neighborhood.

A social identity

Community as social identity focuses on the relationship among people based on a shared characteristic or experience (for example, ethnic identity, religion, or migration status). It isn't necessarily tied to where people live. Instead, it's about what they collectively share or have in common. Members of the community provide support for each other based on their shared social identity and values, and they come together for mutual aid and connection.

Most often, a shared social identity leads to people also physically living near each other and creating a physical space for their social community. One group of people settles in a particular neighborhood and, over time, creates a safe network where they work and live together and build social capital. In this way, community fosters a sense of belonging and connection. It's highly relational and less dependent on physical boundaries. Physical proximity can facilitate connections, but the internet enables the formation of communities built on shared social identities, allowing people to connect regardless of their geographical locations. Plus, it can reveal that some individuals are more closely tied geographically than they initially believed.

A political unit

A community can also be a *political unit* (in which people come together to make governance decisions or mobilize for social action). The community can be a place where people deliberate and make representative decisions about what happens in their lives. These communities mobilize people to have a voice in what happens in their neighborhoods and deliberate on decisions about schools, *infrastructure* (for example, roads), and safety. This is neighborhood democracy and macro social work that focuses on this definition of community focus works on community development and civic engagement as its form of intervention. Local communities can be empowered to make decisions that best serve their residents and resist oppressive or centralized changes like *gentrification* (economic development in under-resourced neighborhoods that displaces long-standing low-income residents).

In other instances, a community emerges around a specific political issue and people come together to mobilize for change. This is where people get together to challenge authorities, systems, or structures that are marginalizing or are not sharing power or decision making on issues that directly impact them. Examples of this include communities advocating for affordable housing or mobilizing to block a hazardous waste plant in their neighborhood.

Looking at approaches to community practice

Macro social work — specifically, community-based social work — focuses on advocating for improvement in social conditions so people have equal access to a high quality of life. There are many models and approaches to community practice, but at the heart of each model is an emphasis on promoting social justice. Community practice approaches emphasize collaboration, power redistribution and sharing, diverse and inclusive leadership, and restructuring of systems and institutions to better serve all people.

Here are the major areas and models of community practice:

>> **Coalition work:** Collaborative efforts between organizations or groups with common interests to work together on specific goals, typically related to policy change or advocacy

>> **Inclusive program development:** Creating initiatives that are accessible and beneficial to all community members, regardless of differences in background or abilities

>> **Movement and progressive change:** Involvement in or support for societal movements and initiatives focused on achieving positive and progressive transformations, often related to civil rights, environmental concerns, or other social causes

>> **Neighborhood and community organizing:** Mobilizing residents to address local issues and improve the quality of life within a specific neighborhood or community

>> **Organizing functional communities:** Bringing together like-minded groups or individuals to collaborate on shared objectives, often with a focus on advocacy or problem solving

>> **Political and social action:** Activities intended to influence political decisions and promote social change through methods like activism, lobbying, and advocacy

>> **Social, economic, and sustainable development:** Strategies and actions aimed at enhancing the well-being, economic prospects, and environmental sustainability of a community

>> **Social planning:** The systematic assessment of community needs and the development of policies and strategies to address those needs, especially in areas such as social services and public welfare

This chapter primarily focuses on community organizing and social action.

Community Organizing

Community organizing is a method of helping people come together to identify and solve problems through a collective process. Community organizing happens within the context of community practice. Aggrieved or marginalized individuals can't compel larger forces or systems to respond to their needs on an individual basis. The system may not be interested in sharing power or listening to the needs of people it deems unworthy. But when citizens come together, they can force the system to listen — or at least make it harder for the system to ignore them.

Macro practice uses transformational change as part of the social reform process. Change doesn't come easily or without negotiation of power. In the world of macro social work, power isn't just about strength — it's about who has control and influence over resources, decisions, and opportunities. Oppression often arises when power is unequally distributed, and that's where social workers come in.

Dealing with power

Macro social work and community organizing practitioners use two main tactics when dealing with power:

» **Consensus organizing:** Consensus organizing works on finding common ground and working together toward positive change. It's all about building partnerships and collaboration. Consensus-based models engage community members and empower them to speak for themselves as stakeholders. They also prioritize collaboration among diverse perspectives and place a strong emphasis on collaboration and compromise so all people's needs are met. It's what they call an *accommodationist approach*.

Consensus organizing is hard work. Think about trying to get all your family members to make a decision on where to eat dinner or which movie to watch. It makes you want to quit before you even start, right? With consensus organizing, you're trying to get people with all kinds of perspectives and viewpoints to agree on something that matters to them. It takes work, skill, and patience, but social workers are trained in methods that work. It isn't just about wearing someone down or convincing them to change. It involves using interventions and methods like group dialogues to help identify the shared values and priorities of the group and create a road map for accomplishing what everyone agrees upon.

» **Conflict organizing:** Conflict organizing acknowledges that change requires challenging the status quo and requires equal measures of power and resistance. Sometimes people in power don't want to give up their power, so they must be compelled to do so through collective activism.

In conflict organizing, people with less power unite to agitate and pressure those in power to change. For example, with abolitionist movements, there was no compromise or collaboration on the practice of enslavement. You can't be a partial slave owner — you're either in the business of enslaving people or you aren't. Enslavers had no interest in giving up the practice of slavery. Abolitionists had to disrupt and demand change in totality, using conflict-based organizing.

Both of these tactics are tools in a macro social worker's toolbox, and knowing when to use each one is an art. Let me give you an example of how each tactic works.

Let's say a neighborhood is facing major problems with gentrification. Long-term residents are being driven or priced out of their homes. Residents of the neighborhood can use a conflict model and picket or sue the developer behind this gentrification effort. Or residents can use a consensus model of organizing and collaborate with the developer to make changes that serve both the existing residents and the developer.

REMEMBER

Where these approaches differ is in the ultimate goal of the organizing efforts. With the conflict model, the goal is usually systemic change. With the consensus model, the goal is to address a specific community need and build community cohesion and voice.

TIP

Social workers have to understand what the *community* wants and what tactic they're comfortable with before deploying their organizing efforts. Otherwise, a community may think the social worker is too accommodating to the powers that be or that the social worker is too aggressive or intense in their approach.

Understanding community organizing models

There are several models and approaches to community organizing. Each model aims to *collectively* address social, economic, and political conditions that impact the community. (Notice the emphasis on the word *collectively* — it's the power of the group and the efforts of the group that bring about the larger change.)

Here are some of the common models of organizing that social workers use to bring about macro-level changes:

>> **Jack Rothman's Three Models of Community Organization Practice:**
Focuses on three models of organizing — *locality development* (building community leadership and promoting social cohesion), *social planning* (addressing social issues, often with varying levels of community involvement),

and *social action* (confronting and challenging inequities and mobilizing communities for collective action and advocacy).

>> **Saul Alinsky's model of organizing:** An approach to organizing that was founded by Saul Alinsky (and outlined in his book *Rules for Radicals*), which focuses on mobilizing communities in the public sphere. It uses confrontational tactics such as protests, rallies, and civil disobedience to pressure decision-makers.

>> **Asset-Based Community Development:** Uses a strengths-based approach to identify assets within the community and leverage them to make change. This model promotes the idea that communities have the resources to solve their own problems and that they can create social capital to make changes. To build up local resources, it uses the following:

- **Asset mapping:** Identifying and assessing available resources within a community or organization to address social issues effectively

- **Community engagement**

- **Capacity-building practices:** Strengthening the skills, knowledge, and infrastructure of individuals or groups to empower them in tackling social challenges and achieving their goals

>> **Grassroots Organizing:** Focuses on empowering community members to become active participants in shaping their own ecosystems. This model mobilizes local residents and builds coalitions and social capital. Organizers develop campaigns that meet the needs of the community.

>> **Faith-Based Organizing:** Uses religious values, principles, and institutions to mobilize the community around social justice issues. This model engages religious leaders and organizes a faith-based community to promote moral and ethical values around political or social issues.

>> **Labor Organizing:** In this model, labor unions and worker organizations advocate for workers' rights and better working conditions. The methods involve strikes, collective bargaining, and political advocacy.

>> **Youth Organizing:** Engages young people in community activism. This model creates youth-led initiatives, builds advocacy campaigns, fosters leadership development, and empowers young people to become activists and address issues that impact their daily lives and their generation.

>> **Transformative, Critical, Feminist, Cross-cultural:** Anti-oppressive organizing models that critically examine social structures that promote inequity (for example, racism, sexism, homophobia) and consciously create organizing efforts that address structural oppression. These models pay attention to the culture of the community and create strategies of engagement that are sensitive to the needs of the community. For example, contemporary community organizing with Black communities includes awareness of the impact of racism on the community, promotion of social justice, leadership development, and building personal and collective esteem and participation.

Identifying the community organizer's role

In the preceding section, I cover the major models of community organizing. Each of these models is action oriented — they're for movers and shakers. They may vary in their area of methodology (conflict, consensus, or hybrid), but they all emphasize the need for momentum and action. The role of the community organizer — in this case, the social worker — is essential in facilitating these changes and actions.

TIP

The major role of a community organizer is to help create power for the collective so the group has the capacity to enact change for social and political betterment. Saul Alinsky, one of the most prominent social work community organizers, describes a community organizer as a social worker who is imaginative, is curious, and has a blurred or enchanted vision for a better world. It takes a bit of delusion and radical hope to imagine a different paradigm for how society should exist. Agitators who make "good trouble" should have a view of the world that challenges the status quo and are open-minded to what's possible.

The consensus organizer's primary role is to empower others. They need to have deep listening skills and be able to broker relationships between opposing or unlikely partners. They do this through strategic planning and trained skills. They need to have a high tolerance for conflict and be able to hold space for different perspectives. Their goal is to find the common ground and value of the group and help put a plan in place to deliver the wishes of the group. They're behind the scenes, and their goal is to leave the community to run on its own. They help develop sustainable change that the community members can own and adapt. Their approaches are collaborative and less confrontational than the conflict organizer.

Community organizers adapt their roles and stances as they implement the change process. They may start off as the clear organizer and leader of the movement and eventually fade into being the facilitator or observer. Or they may be contacted to help with an existing campaign or play a consultant role in the organizing process.

TIP

Here are some of the key roles that community organizers hold in the intervention process:

>> **Initiator:** Part of the preliminary group that identifies the community need and builds an assessment process to prioritize action

>> **Facilitator/enabler:** Facilitates and empowers community members to identify their goals, agenda, and action items

>> **Mobilizer:** Engages community members for collective action and brings on campaigns

- >> **Mediator/negotiator:** Helps resolve conflicts, negotiate agreements, and build consensus among conflicting parties

- >> **Broker:** Connects the community with external resources, services, and institutional/social supports

- >> **Advocate:** Represents the community's needs at the policy and legislative level

- >> **Educator:** Provides training, information, and education to community members to help address the needs they've identified

- >> **Researcher and analyst:** Gathers data and conducts research relevant to the organizing campaign

- >> **Fundraiser and grant writer:** Secures funding for the organizing effort

In each of these roles, the community organizer is service oriented and develops a plan with the community to address an unmet need. The goals are focused on building the strengths of the community.

WARNING

The community organizer has to make sure not to be tone deaf or have a savior complex, trying to impose their will on the community. Savior approaches are usually rejected by the group and, in worst-case scenarios, end up reproducing the very harm or coercive practices they were trying to address in the first place.

Social workers who are trained in macro practice and in community organizing have a clear understanding of their role within the process.

Looking at the basic steps of community organizing

Now that you know the kinds of things that community organizers do, you're ready to roll up your sleeves and start doing the work. Community organizing involves five major steps.

Step 1: Assessing the situation and identifying the issue

The first step is to understand what the community needs. In order to do this, you need a robust assessment plan that involves and includes the folks who are experiencing the need you're trying to address.

You should assess the following entities:

>> Health and human service providers

>> Government officials

>> People who are identified as leaders

>> Community activities

>> Businesses

>> People whose jobs or lives can be impacted by the actions that result from the assessment

You should assess the resources and strengths of the community, as well as the needs and barriers.

Assessment is a critical process that can foster trust with community members and is worth getting right. Without the input of the critical players, you may end up on focusing on the wrong issue or the issue that isn't the most pressing one.

Step 2: Strategic planning

After you've clearly identified the issue, you need to come up with a strategy for *how* you're going to address the problem or meet the unmet need.

Start by organizing a brainstorming meeting with your team to clarify your vision, mission, and objectives for the organizing efforts. Your strategy or process should give your work clear and achievable short-term, midterm, and long-term goals with benchmarks and timelines.

Develop an evaluation plan as part of your strategic planning. Your evaluation plan will enable you to monitor your progress so by the end of your efforts, you can see if you met your goals.

Your plan should take into account the resources and opportunities of the community and should outline where you have gaps that you need to allocate resources to.

Your strategic plan should always aim to reach the people who are impacted by the problem. Otherwise, it won't do any good.

Step 3: Implementing the plan

In this step, it's finally time to put all that assessment and planning into action. You'll carry out the action plan, launch the project, and produce and analyze your first results.

In this part of the process, you have the action plan, as well as the process tasks (like establishing structure, tracking the workflow, and cultivating resources).

If you're working with staff or volunteers, you'll need an administrative structure to keep track of your work and onboard new members and develop leaders.

Being flexible and nimble in this phase of the work is important. There will be political and economic changes throughout the organizing efforts, and you'll need to have a solid infrastructure that can withstand and tolerate the fluxes in social and political conditions.

Step 4: Evaluating the plan

The evaluation process helps you assess the impact, effectiveness, and overall success of your organizing effort. It provides critical feedback about what worked and what didn't. Your evaluation should directly assess the goals and objectives of the organizing effort and help to provide evidence that your understanding of the problem was accurate and meaningful.

REMEMBER

You don't have to rely on memory or anecdotal information to do your evaluation. You'll go to the data to tell the story and learn and improve the work. You should have a timeline of when you'll collect the information.

The methods you use to evaluate can be numerical (quantitative) or descriptive (qualitative). They can include interviews, surveys, process and outcome measures, observations, and community-level indicators. Analyze and interpret the data, looking for patterns, trends, and significant changes.

REMEMBER

Your evaluation *must* include feedback from the people impacted by the unmet need. And be sure to share the results of your evaluation with the community. It's crucial to always keep the individuals most affected by the problem in focus. If you observe that your programs are effective, it indicates their responsiveness to the community's needs. This signifies that you've listened to those most impacted and reaffirmed the significance of their involvement. This, in turn, helps build trust and ensures ongoing proactive efforts to prevent new issues or enable early intervention. Building and nurturing relationships is central to community advocacy and change.

Step 5: Monitoring and maintaining change

Now that you've done this big job of running a successful organizing effort, you have to monitor and sustain the change so the positive outcomes can continue to benefit the community.

Make sure you have an infrastructure to maintain the change and that you're investing in capacity building so community leaders and community members have the resources, training, and supports they need to keep up the work. You do this by fostering partnerships and collaborations with all the stakeholders you interviewed in Step 1 and built relationships with in Step 3.

REMEMBER

Initiatives are successful when they run on their own and can adapt to new challenges. You want to be able to give local ownership. And don't forget to celebrate and mark the success!

Political and Legislative Action and Community Practice

In addition to using social action models like the consensus and conflict organizing models (see "Dealing with power," earlier in this chapter), macro social workers are interested in legislative and political action to enact social changes. They work on empowering people and allocating resources to them so they can live in a just and equitable society. These efforts can target local municipalities, state and national government offices, and politics. This work involves mixing it up with policymakers and maybe even becoming one yourself.

What is legislative action in community practice? It's using advocacy and lobbying efforts to influence lawmakers and helping draft and pass laws to bring about social justice. A social worker can be a lobbyist or an activist who is looking to make an impact at this level. Lobbying efforts go further when professional groups, such as the National Association of Social Workers, can put pressure on or collaborate with lawmakers to enact laws that are focused on social justice issues.

Political action entails meeting with elected officials, building alliances, forming coalitions, and creating awareness around the issue you want to bring attention to. People often feel that the legislative process is something other people do. Persuading public officials to change laws or create laws is a big task, but don't be intimidated by it. Coalitions of people have been doing this kind of work for years, and you'll be trained in the process.

Social workers are well positioned to educate public officials about the need for social change for many reasons. Social workers' knowledge and value base provides a solid foundation for policy work. Social workers are the most likely to understand the changes that need to be made with social welfare policies because they're on the ground seeing the challenges and working with marginalized groups who are most impacted by social welfare policies. Even when they aren't working in direct practice, they're collaborating with social workers who are. Because of this, they're well positioned to also understand what changes need to be made. They can also be a voice for marginalized groups, especially if a group feels silenced and oppressed.

Social work students also have opportunities to engage in policy work and political action through social work programs, clubs, and political action committees. Student representation is an important component of this work because students are impacted by policies every day. Policies impact various aspects of social work education and the profession, including licensure, student loan debt, service delivery, rights and protections, and benefits. Social work students also have opportunities to complete internships or practicums at the state and federal level of government through programs offered with state and federal legislatures. They can work with the National Association of Social Workers (NASW) to address key policy issues nationwide.

REMEMBER

This may all seem very scary, but it's important to know that legislative officials are looking to students to understand the needs of younger generations and to be inspired about new paths for change and advocacy. Not only does change take time, but it requires creativity, curiosity, and sometimes risk taking. Who is better suited than a student or a new social worker ready to take on the world? Some of the most meaningful changes in child welfare policy have come from foster youth working with legislative officials. Now if that isn't inspirational, I don't know what is.

Another form of activism is running for elected office. Social workers can work on any part of this process — they can register voters, help run a campaign, or be the candidate running for office. Galvanizing voters has significant outcomes on elections and is something that social workers have been doing since the formation of the profession.

Issues like restricting voting rights, limiting health-care access, and curtailing civil rights issues are constantly being debated and voted on. These issues deeply impact the lives of the people we work with, so we have to get involved in the political arena.

Social workers galvanize voters and speak out on issues that are core to social work values and principles. In social work, we say the personal is political — we must be involved in political action as part of our professional work. In fact, we're inherently involved in political action. Macro social workers are some of the most visible community practitioners in the political action arena.

Serving in public office is something you may find intimidating or not even possible. But over time, many community organizers become known as public servants in the community. They may organically rise into the political space and end up running for office. Those in public office say they got tired of fighting against policies and decided to jump in the ring and help create or change policies.

Defining and understanding power

In macro practice, understanding, leveraging, and redistributing power from those who have it to those who don't is important. Giving people agency over their lives, situations, and communities allows them to live better lives. Social workers use the term *empowerment* when they talk about helping people in this way. We can empower communities using confrontational or collaborative tactics.

Confrontational tactics

Confrontational or conflict-based tactics use anger and rage as the motivations for contesting and protesting conditions that deprive people of their fundamental rights or ability to live in a fair and equitable system. We *should* be outraged by poverty, violence, and disenfranchisement — there is no reason these conditions should exist.

According this approach, powerful groups must be compelled to make changes they don't want to make. The conflict-based understanding of power is adversarial and clear-eyed. The target is the one who has the power, and the goal is to take the power away from them and give it to the people impacted by the oppressive structure.

Essentially, according to this approach, people and systems that extort and harm others don't need to be negotiated with — they need to be confronted with collective power and forced to change for the better. Tactics such as rallies, sit-ins, marches, and lawsuits create public spectacles that eventually create social movements that change whole systems. Labor movements and civil rights movements are examples of these conflict/confrontational tactics.

Collaborative tactics

Collaborative or consensus-based approaches believe that power can be shared and grown between opposing sides. They say that people will act in reasonable ways when they're given options that work for them and when they aren't cornered into a defensive posture. It's a matter of finding common values and ground between the target and the community and getting a workable solution that builds partnership and collaborations. They form coalitions and groups based on these shared values and build power through dialogue, creating a process where they can get the best out of all involved. They do this by empowering people in the community to be at the table when decisions are being made and giving people roles to take action.

Consensus building can seem like wishful thinking. It take lots of time and hard work, but it works, and there are many models of consensus-based or shared power models of community work. This is a particularly a helpful way of doing neighborhood work.

Advocating for change

How do get powerful individuals and systems to make changes they aren't interested in making? Through planned advocacy work. This section explores effective strategies for driving change within community practice, emphasizing the importance of a change-focused perspective. By understanding the issues, setting clear goals, utilizing available resources, and maintaining adaptability, you can navigate the path toward influencing those who may otherwise be resistant to change.

REMEMBER

Advocating for change using principles of macro social work and community organizing will make your efforts successful. You'll be joining a long tradition of social work practice in the public sphere, and you'll have a good playbook and passionate partners. There is no cause too small, no problem too big.

Understanding the problem and targets

To effectively advocate for change, it's crucial to develop a comprehensive understanding of the problem and identify the specific targets for transformation. Determine whether your efforts will be directed at multiple targets or channeled toward a representative figure, such as a senior executive or policymaker. This initial step lays the foundation for an advocacy strategy centered on instigating change.

Setting goals and resources

Advocating for change demands clear goals. Social workers develop goals that are specific, measurable, achievable, relevant, and time-bound (SMART). These goals help you stay on track and ensure you aren't pulled in multiple directions throughout the advocacy process.

Conduct an inventory of your available resources and assets, which may encompass funds, connections, media contacts, facilities, and access to information. An in-depth understanding of your available resources is essential for crafting and executing an impactful advocacy campaign.

Identifying support and opposition

Determine who within your community will provide support for your advocacy efforts and who may resist them. This information will shape your advocacy approach, whether it leans toward persuasive diplomacy or assertive demonstrations.

You also want to see what kind of appetite people have for your planned efforts. You may be angry and ready to rally, but the community members may be more passive or consensus-driven and be unsupportive of your tactics. You want to move in tandem with the community.

While planning, consider the scale, duration, and necessary resources for your chosen advocacy method, while remaining adaptable as circumstances evolve.

Strategic planning

Develop a comprehensive strategy for advocating change by outlining your goals, resources, and potential obstacles. Define long-term objectives for the conclusion of your campaign, set intermediate milestones along the way, and establish short-term goals to guide your daily actions. Engage in activities such as elevating public awareness, conducting educational campaigns, and building coalitions with like-minded entities to strengthen your position.

Managing responses

Throughout your advocacy campaign, be prepared to effectively manage responses as they arise. Celebrate and publicize good news to generate momentum, thoroughly investigate rumors of unfavorable developments to maintain transparency, and promptly address unmet needs. In the face of negative news, deliver a swift response to mitigate its impact and sustain public support.

Chapter 13

Enhancing Leadership Roles in Organizations

When I talk to prospective social work students, I always ask what makes them interested in social work or the helping field. A good number of people tell me they want to open a nonprofit organization. I love this answer because it means they're interested in doing public service and willing to be a leader. What I don't say is, "What you're thinking about probably exists, and what you actually want to do is be a nonprofit leader." (I'm not a dream crusher, I promise.)

Approximately 1.54 million nonprofits are registered with the Internal Revenue Service (IRS). That's a *lot* of nonprofits. Many people and organizations want to do good work. It's important to understand that having a good idea or identifying a gap or a need in service is the *start* of the process not the end. What you may think is brand new or innovative may already exist, and what you need to do is join the group that's already doing that work. Or you may discover the group is doing some aspect of what you were proposing, and you can add another dimension to it.

For instance, maybe you want to open a shelter that allows pets. You discovered that people stay in unsafe relationships or refuse shelter services because they can't bring their pets with them. Instead of starting a whole new shelter, you could approach the existing shelters in your community and talk to them about adding a program that allows people to bring their pets.

Or maybe you have an idea to start a medication-assisted treatment center for people who are struggling with substance use. Your town may have abstinence-only programs where people can find help if they try to quit cold turkey or with the help of groups like Alcoholics Anonymous or Narcotics Anonymous. The abstinence-only folks can't graft you into their program — your mission and approach are too different. Your idea is novel and needs its own start.

Nonprofit management is one of the foundational roles in social work. Many other majors (even business schools) have implemented nonprofit management or sustainable leadership as one of their core offerings. These other professions are emerging programs, but the social work profession has been doing this work since its inception as a profession. Social workers are trained to be effective leaders with management and leadership skills.

In this chapter, I discuss the purpose and structure of nonprofits. I also discuss the leader of the organization as the change agent. I share what makes a nonprofit, why it exists, and the process it uses to enact change. Then I shift over to the leaders of the organization and talk about what makes a good nonprofit leader and how leaders can create a healthy organization that takes care of its staff as well as it takes care of the people it serves.

Understanding What Makes Nonprofits Unique

A for-profit business is in business to make money. Coca-Cola makes beverages and Nike makes athletic gear, but they make those goods in order to make money.

The central goal of every *nonprofit* organization is to promote the mission of the organization, not to generate money. Any money the organization takes in is a resource; it isn't the end goal. The mechanism for delivering social service to meet unmet needs and alleviate human suffering is the nonprofit itself. The nonprofit is the level of intervention. Whatever extra money is made or generated must be reinvested back into the organization.

The IRS has more than 30 categories or classifications that allow an organization to be classified as a nonprofit. This designation exempts the organization from paying federal and state taxes. Charitable organizations can receive gifts that are tax-deductible from donors. These tax benefits are meant to encourage the public to support nonprofit organizations.

REMEMBER

Human service nonprofits are the largest subsector of nonprofit organizations, and they're where social workers have the biggest role and the most visibility. These nonprofits make up one-third of all the public charities in the United States. They provide a wide range of services and support in areas such as homelessness, services for children and older adults, people with disabilities, education, medical services, and workforce development.

Nonprofits are funded by private sources, government grants, and fees for service. (They usually charge insurance companies for their fees and not the consumer directly.) They're governed by a board of directors that has the ultimate financial responsibility for the agency. Boards help set the mission and goal of the organization, create a strategic plan, approve organizational programming, and establish organization effectiveness measurements. The executive director (ED) or the chief executive officer (CEO) of the nonprofit reports to the board of directors and helps implement the vision and mission of the organization. It's a big role, and most social service agencies are led by executive directors trained in social work.

Seeing How Nonprofits Operate

One of my favorite professors once said, "Organizations are sexy." She got the whole class's attention. We'd never heard organizations described this way. In fact, when people think of organizations, they usually think of dense bureaucratic systems that have lots of paperwork and grumpy staff. My professor went on to explain that organizations have the allure of solving problems faster and more efficiently. They reproduce the work of one person by thousands — and what one person can do, the organization does in a tenfold way. Isn't that sexy?

Well, we weren't as turned on by this notion as our professor was, but we got the point. Change, lots of change, can happen when there's a collective or strategic process. An individual can only do so much. Pioneer social workers and activists wanted to build a net for people who were falling through the cracks. They saw that one-on-one work needed to be multiplied to reach large groups. So, they started establishing charitable organizations, through activism and legislative changes.

Before and even after charitable organizations were established, people who have been sidelined or marginalized have been helping each other through a process called *mutual aid.* They've formed helping groups through their faith groups, men or women's groups, or occupational groups. They had to use these methods because charitable organizations had limited resources and consistently left Black Americans and Native peoples out of their helping process. Today, social workers are adding this critical note about our own helping history when we tell our story. This helps remind the current generation of nonprofit leaders to be intentional about not leaving out groups that need help the most.

Social workers, sociologists, and economists have developed theories to explain why nonprofits exist and their function in society, including the following:

>> Nonprofits are the result of historical social movements.

>> The IRS tax structure provides benefits for nonprofits.

>> Nonprofits provide a buffer or link between people and a larger institution — they help connect one to the other.

>> Nonprofits give voice to people from diverse backgrounds who haven't had their needs met.

>> Nonprofits provide creative and efficient solutions to emerging needs.

>> Nonprofits help when there is government and economic failure and fill in the gaps.

>> Nonprofits promote altruism.

These theories highlight that nonprofits exist to solve social problems. They can help solve issues like homelessness, child hunger, and human trafficking. They may start off as grass-roots organizations that bring attention to a social problem, like domestic or intimate partner violence. After social awareness and government support are provided, nonprofits provide help to the population in need in a strategic way. Help for victims of intimate partner violence started as women creating safe local houses for women and helping women disappear to save their lives. As the issue gained attention and public and legislative support, nonprofits were able to create safe community shelters and robust programming.

Nonprofits also offer public good and should be benevolent. Society should be better because the nonprofit exits. The nonprofit shouldn't an agent of social control or harm. For example, in the past, "help" used to be provided in the form of asylums for people with severe mental health issues. Most of these spaces were basically prisons — they were warehouses for people. This was a moral failing by the helping sector. Nonprofits make social change or intervene at the macro level.

They're a collective force. It goes back to my professor's comments about organizations being sexy — they're an agent of change because they compound impact of the help they provide.

Getting clear on your mission, vision, and values

REMEMBER

For a nonprofit, the mission is the calling and heartbeat of the organization. It captures the essence of the organization's purpose and doesn't change much. If the organization becomes broader and bigger over time, it can change the scope of its mission. But the social problem or the work it's addressing stays the same.

If an organization strays too far from its founding purpose, it can run into a problem called *mission creep*. For more on mission creep, see the nearby sidebar.

Mission statements are usually short and bold — for example, ending homelessness; eradicating poverty; protecting children and families; ending sexual violence; or in the case of the organization I work for, changing our selves, the future, and the world. Big stuff, right? A mission statement should be big and inspiring. That's the point of making changes at the macro level.

AVOIDING MISSION CREEP

Mission creep is the erosion of the original purpose of the organization. Why would an organization have mission creep if the mission is the heartbeat of the organization?

Nonprofits have to constantly seek funding from major sources like foundations and government entities. Funding priorities change every five years. To stay afloat, organizations may have to expand their programming or adopt totally different interventions.

For instance, let's say a nonprofit is set up to provide recovery supports and temporary shelter for families. A government entity like the U.S. Department of Housing and Urban Development (HUD) may shift its funding structure and no longer fund temporary shelters. It may want all transitional shelters converted to into permanent housing. So, the nonprofit has to decide if it will change its mission from providing temporary shelter to one that gives permanent housing. That means the organization may become a housing development organization and not a recovery-centered organization.

This situation may be seen as mission creep — or it could just be adapting to a better model. The nonprofit's board has to decide if this change is interfering with the mission or if it's simply doing something new to meet its mission.

The vision and values of the organization usually follow the mission statement:

>> **Vision:** The *vision* is the description of the future. Where does the organization see itself in one year, five years, or ten years?

>> **Values:** The *values* are the guiding core principles that are central to the mission. For instance, if the mission is to end homelessness, the value is to give people affordable housing.

Doing some strategic planning

REMEMBER

Nonprofits use a strategic planning process to develop programs and goals that enact the mission and values of the organization. The *strategic plan* is the road map for the organization and sets measurable benchmarks. It's also a planning and communication tool that organizations use to show funders that they have concrete and measurable objectives for their work.

For example, an organization that serves homeless people can't just say it plans on ending homelessness. The organization must provide a plan where it shows that it's investing in building affordable housing, meeting the needs of the residents, and being attuned to the larger community.

As part of the strategic plan, nonprofits must assess information within and outside the organization. This helps the nonprofit understand the threats to the organization and the distinctive strengths of the organization. It also helps the nonprofit stay informed on cutting-edge work, competitors, and issues that are impacting organizational culture. Information gleaned from the assessment helps inform the future goals or direction of the organization. The goals usually center on core programming, organization infrastructure, finances, and organization culture.

Developing and implementing a program

After broad goals are established, organizations establish programs with specific objectives to meet those goals. The nonprofit keeps the following questions in mind as it develops the new program:

>> Does the new program have a competitive edge?

>> What makes this program stand out to funders?

>> Does the organization want to offer this program or is it being pressured to offer it because of funding needs?

>> Does the organization have capacity to develop the new program?

These questions help programs be innovative, non-redundant, and useful to the communities they serve. There is no need to have multiple providers fighting for the same pot of money to offer the same program down the block. Nonprofit organizations should offer programs that are complementary to one another and meet unfilled needs in the community. This is something they usually have to demonstrate to potential funders. They should develop the program with these principles in mind.

TIP

Many nonprofits use a *matrix map* (like the one shown in Figure 13-1) to help them visualize the organization programs and activities. A matrix map assesses for the impact of the new program using criteria the organization sets, typically against the mission of the organization and the finances of the organization. The matrix map assesses the following:

>> How aligned is the new program with the mission of the organization?

>> Can the organization deliver the program effectively using the best science and community engagement practices?

>> What is the scale and depth of the program?

>> How much community impact will it have?

>> How much funding will it need?

>> How profitable will it be?

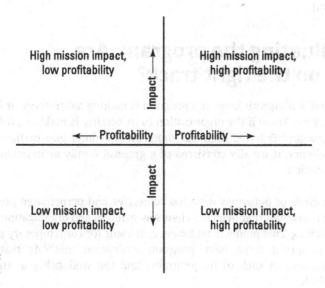

High mission impact,
low profitability

High mission impact,
high profitability

Impact ↑

← Profitability   Profitability →

Impact ↓

Low mission impact,
low profitability

Low mission impact,
high profitability

FIGURE 13-1:
A matrix map.

The best programs are ones that are *profitable* (income generating), have high impact, and are mission centered. Organizations should invest in these programs and see them as a major assets. Some programs are not profitable but are central to the mission of the program; they speak to the soul of the organization and are valuable. Organizations should keep these programs but must not allow them to drain the organization of all its funds. The programs that an organization should stop or roll out are those with low impact and those that have low mission alignment — they're a waste of time and resources.

After a new program has been established, it needs to be implemented thoughtfully and strategically. It should be sufficiently resourced, have clear roles and appropriate staff, and have clear criteria for outcomes. It should be developed with the end in mind.

For example, if a nonprofit determines that it wants to address human trafficking and expand its program to include a drop-off center, it needs to think about where that center will be located, who will staff it, how it will work with other community organizations, and what its measure for success will be.

REMEMBER

The program should also adapt to changes as the nonprofit rolls it out. The best-laid plans are just that: plans. Working in the human service sector means that you have to be flexible and dynamic. Maybe the organization placed the program in a centrally located location because it wanted it to be accessible to clients, but potential clients may think it's too visible and not use the resource because they feel it's too risky. The organization will have to adjust and consider another location.

Evaluating the program: Are we on the right track?

How will a nonprofit know if a program is making a difference or being effective? How do you know if the organization in its totality is making a difference? In the past, nonprofits based their outcomes on anecdotal information and testimony from clients. It usually consisted of a grateful family or individual and a savior organization.

These kinds of outcomes were too subjective and perpetuated problematic hero/savior narratives that depicted clients as helpless and organizations as benevolent benefactors. This model is no longer sufficient for contemporary practice. Today, each nonprofit must have program evaluation methods that measure the effectiveness of each of its programs and the well-being of the organization as a whole.

Organizations use a range of methods to measure organizational effectiveness. Financial and programmatic outcomes are the most common methods of evaluation.

TIP

Charity Navigator (www.charitynavigator.org) is an industry-standard charity rater that uses financial information as one of the methods to assess the effectiveness of an organization. It rates an organization's finances based on its expenses, *liabilities* (debts), capital, *fundraising efficiency* (how much money it spends to make money), administrative costs, program expenses, and growth. It also looks at accountability and transparency measures. An organization can earn a total of 100 points. Nonprofits use the information from Charity Navigator to understand the landscape of the services being provided. Similarly, organizations use financial metrics to report how financially stable or profitable a specific program is.

REMEMBER

Nonprofits use financial ratios to assess the financial health of the charitable organization. Financial ratios take into account the program expenses ratio, administrative expenses ratio, fundraising efficiency ratio, working capital ratio, and liabilities-to-assets ratio to evaluate the financial health and transparency of charitable organizations nonprofits.

Nonprofits also use a logic model (like the one shown in Figure 13-2) to link the activities of the organization to the expected outcomes. Outcomes are measured by the resources invested in short-term, medium-term, and long-term goals, along with associated activities and actions. These efforts should result in expected change in the social problem or issue the program is addressing. For example, if the organization is providing services for people with substance use issues, the outcome would be a reduction in the use of substances or overall health of the clients served.

Thinking of Logic Models as a Series of *If . . .Then* Statements

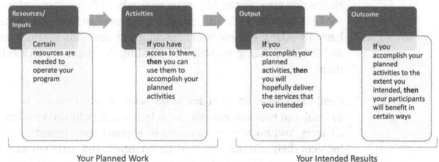

FIGURE 13-2:
A logic model.

Source: Centers for Disease Control and Prevention (www.cdc.gov/tb/programs/evaluation/Logic_Model.html)\
U.S. Department of Health & Human Services\Public domain

TIP

Logic models are very useful because they can clearly and coherently show causal pathways and the step-by-step correlation between the efforts of the program and the results of the program. Logic models can be as simple or as complicated as the organization. The Administration of Children & Families, which is part of the U.S. Department of Health and Human Services, provides a useful template to demonstrate the logic model; you can download it at www.acf.hhs.gov/media/4499.

Looking at What Nonprofit Leaders Do

REMEMBER

Nonprofit CEOs (also known as executive directors) have many roles, but the main one is that of enacting the mission and program of the organization as a formal employee of the organization. The CEO is the chief liaison between the board of directors and the staff. As such, they must always have the mission of the organization on their mind and serve as the public champions for the program. In addition to being the chief mission officer, the CEO must also have strong management and financial stewardship skills. Fundraising and maintaining fiscally sound practices are a core function of their role.

Some CEOs come to hold the position of CEO because they're champions of the cause or the public face of the organization's grass-roots efforts. Financial management is often new to them and something they struggle to embrace. But leading the organization in the CEO capacity entails financial management — there's no way around it. Nonprofit leaders must ensure that the organization adheres to the highest ethical standards in financial practices and keeps strong accountability measures in place so the agency is protected and seen as a public force for good.

Nonprofits are constantly procuring funds, and this is one of the biggest roles for the CEO. In order to do the job well, CEOs need to have strong relational skills and have a working knowledge of funding sources. This means knowing local, state, and federal funding sources and creating development strategies geared toward them.

Good CEOs serve on local and state-level committees and boards so they're seen as local and national experts. Legislators and policymakers tap them to serve on advisory committees or seek their support and expertise on legislation that impacts their mission. This is the advocacy and activism part of the role. CEOs have first-hand knowledge of what their clients and staff need and can articulate that to decision makers.

Social workers who serve as CEOs always have a change of clothes in their offices and cars. They may be meeting with a funder in a formal setting and wear corporate clothing. Later that day, they may head over to the community to do hands-on work and change into more casual clothing. CEOS must wear many hats.

In the following sections, I fill you in on what makes an effective CEO, how CEOs motivate their staff, and the organization culture they can create.

Recognizing what makes a good leader

CEOs of nonprofits oversee the team that runs the day-to-day operations, and they're responsible for the financing management of the organization. They do this while constantly focusing on the vision for the company and being the public face of the organization.

TECHNICAL STUFF

People often confuse leaders with managers. Managers focus on the day-to-day operations or day-to-day function of an organization. Leaders set the vision and the change process. Managers figure out how to get the trains there on time, whereas leaders determine where the train is going. Nonprofit CEOs are *both* leaders and managers. Typically, they spend 70 percent to 90 percent of their time leading and 10 percent to 30 percent of their time managing.

A strong nonprofit CEO trained in social work should:

>> Stay focused on the organization's mission and culture.

>> Cultivate a strong working relationship with the board of directors.

>> Have a strong relationship with external stakeholders like funders, constituents, and clients.

>> Communicate effectively.

>> Have a good grasp on the political climate locally and nationally.

>> Have emotional intelligence — they're self-aware, they have social awareness and skills, and they can self-manage.

>> Use anti-oppressive and community-engaged approaches to create a plan and execute change.

REMEMBER

Emotional intelligence is especially important in human services work. Leaders must treat their staff with respect using humanistic approaches. Staff members are often the ones doing frontline work that's emotionally and physically taxing. They need an organizational culture and a leader who cares about them just as much as they care about the work they do. Leaders are most successful in enacting change when they pay attention to the glue that holds the place together: the organizational culture.

NO SUCH THING AS A "BORN LEADER"

You can find plenty of books on what makes a strong leader. These books focus on the characteristics, temperament, and personality of leaders. They ask you to assess to see what type of leader you are. The traits championed by these books tend to fall into the "strong male" stereotype.

Personality-based leadership models make the fundamental assumption that people are born with the characteristics to lead — you either have what it takes or you don't. But this approach is too deterministic and oppressive. Many people would have these so-called leadership traits if they were given the chance and the means to succeed.

Social workers recognize that power, authority, and access are automatically given to some people and intentionally withheld from others. So, the leadership models that assert that leadership is based on personality traits and characteristics are limiting. Leadership researchers also are echoing the criticism of the trait-based approach and have shifted their focus from traits to behaviors (what good leaders *do*) and to contingency models (what good leaders do in different situations).

Motivating people to change

Part of leading is creating a vision for the organization and moving the organization toward that vision, which often involves change. And if there's one thing most people are resistant to, it's change. So, a nonprofit leader has to find a way to motivate their team members to do it.

They can do this by building urgency around the need and sharing the vision to solve the problem. They also have to get buy-in from key members of the organization so those people can positively influence others to join the efforts — sort of like peer pressure.

After building a collective coalition for change (that sounds better than peer pressure), the leader must clearly articulate the short-term and long-term wins and empower people to make changes. In other words, give people the vision, and then give them the space to implement the changes and get wins.

Leaders in social work, though faced with distinct challenges from front-line workers, benefit from cultivating emotional intelligence to enhance organizational and client outcomes. By fostering self-awareness, regulation, and empathy, they facilitate constructive interactions and are better equipped to make tough decisions during crises, fostering trust and motivation for both staff and clients.

When there are small wins or gains, don't forget to celebrate and reward them! Use the momentum from these achievements to get more wins and keep moving toward the vision you set.

That said, organizational and cultural change takes time. So, don't celebrate too soon and think the job is done. Highlight the changes and start making them a permanent part of the organization.

Knowing the organizational culture

Organizational culture entails the shared values, beliefs, rituals, code of conduct, and interpersonal interactions. It's the invisible thread that holds everything together.

Think about a job you've held where you loved going to work. You looked forward to the workday, even if the job itself was tough. Now think about a job where you dreaded going to work and wished you could call in sick every day. I bet the organizational culture had a lot to do with how you felt in both of those jobs.

Many human-services agencies struggle to retain good staff because people get overwhelmed by the organizational climate. They literally can't bear to stay in the job and end up quitting. When good people leave an agency, they take with them the financial investment the organization has made them, part of the organization's history, and their own talents and gifts. Here are the most cited or common issues human-services organizations face:

>> High turnover rates.

>> Role ambiguity — they don't know the job.

>> Role overload — they have too much work.

>> Poor supervision and mentoring.

>> Workplace violence.

>> Poor wages.

>> Lack of diversity.

>> Unfair or inequitable practices.

This information is critical. I have served on the board of directors and worked for organizations that have high visibility and surprisingly very poor organizational cultures, riddled with the same problems listed here.

TIP

The good news is, good CEOs can turn tough organizational climates around! They can do this by:

>> Advocating for good living wages and benefits for all staff

>> Having clearly defined job roles and responsibilities

>> Providing quality supervision and development opportunities

>> Prioritizing diversity and equity in the workplace

>> Having open, transparent, and accountable policies

>> Creating rituals like monthly celebrations or traditions

>> Acknowledging and rewarding good work

>> Acknowledging loss and change

These practices address the tangible needs (those having to do with money and time), as well as the overall well-being of the staff. When people feel happy and respected, they'll do good work and stay at their jobs longer.

Chapter 14

Going Broad with Global Social Work

 social work is a global profession. The International Federation of Social Workers (www.ifsw.org) serves as the international representative organization for social work and has 147 participating countries representing more than 5 million social workers worldwide. This significant number underscores the profession's global reach.

International social work is a specialized practice area that looks at improving the physical, mental, and material lives of people across geopolitical settings. This work happens at the local, state, national, provincial, and regional levels with individuals, groups, and communities. It is as broad as social work gets, and the impact is just as big.

International social work practice can happen in two settings:

» **Domestically:** Domestic global social work involves working with immigrants, refugees, and migrant minorities within your own country, with a primary focus on addressing cultural and racial diversity issues. This type of social work primarily occurs within multicultural, multilingual settings, often in urban areas or neighborhoods with diverse ethnic populations. For example, in my city, there is a large Bhutanese and Nepalese resettlement program, so local nonprofits and social workers respond to the needs of this population in our local American context. Social workers who work with this community consider themselves to be global social workers.

>> **Internationally:** What people have in mind when it comes to global social work is social work practice that operates across borders or in a foreign country. In this kind of practice, social workers provide services in a cross-national and cross-cultural context, working for nongovernmental organizations (NGOs), in aid and relief programs, in emergency or crisis work, in environmental sustainability programs, or in resettlement camps. It's social work practice in another country. This kind of work is ideal for social workers who love learning about other cultures, can handle change, and are flexible when it comes to their living conditions.

TECHNICAL
STUFF

Although I'm defining global social work in these two distinct ways, there isn't a universal definition of the term or the role of the global social worker. This is because the world is a pretty big place, and there are competing educational organizations, accreditation bodies, and varying roles for social workers in different countries. Plus, the recognition and regulation of social work as a profession — including licensing, titles, protection, and public acknowledgment — vary significantly from one country to another.

Regardless of the challenges, social work is concerned with promoting justice and equity worldwide, not just within local communities. At the core of global social work is a steadfast commitment to upholding human rights and fostering social justice. Global social work is a rewarding field of practice for people who have a passion for travel, an appreciation for different cultures, a natural curiosity about the world, and a desire to make a meaningful impact on a global scale, beyond their immediate surroundings.

In this chapter, I explore how a human rights–based approach influences the practice of global social work, delve into key focus areas within global social work, and provide tips on how you can actively engage in global social work in your community or abroad.

I have firsthand experience working with immigrants and refugees, as well as firsthand exposure to social work practices in different countries. Plus, I personally benefited from the efforts of social workers when my family immigrated to the United States. Throughout this book, you encounter the perspective that social work views political and social issues as deeply personal matters. This sentiment holds especially true for me in this context. I'm not merely writing on behalf of others; I'm sharing my insights as someone who has held several roles in this practice, including clinician, activist, and educator.

Understanding the World and Your Place in It

If you want to do global social work, you need to know where various countries are located. It sounds basic, but you'd be surprised by how many people don't know basic geography, including immigration officials. I can remember my family's hearts sinking when our immigration case went before a judge, and he asked, "Where is Ethiopia again?" When you're in a position of helping or you have authority over the lives of people in these contexts, you need to know where they're from and what conditions pulled or pushed them out of their country of origin. Their status and ability to live and work in a particular place may depend on your service and knowledge of their home country.

If you spend any time talking about global issues, you'll hear people talking about the *Global North* and the *Global South*. For a while, I thought these folks were talking about North America and South America because, well, Americans always think we're talking about America. Eventually, I began to understand that *Global North* and *Global South* are terms used to discuss resourced and less resourced countries. (In the past, you may have heard terms like *first-world countries, second-world countries,* and *third-world countries* to discuss the same issues.)

REMEMBER

Global North and *Global South* are commonly used to describe the division of the world based on economic, political, and developmental characteristics. They serve as shorthand for describing broad economic and political trends, disparities, and power dynamics. *Global North* typically refers to economically developed and industrialized countries, primarily in North America, Western Europe, and parts of Asia. In contrast, *Global South* represents less economically developed nations, often located in regions such as Africa, the Middle East, Asia, Oceania, Latin America, and the Caribbean.

The use of these terms rose in prominence in the 1980s when the Brandt Report distinguished countries based on their levels of *gross domestic product* (GDP) per capita, meaning the total monetary value of all goods and services produced within a country. The Brandt Report noted that countries with higher GDPs as being concentrated in the Northern Hemisphere and the ones with lower GDPs as being in the Southern Hemisphere. The Global North is associated with economic prosperity, advanced technology, and political influence, while the Global South is linked to challenges like poverty, underdevelopment, and historical legacies of colonialism.

The countries that fall into the Global South were below what is now called the *Brandt line.* This line separates the Global North and Global South as an imaginary demarcation line, stretching from the Rio Grande down to the Gulf of Mexico, spanning across the Atlantic Ocean, traversing the Mediterranean Sea, and extending over the vast landscapes of Central Asia until it reaches the Pacific Ocean.

In recent years, there has been a notable shift in the language and conversation about the Global North and Global South. Although the terms are common, the categorization is overly simplistic and inaccurate. This interrogation of the terms acknowledges the limitations and simplifications inherent in these labels. The global landscape is far more complex and diverse than these categories suggest. For instance, within the Global North, there is a wide range of economic development levels, political systems, and cultural diversity. Similarly, within the Global South, countries exhibit varying degrees of economic growth, political stability, and unique national priorities.

TIP

If you intend to work in a global context as a social worker, you must be mindful of these geographical descriptions and distinctions. Be prepared to challenge stereotypes and the limitations of binary categorization that attempt to oversimplify the complexities of the entire world. You should also aim to articulate how you perceive and describe the world in a nuanced and culturally sensitive manner.

REMEMBER

If you want to challenge something, you must first have a solid understanding of what you're challenging. Otherwise, you risk losing credibility.

So, the first lesson in global social work practice is all about geography. It's about understanding where different regions are located on the map and getting familiar with the terminology used by professionals working in international contexts.

The United States, with its unique geographical isolation, vast size, and incredible diversity in terms of both its people and topography, can sometimes lead those living within its borders to view it as the whole world. But when my students go on study-abroad experiences, it's truly a joy to witness their eyes light up and their perspectives shift as they're exposed to new places and cultures.

During these trips, we delve deeper into understanding the social issues and challenges that different countries face, as well as the role of the social work profession in addressing these issues. What becomes abundantly clear in our work is that social problems stemming from poverty, inadequate health-care systems, gender-based violence, inequality, and environmental degradation tend to be universal in nature. However, the severity of these problems and the infrastructure in place to address them can vary significantly from one host country to another. Sometimes, the United States leads the way in these initiatives, while at other times, there is so much to learn from the approaches taken by other countries.

THE MAP THAT LEADS TO YOU

Global social work starts with geography and geopolitics. The map of the world gives people a sense of where they belong on the earth and orients them to the physical boundaries of nations. Mapmakers have tremendous power to determine who and what is captured and seen.

Currently, we use longitude and latitude lines to precisely locate geographic structures. The originators of this map structure were Flemish cartographers who decided to make Europe the center of the map — in doing so, they literally made the world Eurocentric. This type of mapmaking exaggerates the sizes of land masses near the poles of the earth so Greenland and Antarctica seem much larger than they are. Using this map, Greenland and the entire continent of Africa seem to be similar sizes, when in reality, Greenland measures 0.8 million square miles and Africa measure 11.6 million square miles.

Think about how these distortions shape what's presented to people. Maps can center or decenter people and places, which has a profound cognitive and psychological impact on everyone.

Understanding the Role of the United Nations

Social workers who want to do global social work (really all social workers) need to understand the role of the United Nations (UN), particularly the Universal Declaration of Human Rights and the Sustainable Development Goals (SDGs). These are pretty significant in the world of international aid and development work. A substantial chunk of the funding, how we assess progress, and opportunities for collaboration across different fields are closely connected to the initiatives established by the UN and the SDGs.

Unfortunately, many Americans, including social workers, may not fully appreciate the depth and breadth of the UN's human rights perspective and documents, as well as the importance of the SDGs. In this section, I work on changing that.

Getting acquainted with the history of the United Nations and what it's doing today

The UN was created at end of World War II. It serves as the primary international arena for governments to come together to discuss common concerns, create common goals, and solve pressing social concerns. Except for Palestine, the Vatican, and Taiwan, every country in the world is a member of the UN.

In the UN, governments negotiate to make treaties, protocols, and declarations. However, professional and service representative groups and NGOs play a significant role in informing policies and representing civil groups. The UN grants these groups consultation status and allows them to have a seat at the table for policy formation and in an advisory capacity. The International Federation of Social Workers, the International Association of Schools of Social Work, and International Council on Social Welfare have been given consultative status, which gives social workers an opportunity to speak to humanitarian and social justice issues from our specific orientation on a global scale.

Social workers who specialize in global social work practice play a crucial role in implementing the humanitarian goals of the UN. They actively advocate for and influence policies, including development goals, that align with the UN's mission. They specialize in addressing the complex needs of vulnerable populations around the world, such as refugees, and work diligently to uphold human rights, contributing directly to the UN's objectives by advocating for social justice, equitable access to resources, and the well-being of marginalized communities. The social work profession's commitment to social justice makes it a natural partner for the UN's humanitarian and development objectives.

The UN consists of what they call six principal organs:

>> General Assembly

>> Security Council

>> Economic and Social Council

>> Trusteeship Council (currently inactive)

>> International Court of Justice

>> Secretariat

These organs work together to address international issues, promote peace, and facilitate cooperation among member states. From these six organs the General Assembly, the Economic and Social Council, and the International Court of Justice have particular relevance to social workers:

General Assembly

The General Assembly is the primary deliberative and policymaking organ of the United Nations, where all member states have a voice. It plays a vital role in shaping the organization's direction and policies, making decisions on critical global issues, and adopting resolutions on matters such as peace and development. It has annual meetings in its headquarters in New York City; these meetings make the national and global news.

Economic and Social Council

The Economic and Social Council (ECOSOC) serves as a key forum for discussing economic, social, and environmental issues. ECOSOC's significance lies in its allocation of up to 70 percent of the UN's human and financial resources to various UN programs and specialized agencies, thus enabling the organization to tackle pressing global challenges effectively.

International Court of Justice

The International Court of Justice (ICJ) serves as the principal judicial organ of the UN, resolving legal disputes between states. Its role is crucial in maintaining international law and promoting peaceful settlement of conflicts among nations. Social workers who work in conflict areas or do restorative work will often work with this organ of the UN. The UN's emphasis on human rights and humanitarian issues in Geneva underscores its commitment to protecting and promoting the rights and well-being of individuals worldwide.

The Universal Declaration of Human Rights

The United Nations has played a pivotal role in the development and promotion of human rights, encapsulated in what is commonly known as the Universal Declaration of Human Rights (UDHR). This landmark document, adopted by the UN General Assembly in 1948, outlines a comprehensive framework for human rights protection.

The UDHR outlines 30 rights in total. These rights cover a wide range of civil, political, economic, social, and cultural rights that are considered fundamental to all individuals, regardless of their nationality, race, religion, or other characteristics. The 30 rights are organized into three broad categories:

>> **Political and civil rights:** These rights encompass the idea of negative freedoms. They safeguard individuals from government abuse and ensure fundamental liberties such as freedom of speech, religion, and the right to a fair trial.

>> **Social and economic rights:** These rights are considered positive freedoms, which necessitate government action to guarantee them. They include the right to work, the right to equitable compensation, the right to housing, and

the right to education. The concept behind these rights is to create conditions that allow individuals to fully participate in society and lead dignified lives.

>> **Collective rights:** These rights acknowledge the significance of group-based identity and protection. They encompass the rights of Indigenous peoples, minorities, and other marginalized groups, recognizing their unique cultural, linguistic, and social attributes.

The UDHR underscores that these rights are universal principles that all governments should aspire to uphold and protect, irrespective of cultural, political, or economic differences. In essence, the UN's advocacy for human rights seeks to create a world where every individual enjoys these fundamental rights and freedoms, fostering a more just and equitable global community.

The National Association of Social Workers, the Council on Social Work Education, and the International Federation of Social Workers have all adopted and endorsed the UDHR. These organizations recognize the importance of human rights in the field of social work and promote its principles and values in their codes of ethics and educational standards.

Plus, the Social Work Code of Ethics, as defined by the National Association of Social Workers, incorporates principles that align with the UDHR. The NASW Code of Ethics doesn't explicitly mention the UDHR, but it does emphasize the importance of upholding and promoting the dignity and worth of all individuals, respecting their rights and liberties, and advocating for social justice and equality. These principles are in harmony with the values outlined in the UDHR. Social workers are expected to abide by the NASW Code of Ethics in their professional practice. So, in essence, all social workers in the United States principally apply the human rights perspective outlined in the UDHR.

Sustainable Development Goals

So, how is the UDHR implemented or put into action? Through strategic global initiatives and goals. As a convening entity, the UN was the natural place to discuss how to solve the root causes of social development problems and provide a road map of solutions, all underwritten by a human rights perspective.

In 2000, the Millennium Developmental Goals (MDGs) were established; they ran until 2015. The MDGs were criticized for their narrow focus and limited success in addressing all aspects of sustainable development. They also lacked inclusivity, because they primarily targeted developing countries, leaving out middle-income and developed nations. In 2015, the MDGs reached their target date, and although some progress had been made, many goals had not fully been achieved.

In 2015, the international community adopted the Sustainable Development Goals (SDGs) as a successor to the MDGs. The SDGs (which you can find at https:// sdgs.un.org/goals) are more comprehensive and ambitious, addressing a broader range of global challenges, including poverty, inequality, climate change, and environmental sustainability. The SDGs aim to leave no one behind and are universal, applying to all countries, not just developing ones. They were also explicit about eradicating social problems, not just making them better.

The formation of the SDGs was guided by five principles:

>> **Leave no one behind.** The SDGs ensure that all individuals, regardless of their circumstances, benefit from development.

>> **Put sustainable development at the core.** The SDGs integrate economic, social, and environmental sustainability.

>> **Transform economies for jobs and inclusive growth.** The SDGs promote economic growth that benefits everyone.

>> **Build peace and effective, open, and accountable institutions for all.** The SDGs foster peace, justice, and strong institutions.

>> **Forge a new global partnership.** The SDGs encourage collaboration among a wide range of stakeholders, including governments, international organizations, civil society, the private sector, and local communities.

From these principles, 17 SDGs were developed. The SDGs encompass a wide range of issues, from eradicating poverty and hunger to promoting gender equality, clean energy, and sustainable cities. During the deliberation and adoption of these goals, the International Federation of Social Workers, the International Association of Schools of Social Work, and the International Council on Social Welfare endorsed initiatives and pledged the support of the social work profession to these goals.

It isn't hard to see the connection between the SDGs and the mission of the social work profession. In fact, these goals make social workers critical players in addressing social problems because of the tremendous mission alignment.

TIP

I've seen health care, gender-based violence, education, and poverty be the most salient and common issues in global social work. If you're thinking about working oversees, consider specializing in one of these areas, volunteering with an organization that does work in this space, or securing an internship or fellowship on these topics. The skills you gain will be transferable and will lead you to secure a job in an international setting.

Digging Deep into Colonization and Global Inequality

In the realm of global social work, understanding the profound and enduring impacts of colonization and imperialism is paramount. These historical processes, driven primarily by European powers from the 15th to the 20th centuries, have left an indelible mark on the world, contributing significantly to contemporary global inequity. This section explores the implications of colonization and imperialism from the perspective of social workers working in a global context. It emphasizes the essential need for partnerships with local communities to combat the persistent consequences of these historical injustices.

Understanding the impact of colonization and imperialization on global inequity

Social workers operating in formerly colonized regions must have a deep understanding of how colonization and imperialism have shaped the societies they serve. This understanding is vital for culturally sensitive and effective practice. Formerly colonized regions are nearly all developing countries. They continue to feel the economic inequity and disparity brought on by colonial and imperial powers that owned, exploited, and abandoned them. If you're a social worker trained in the United States or from western perspective, it's imperative for you to have an awareness of this legacy and history for the following reasons:

>> **Historical trauma and cultural sensitivity:** Colonization and imperialism inflicted profound cultural trauma by imposing Western values and norms, erasing Indigenous cultures, and fostering dependency on foreign systems. Social workers must approach their practice with sensitivity to these historical wounds, recognizing that communities carry the scars of past oppression. As an aid worker, you may serve as a representative of an institution that once oppressed and exploited people or is in the process of recovering from its legacy of harm.

>> **Economic exploitation and dependency:** The economic exploitation inherent in colonization and imperialism resulted in profound economic disparities in Indigenous regions. Postcolonial nations often struggle with economic dependence and the unequal distribution of wealth. Social workers should be aware of these dynamics and advocate for economic justice and development that is attuned to this power imbalance.

>> **Cultural influence and identity:** The legacies of colonization and imperialism are still evident in the cultural norms and identities of societies. This shows up

in how people view a culture as sophisticated, advanced, or developed based on western standards. Social workers must be attuned to how these preferences and biases shape the values, beliefs, and behaviors of the communities they work with and how aid workers measure success based on the same imperialistic western standards.

>> **Conflict, borders, and ethnic tensions:** Arbitrary borders created during colonization and imperialism often divided ethnic and cultural groups, leading to lasting conflicts and tensions. Social workers should understand and not minimize these divisions and their long-lasting impacts on the sociopolitical climate.

>> **Environmental and health consequences:** Environmental degradation and health disparities are among the enduring consequences of these historical processes. Social workers will encounter communities grappling with the environmental and health fallout from this legacy.

>> **Reparative justice:** The pursuit of reparative justice is essential to healing historical injustices. Social workers can advocate for *reparations* (financial or material compensation provided to individuals or groups who have suffered historical injustices or harm, often as a form of acknowledgment and restitution for past wrongs), truth and reconciliation processes, and initiatives to rectify past wrongs. This means they have special training in truth and reconciliation processes specific to the sociopolitical issue they're addressing.

Partnering with local communities to address inequalities

Effectively addressing the multifaceted consequences of colonization and imperialism requires collaboration with local communities. This partnership is not only a best practice but a moral imperative. Local communities have invaluable insights into their own histories, needs, and strengths. They're the experts in their experiences, and they can provide crucial guidance to social workers. Facilitating partnerships and collaborations is a skill set that social workers are trained in; it's an area of expertise that is sought after by governments, NGOs, and humanitarian relief efforts. Local partnerships empower communities to take ownership of their own development and healing processes.

Through collaborative efforts, social workers can help communities identify and mobilize their resources, build resilience, and advocate for their rights. By involving communities in decision-making, interventions become more contextually relevant, sustainable, and respectful of local traditions. Social workers do this through a deliberative process that they're experts in. Fostering partnerships with local communities is not just advisable but imperative. These partnerships are the cornerstone of social work that empowers communities to combat the historical injustices perpetuating global inequity, thus fostering a more equitable and just world for all.

Working with Immigrant Populations

Social work with immigrant populations in the United States is a dynamic and complex field that navigates the intricate intersection of culture, policy, and human rights. In this section, I explore the prevailing attitudes in the United States toward immigration and immigrants, examining the complex interplay of factors that push individuals and families to migrate, as well as those that pull them towards the United States. I also delve into the essential role of social workers in serving immigrant and refugee families, highlighting the various ways they address acculturation challenges, trauma, legal processes, and overall well-being within this diverse and dynamic population.

How Americans view immigrants

The United States is a destination for people from around the world. Unfortunately, America sends mixed messages about welcoming immigrants and outsiders. On the one hand, it views itself as a haven for those in need and a place that welcomes strangers as a symbol of hope. U.S.-born citizens often feel nostalgic about their family's initial journey and settlement in America, recognizing that their own ancestors were once immigrants.

However, the United States sometimes suffers from intermittent amnesia when it comes to retelling its own history. U.S. history books typically mention that the original settlers were escaping persecution in England and forging a new path in a new land. What these history books often omit are the conquests and colonization of lands and the displacement of Indigenous peoples. They also tend to overlook the long history of chattel enslavement and continued racial oppression even after the abolition of slavery.

TECHNICAL STUFF

Chattel enslavement refers to a system in which individuals are treated as *chattel* (property) rather than merely as forced laborers. In chattel enslavement, people are legally owned by other individuals and are bought, sold, and inherited as if they were objects or possessions.

I mention this because this amnesia carries over into how people currently perceive immigrants and influences political debates about what types of immigration and immigrants are considered positive or negative. The immigration narrative that closely resembles the nostalgic original migration story, primarily involving white Europeans coming to America, is typically regarded as favorable. On the other hand, migration from the Global South or from regions with predominantly Black and Brown populations is often viewed less favorably and, in some instances, subject to discriminatory and stigmatized treatment.

Following are some generalized attitudes that people in the United States may express regarding immigration, both positive and negative.

REMEMBER

Positive attitudes about immigrants include the following:

» Immigrants add value and culture.

» Immigrants contribute positively to the U.S economy by having skilled and specialized labor.

» Immigrants are willing to work in unskilled labor areas that most Americans don't want to work in.

» Good immigrants are the ones who adapt to American culture.

Negative attitudes about immigrants include the following:

» Immigrants are dangerous.

» Immigrants take jobs from Americans.

» Immigrants are a drain on the economy and steal benefits and resources from Americans.

» Immigrants contaminate American culture and values.

» Most immigrants are here illegally and should be deported.

The political sentiment regarding immigration — particularly the distinction between "good" and "bad" immigrants — significantly affects the sense of belonging for those who are migrating. They may be warmly welcomed or become targets of discriminatory policies, violence, and *xenophobia* (prejudiced and irrational fear or hostility directed toward immigrants and individuals perceived as foreign, often rooted in ethnocentrism and a belief in the superiority of "American" culture or group). Currently, there is a considerable amount of political attention focused on undocumented immigrants and the legal immigration process. Immigration laws prioritize admission based on family ties and employment status. These laws primarily concentrate on penalizing employers who hire individuals without legal status, increasing border control measures, and adopting fluctuating policies regarding amnesty for long-term residents without legal status.

There is an ongoing call and debate surrounding human rights and compassionate immigration policies. However, the prevailing message and negative attitudes toward immigrants often resonate the loudest, contributing to a significant social stigma for immigrants. These negative perceptions can lead individuals to conceal their immigration status, refrain from seeking assistance when needed, and, at times, subject them to direct violence. It is crucial to remain cognizant of the national climate and prevailing attitude concerning this topic because they have a direct impact on how social services are provided and received.

Pushed or pulled into the host country

For social workers dealing with immigrants, the push–pull theory offers a valuable framework for understanding why individuals leave their home countries.

Even if the United States is an appealing destination, that doesn't automatically mean that everyone who arrives here intends to stay permanently. People come to the United States for various reasons. They may be pushed from their home countries due to political and social oppression, or they may be pulled to the destination country by the prospect of economic and social betterment. Social workers are interested in how these dynamics play out at multiple levels:

>> **Macro (community) level:** At the macro level, rising levels of economic inequality and poverty rates can drive people to migrate to more developed countries. Factors like climate change, natural disasters, and resource depletion can also push individuals to seek safer locations. Additionally, political turmoil and identity-based violence can force people to flee their home countries in pursuit of political asylum or refugee status in host countries.

>> **Mezzo (family or group) level:** At the mezzo level, the level of attachment an individual has to their home country and the opportunities available within their homeland significantly influence migration decisions. People with strong national identities, strong family ties, and ample economic prospects may visit other countries without necessarily intending to settle or permanently migrate. *Chain migration* (in which immigrants move to locations where friends, family, and established ethnic communities exist, often for safety and support) is also common.

>> **Micro (individual) level:** At the micro level, demographic characteristics such as age, gender, education, and health play a role in determining an individual's readiness to undertake such a significant life change. Those who want to leave their home country may face obstacles due to limited resources, health issues, or fear. Conversely, individuals with educational opportunities, youthfulness, and male gender (given cultural safety or social acceptability) may be more inclined and able to embark on this journey.

TIP

Social workers who work with immigrants are often focused on helping people adjust and adapt after they get to the United States. In the initial stage of working with immigrants, social workers need have an understanding of the conditions and reasons for migrating. They should ask the following questions to get an understanding of someone's personal migration story:

>> What political, economic, social, and relational factors contributed to the decision to migrate?

>> What was their situation in their home country?

>> What was their transit to the destination country?

>> Are they able to go back or visit their home country?

>> Do they live in two countries?

>> Do they want to return home?

The answers to these questions will help clarify the person's legal classification, legal status, and how help can be given. For example, there would be a significant difference between providing help to someone who is escaping political or religious oppression and can never return to their country of origin and providing help to someone who is a college student who is here on a student or employment visa.

How to serve immigrants and refugees

TIP

So, what do you need to know or keep in mind when working with immigrants and refugees in the United Sates? Well, there are lots of things to know, but here are my best tips:

>> **Know the legal status of the person you're working with.** Their legal status significantly impacts their quality of life. It impacts their ability to work, to have identity documents, and to access to resources.

It's especially important to understand the immigration context versus refugee context. Refugees are leaving unsafe and often traumatic conditions. Immigrants may be pulled to the host country for family or economic reasons. Their legal status and ability to navigate resources is contingent upon their status. For people without status, they may remain hidden or be very reluctant to come forward for services.

>> **Conduct a robust assessment and get the client's and their family's story.** Find out their reasons for migration, their legal status, how long they've been in this country, what language they speak, any important

cultural traditions they have, the varying roles of family members, their values, and the significant cultural intuition.

A *cultural genogram* is a useful tool that social workers use to capture this information. A cultural genogram is a visual tool used to map and understand the cultural and familial background of an individual or family. It combines the traditional genogram format, which depicts family relationships, with information about cultural heritage, beliefs, customs, and other cultural factors. This tool helps social workers gain insight into how culture and family dynamics intersect, allowing for more culturally sensitive and effective interventions.

» **Become familiar with the pathway for citizenship (for example, how people get lawful permanent resident status or a green card and get naturalized) and build good relationships with immigration legal clinics and lawyers for referral and resources.**

» **Be aware of resources for people without status and documents and the rights they have, especially educational rights for children and their ability to enroll in primary, secondary, and higher education.**

» **Have a strengths-based approach and value and appreciate immigrants as an asset to the community.**

» **Help immigrants navigate social services, health care, and education.** Affirm and respect their cultural identity, and connect them to community resources.

» **Seek out specialized trainings and practice models for work in this population.** For instance, working with recent immigrants and second-generation migrants involves recognizing their distinct needs and circumstances. It's essential to tailor support to their nuanced requirements, because they aren't a homogeneous population.

» **Become aware of city, state, and federal laws that impact immigrants or attempt to discriminate or target them in oppressive ways.** Advocate for just and humane laws that are consistent with social work values and principles.

WARNING

A critical consideration for social workers is the power differential inherent in this helping process. Due to the myriad obstacles and barriers faced by immigrants, helpers can either empower individuals and have a profoundly positive impact or become gatekeepers who perpetuate myths about deserving and undeserving immigrants. In the latter case, they may withhold assistance or unfairly penalize immigrants and their families. This type of assistance is oppressive and runs counter to social work principles.

TIP

Social workers should adopt a cultural humility approach that centers the client's experience and assumes a stance of being a learner as the helper. There's a significant distinction between asking someone about their experiences and culture and telling someone what they must do to conform, adapt, or fit into a particular American mold. Social workers who work with immigrants need to engage in self-reflective practices. This involves understanding their motivations for offering help, recognizing any conscious or unconscious biases they may harbor, and evaluating whether their approach to helping is collaborative or authoritarian in nature.

Becoming a Global Social Worker in Another Country

If cross-cultural and cross-border work sounds interesting to you, you may want to consider a job in global social work where you live outside of your home country and provide social work services in a global context. This is usually the case for someone who loves other cultures, traveling, and humanitarian missions.

REMEMBER

International social work practice is not merely an opportunity to live abroad and travel while having a job on the side. You should consider the job and the mission of the work as the primary motivators and the opportunity to immerse yourself in another culture and the world as secondary.

Global social work is not volunteer, mission, or charitable work. Given the vulnerability of the people or places you'll serve, you must be very clear about your role as a professional in a helping context. This isn't just a time for personal growth — it's a time for you to develop your practice skills in cross-national and cross-cultural contexts.

TIP

If you want to become a global social worker working in another country, keep the following tips in mind:

>> **Obtain a social work degree at the bachelor's or master's level.** Specialize in one of the 17 SDGs, particularly, poverty, health and well-being, education gender equity, clean water and sanitation, or reducing inequality.

>> **Take a course on global social work.** Try to have international or cross-cultural fellowship or internship experience during your educational experience.

>> **Begin taking immersive language lessons.** You should have at least basic communication skills in the host language. With some jobs, you may need to pass language fluency exams.

>> **Learn the history, geopolitics, racial and ethnic politics, and cultural and social norms and expectations of the host country.** This will help you understand power relations between and within the country.

>> **Adapt a cultural humility perspective that honors local knowledge.** That way, you won't reproduce a power imbalance and social injustice.

>> **Begin doing reflective emotional work on what it will feel like for you to have a minority status or even more minoritized status if you have intersections of minoritized identities.** For example, I lived in Beirut, Lebanon, as an American-identifying Ethiopian person. It was a layered experienced for me to be a Black female in a Middle Eastern context.

>> **Consider how you will work through emotional reactions to having a position of privilege and oppression in your new context.**

>> **Think about your physical safety based on your identity and how you can increase your safety.** Do you need to live in a cohort or community setting with other professionals, or can you safely live alone with precautions in place? Which countries will never be safe for you to work in? (Perhaps you're a member of a sexual minority group and certain countries' laws are deadly for you.)

>> **Physically prepare to move to another country.** It's usually a six-month process. Try to find a job where the job site will house you and pay for relocation costs.

>> **Have a budget and your finances in place.** You need extra funds for emergencies.

>> **Understand the scope of what social workers can do in the host country.** Make sure your level of credentials and licenses transfer.

>> **Think about how you'll stay connected to your family and friends at home after the honeymoon period of living abroad wears off.** You'll be homesick, and you need to plan for it.

>> **Find a way to capture your experiences.** Find a medium that works for you — journals, photos, social media posts, or blogs. Just make sure you capture this time.

>> **Get specialized training after you get settled in your host country and begin forming community and a life for yourself.** This is your real life now, not a vacation.

>> **When possible, travel and get to know your host country, as well as neighboring countries.**

TIP

Here are some agencies that employ international social workers:

>> **International Rescue Committee:** www.rescue.org

>> **Médecins sans Frontières (Doctors Without Borders):** www.msf.org

>> **Save the Children:** www.savethechildren.org

>> **United Nations:** www.un.org

>> **U.S. Agency for International Development (USAID):** www.usaid.gov

TIP

The following organizations can give you information on training and jobs:

>> **Council on Social Work Education:** www.cswe.org

>> **European Institute for Social Work:** www.socialeurope.net/english-1

>> **Global Impact:** https://charity.org

>> **Global Social Service Workforce Alliance:** www.socialserviceworkforce.org

>> **International Association of Schools of Social Work:** www.iassw-aiets.org

>> **International Council on Social Welfare:** www.icsw.org

>> **International Federation of Social Workers:** www.ifsw.org

3
Life in the Trenches

Get a sense of what you'll face when you're employed as a social worker and what you can do to set yourself up for a successful and satisfying career.

Learn about the scope of your professional responsibilities and what you need to keep in mind when you face ethical dilemmas and tough cases and situations.

Plan for professional development and learn the pathways for career and financial growth.

Chapter **15**

Starting Your Life as a Social Worker

I f you're considering a career in social work, you're probably wondering what your day-to-day work will look like. If so, you've come to the right place!

In the first part of this chapter, I cover issues that come up in the very beginning of the employment process and what you can expect from working in a helping profession. When you understand the agency's purpose and your role and function within the organization, you'll be able to thrive and flourish and avoid the occupational hazard of burnout.

In the second part of the chapter, I talk about everyone's favorite part of the job: paperwork. Paperwork is critical because it protects you, your clients, and the organization you work for.

The daily minutiae isn't glamorous, but the result of all this hard work changes lives.

Knowing What to Expect on the First Day

You've decided to pursue social work career and landed your first job. Congratulations! In this section, I explain the onboarding process in social work jobs, which includes everything from understanding the organization and its mission to making sense of human resources (HR) and your job benefits. If you're about to start a new job, read on!

Getting clear on the organization's mission

An organization's *mission* articulates the organization's purpose, its vision, and direction. Some common missions in social work jobs are:

» Protecting people across the life span

» Helping families

» Ending or eradicating major social problems like poverty and homelessness

» Developing communities

» Advocating for change through social movements

As you can see, these missions vary quite a bit, and so do the jobs.

Understanding the mission or purpose of the organization is critical:

» **The mission tells you what you're meant to be doing.** Think of it as the North Star, guiding you every step of the way.

» **The mission sets limits on what you should and shouldn't be doing.** If the organization's mission is to help children who are being trafficked, and you're focusing on the grandparents' needs, you're getting off course. That doesn't mean you should ignore the grandparents if they're needing help, but you can give them resources of other organizations to turn to.

» **The mission guides you when you're working as part of an interprofessional group.** Maybe you're working in a hospital, in a school, in a correctional setting, or in the miliary. These settings have very specific missions (like education, physical health, safety, and security), and their missions aren't necessarily driven by the core social work values. As part of an interdisciplinary team, you have to be knowledgeable and skilled in navigating the system you're in and do your part by helping to address the overarching mission of that system.

For example, in a school-based setting, the mission is to make sure children are educated. A social worker may help the child with their social and emotional skills because those are good life skills, but they must tie those goals to the child's *educational* goals because that's the mission of the school.

You may work in spaces where it feels like your role as a social worker is at odds with the mission of the system, but you're there because of inequities. This can happen in jails or prisons, for example, where the goal of the site is public safety and the goal of the social worker is the well-being of the incarcerated person. Being cognizant of the mission differences can help you understand how to navigate the different systems and succeed in your role.

TIP

People are usually the most satisfied in their work when the mission of the organization is aligned with their personal values and when their skill set and job role match the mission.

Going through orientation

Most jobs have a formal orientation process where you're introduced to your job role and to the organization. The orientation can be a one- to two-day training or it can last up to three months, depending on the regulatory structures for the job. Almost all job orientations discuss the mission and history of the organization, physical and environmental safety, workplace protections against harassment and discrimination, and how to sign up for benefits like health care and retirement plans.

REMEMBER

Some jobs may also require routine drug and alcohol screening as part of the job; this can occur in agencies that see clients for substance use disorder. Don't be alarmed if you're asked for a urine sample — it isn't out of the ordinary.

In child welfare work, child protective workers are trained for up to three months on the typology of child abuse, how to asses for risk and safety, how to do effective interviews, how to engage children and families for treatment, and how to prepare paperwork for court cases. This job is a serious one, and people need time to be oriented into the regulatory and humanistic parts of the job. Places that serve survivors of intimate partner violence also have a lengthy training process, where new employees must learn local, state, and federal guidelines to ensure competence in interventions and support. Health-care settings may also have long orientation processes, where they train social workers on medical conditions, health records and documentation, and discharge planning.

For places with a long orientation process, you can't just start the job with your social work education alone. You need to be trained on the methods the job sites use. Your employer uses the extended orientation process to train you in the job-specific modalities.

For some people, this extended orientation process is appealing — they get specialized training and become certified in a process as a result of the employment. That's actually a perk of the job.

Understanding your role within the organization

Understanding your specific job and role within the organization is essential. If you're working for an established organization, your role within the organization may be clearly outlined on an organizational chart. If you're working for a newer or smaller organization, your role may be less clearly defined.

For nonprofits and governmental agencies, the board of directors oversees the agency and the executive director (ED) reports to the board. The ED usually serves as the head of the organization — sort of like the president or CEO. The ED usually has an executive team consisting of program directors, financial officers, and HR. From there, depending on how big the agency is, the program directors oversee various programs, and middle management and frontline employees deliver the program.

Entry-level jobs, even for people with an MSW degree, start at the frontline, with direct contact with people and systems. They work with kids, families, and groups. This is where you'll get experience and see what social work is all about. You get a chance to roll up your sleeves and do the work.

REMEMBER

Social work isn't always one-on-one work. It can be community based or activism related. Even in those roles, for established organizations, early career work involves gathering data, developing reports, canvassing, talking to stakeholders, and doing capacity building projects. These roles are the building blocks for taking on leadership roles where you'll be the lead — the person who oversees the strategic plan and hires other folks to execute the mission.

Regardless of where you're working, having a strategic plan with roles and responsibilities as fleshed out as possible is key. That way, you'll have a sense of the scope of your work and not be tripping over your coworkers.

WARNING

Research shows that people who have demanding jobs with lots of roles and no way to mitigate their stressors have high instances of burnout. You can avoid this by having a clear sense of your role and job responsibility.

TIP

Make sure your role and duties are written out and given to you when you're hired, and file them away somewhere safe. If an employer forgets to provide you with a job description, don't hesitate to ask for it — this is a common request. If you discover that there isn't a job description or it's still in development, request a timeline for its completion and follow up on it. This practice not only protects your interests but is also a good HR policy that all companies should follow. New employees can often remind the organization of elements they intended to include in the onboarding process but may have overlooked.

Refer to that piece of paper when you feel like you're being asked to work significantly beyond what you were hired for. A clear job and role description helps protect you. It also helps you think about what you want to be doing in the future as you master your job.

TIP

Make sure to discuss any changes in your role as the agency grows and changes.

Making sense of the supervision structure

Supervision can make or break a job. Good supervision can be the element that helps staff stay motivated and safe. A lack of supervision can decrease morale and lead to good people leaving jobs prematurely.

REMEMBER

Supervision is a form of apprenticeship and a hallmark of the social work profession. It's a conduit for developing professional practice skills and for professional advancement.

When you start your job, you want to ask about what kind of supervision is available for you to help you execute the day-to-day part of your job. You also want to ask about the supervision you'll receive in order to grow your professional skills as a social worker.

Supervision for doing your job: Accountability

Let's start with the supervision you need for doing your job, known as the *accountability* part of your job. In social work, you may have a job that has complex parts and reporting structures. For instance, you may be working with a foster-care agency where you're handling sensitive family information, and your paperwork will be part of the file that goes before the judge for adoption or parental termination processes. You want to make sure you have all the right processes and paperwork in place to facilitate the best outcome. You also want to mitigate risk and minimize damage to the client, the job, and yourself. This is where good supervision comes into play.

As a new employee, ask about the documentation or processes for the role, how your performance will be evaluated formally and informally, what you should do when you make a mistake, and what you can do to enhance your role. If the role has lots of high-stakes and time-sensitive parts, ask for close and even daily check-ins until you get into the swing of things. Ask for decision trees — or create your own decision tree — to help you with the critical aspects of the job, until you've internalized them.

Decision tree mapping is a valuable tool for new social work employees, especially in the context of child welfare case work. Child welfare involves numerous contingency-based decisions where each step in the decision-making process is intricately interconnected. A decision tree is like a road map that helps social workers navigate this complex landscape. It outlines various possible scenarios and their corresponding actions, creating a clear and logical guide for social workers to follow. For example, when dealing with a child protection case, a decision tree might help determine whether a child should be removed from their home, placed in foster care, or receive in-home support services. It ensures that the decisions are process-oriented, reducing the likelihood of overlooking critical information and ensuring that actions are taken in a well-informed and structured manner.

Establishing good work habits from the beginning will help you gain confidence. Soon *you'll* be the seasoned worker who supervises people and rattles off options and acronyms.

Supervision to grow: Professional development

Supervision also provides social workers with the opportunity to grow in their professional role and skills. There are three types of supervision. Individual, group, and peer supervision.

INDIVIDUAL SUPERVISION

Individual supervision is when you go in and meet with a designated supervisor or mentor to discuss not just what you're doing but how you're doing it. Social workers are trained to use a helping process called the *generalist model* (see Chapter 3), which sets the framework for the intervention to be theory driven and evidence or scientifically supported. When you start your job in social work, you'll put those theoretical skills into practice. You'll get exposure to doing this in your internship while you're still in school, but the training wheels come off when you officially get hired. Although you'll be working for real, you aren't left on your own to sink or swim.

Individual supervision gives you the opportunity to talk about your work and discuss any challenges or ethical dilemmas you've faced. These discussions help you grow so you feel more empowered and confident in your decision making and skills.

Your immediate supervisor can serve in this mentoring role, or your workplace may pay for you to get outside supervision as part of your benefits. If you can get supervision outside the workplace or in another department, that's helpful — sometimes supervisors in your own workplace can be defensive or the power structure may be too complicated for you to be as open as you'd like. And sometimes they're simply too busy, putting out fires, and feeling overwhelmed with the day-to-day demands of the job and the limitations they face with resources and other external stressors.

The time you spend in supervision can count toward your licensure hours and requirements if you choose to pursue licensure as part of your career trajectory. (Turn to Chapter 17 for more information on licensure.)

GROUP SUPERVISION

Group supervision is a collective approach where the team discusses a case or issue and you get multiple insights and perspectives. It gives people the space to discuss shared experiences, helps normalize the jitters or nuanced job experiences, and helps people get multiple resources. A combination of group and individual supervision is ideal.

PEER

Peer supervision is when you seek consultation by your peers. Here are some situations in which consulting with a peer may be useful:

>> **When you're dealing with an ethical dilemma:** For example, you're at work and you have a client who asks you to make an exception to a company policy to help them with an immediate need, but your supervisor isn't available to help you.

>> **When you're facing issues that are outside your scope:** For example, you've been working with a client for individual therapy and they want to shift the therapy to couples therapy and aren't sure if you have the training for this type of work.

>> **When you need to draw on someone else's expertise to enhance your work:** For example, if you're creating a new program and you want to make sure it addresses the area of diversity and equity in a holistic manner, you may seek out a peer who specializes in organizational diversity, equity, and inclusion (DEI) work. They can help you think through different dimensions of diversity and be a resource for you.

Looking at the benefits and HR process

As with any job, when you get hired to work in a social work position, you'll want to discuss the benefits that are available to you and take advantage of the perks of the job.

If you're working for a well-established humans service agency, government agency, school, or hospital, you'll likely be part of an established bargaining unit or union, which will do the work of advocating for fair wages and good benefits. If you're working for a startup or a newer agency, the organization is in growth mode and may only offer health benefits and not much more.

TIP

If your workplace doesn't offer retirement benefits, talk with a financial advisor about setting up a retirement account on your own.

Social work jobs typically have excellent perks and benefits. These are some of the perks you may receive:

>> Sign-on bonuses

>> Compensation or reimbursement for licensure

>> Career training in specialized interventions or subspecialties

>> Full or partial tuition reimbursement for educational advancement

>> Eligibility to sign up for federal loan forgiveness programs

>> Flexible and family-friendly hours

>> Family planning and childcare assistance programs

>> Paid time off and opportunities for overtime compensation

>> Wellness programs and mental health support

REMEMBER

Of course, the biggest perk is doing a job that makes a difference. But financial stability and work-life balance are huge.

Doing Paperwork: It Never Ends

Paperwork may seem like the worst part of the job. You may even wonder if it was created to torture you. I promise, all that paperwork matters to you and the system you serve. Paperwork creates a clear path and trail for how things get done, what gets done, and where it gets stored and retrieved after it's done. It standardizes practice so employees are treated in a fair and equitable manner and are protected from litigations. For clients, paperwork outlines their rights, documents their treatment, and can be used to make the case for future decisions about needing more intensive treatment or for discharge.

As social work educators, we often tell our students, "If it isn't documented, it didn't happen." You may be tempted sometimes to overlook or cut corners with paperwork, but the consequences are serious. If information is left out from documentation, no one knows about it and that could result in poor outcomes for clients and organizations.

REMEMBER

In macro social work, paperwork is not necessarily seen as the enemy — it's actually embraced by social workers. Paperwork details strategic plans, prioritizes activities involved with social movements or action, plans interview or data collection for reports and analysis, and may serve as the evaluation process and tool. Keeping up with the paperwork may be a challenge, but the paperwork itself is not seen as barrier — it's the bread and butter of the intervention.

In this section, I explain what you need to know as an employee regarding documentation and what you actually document in your work.

Understanding documentation: If you didn't write it down, it didn't happen

How you account for your work matters. High-quality, thorough documentation provides the evidence for proper and transparent practices for clients, funders (who provide money for the organization to operate), insurance companies, courts, and future service providers or stakeholders. How do you know what needs to be documented? It depends on who you're accountable to and what the work site needs in order to mitigate risk.

TIP

What needs to be documented is determined by the National Association of Social Workers (NASW) Social Work Code of Ethics (www.socialworkers.org/About/Ethics/Code-of-Ethics). Two sections in particular — "Social Workers' Ethical Responsibilities in Practice Settings" and "Social Workers' Ethical Responsibilities as Professionals" — detail what the public can expect from social workers and what social workers need to consider in their work with clients.

Other entities that require a particular form of documentation are funders, the accreditation bodies for your area of specialty, and state and federal policies and laws. For example, if you're working in an interdisciplinary setting, like a hospital, you may have to document your work using the standards for health-care providers, your state's department of health, insurance companies, and of course, the Social Work Code of Ethics.

For some social workers, it can feel like a 10-minute conversation may require 45 minutes of documentation because of the documentation requirements of each separate entity. The good news is, most agencies have worked out a process for meeting the requirements for all these entities in a cohesive and comprehensive manner. There's a lot of overlap in the data each of these agencies needs. If one agency needs a different source of information, it usually enhances the work and makes you a more thorough social worker. (It may not feel like it when you're staying late to do the paperwork, but in the end, the client is served better and, over time, what used to take 45 minutes will take 10 or 15 minutes. Eventually, you'll be training other people on the process.)

If you're doing macro-level social work, you may have to account for your work by providing certain deliverables to grantors or funders at particular cycles of the project. Timelines and deliverables are usually built into projects. There is also a cycle of paperwork for legislative processes and advocacy; there are times of the year when elected officials write, amend, and vote on laws and policies. Social workers who work in these spaces are acutely aware of these timelines and work on documentation in alignment with these cycles.

If you need a reminder of why documentation matters, just remember that documentation:

>> Is part of the social work tradition and standard of practice

>> Provides an accurate and standardized account of the information you've gathered

>> Provides the necessary information to meet standards, covering ethics, legal compliance, billing accuracy, and agency-specific requirements

>> Provides information that will withstand scrutiny by external reviewers, such as accreditation bodies, ombudsmen, lawyers, insurance companies, and quality assurance/improvement officers

>> Provides a historical account of the issue

>> Provides a current account of the issue

There is an element of testimony in writing things down. Narration is important for legal or compliance purposes, but it's also important for making a person's story come to life. Our words give voice and flesh to people who are often marginalized or only talked about in narrow, flat, or negative ways. Whenever you have a humanistic encounter, write it down and make sure that the next person who serves the client or system knows what's going on.

REMEMBER

The other critical purpose of proper documentation is to mitigate risk. Social workers are asked to account for their work by:

>> Making routine appearances in court as part of legal or advocacy work

>> Allowing their files to be audited by funders

>> Allowing their paperwork to be audited by an internal risk management committee

>> Facing lawsuits for misconduct, incompetence, or impairment (rare, but it happens)

By having a routine and thorough documentation process, you won't need to fear these incidents. You'll be prepared.

Getting clear on confidentiality and clients' rights

The trust and respect between a client and their social worker are essential for the helping process. People see social workers at the hardest times of their lives and are asked to disclose sensitive things about their lives. What social workers do with their private information matters because:

>> Our values and principles state that we treat people, communities, and systems with respect and dignity, and we honor what they share with us.

>> The information our clients share impacts the service delivery and treatment process.

>> There is a power differential between the person who is sharing the sensitive information and the person or system that collects and stores the information.

When someone or a system has sensitive information about you, they can use it to help you, harm you, or share it with someone who can help or harm you.

REMEMBER

Because of the high-stakes nature of confidential information, there are protocols having to do with clients' rights, standards of practice regarding privacy and confidentiality, and the sharing of information with outsiders and third parties. Client privacy, consent, confidentiality, and privileged communications are such an important part of social work practice that there are 18 specific standards in the Social Work Code of Ethics addressing these issues. In addition to the Social Work Code of Ethics, there are state and federal regulatory laws that outline the standards for protecting, storing, and sharing private information. Social work students are taught the ins and outs of these laws and processes and see it action during their internships.

TIP

As a rule, clients need to be informed about their rights when it comes the kinds of services they can expect, what's being done with their information, where their information is being stored, the consent process for sharing information, and what they can do if they feel like their rights have been violated. Social workers who are providing services need to share with clients what stays private and confidential and under what conditions they break confidentiality.

REMEMBER

Social workers must break confidentiality and make formal reports to responsible entities in the following situations:

>> When they suspect child abuse or neglect

>> When someone is a serious danger to themselves

>> When someone threatens to harm another person in a violent way, it is foreseeable (meaning it is very likely to happen), and it is imminent (meaning it is happening soon)

You need to have a strong understanding of these standards not only to do good work but also to protect yourself, your clients, and others. Chapter 16 covers what to do in tough situations like this.

TIP

How can you ensure that you're being ethical and providing good care when it comes to client records and confidentiality?

>> Familiarize yourself with laws, regulations, and ethical standards that discuss client confidentiality, privacy, and relevant third parties.

>> Have the appropriate credentials and competence to deliver services.

>> Accurately document the services you provide.

>> Provide clients with access to their records consistent with agency, state, and federal policies.

>> Get appropriate consent for disclosure of third parties like insurance companies, other providers, and family members.

>> Terminate services ethically and consistent with state and federal policies.

>> Properly record, maintain, store, and retrieve client information.

>> Use strengths-based language and ensure that what you write and say about your clients and their lives doesn't libel or slander them.

>> Maintain proper boundaries and avoid conflicts of interest.

>> Get ongoing training on professional ethics, liability, and pertinent federal and state regulations.

Knowing how to document your work

You can document your work and services electronically or on paper. More and more, documentation is being done electronically through the use of protected and encrypted data management systems and electronic health records. Electronic documentation needs to have layers of security and backup plans in case the device holding protected information is stolen or lost.

Some organizations and individuals still maintain paper records because it's too costly or complicated to use electronic records. In that case, legibility of documents and securing documents needs to be part of the data storage plan.

REMEMBER

When you're documenting or writing notes, keep your audience and the purpose of the note in mind. Share enough to convey what's happening but not so much that it divulges or infringes on the client's intimate details. My mentor told me to think about client notes as having the potential to be seen by the public. If you were carrying your notes in a bag, and you dropped your bag and your notes were scattered all over the street, what would you feel comfortable with other people seeing and what would make you feel embarrassed? This image has consistently instilled in me a sense of responsibility toward my clients, serving as a reminder to maintain transparency in my interactions. It ensures they don't feel betrayed or experience any inaccuracies or oversharing when they request access to their health records.

When you write your notes is also important. Agencies and regulatory bodies usually dictate the maximum time limit for writing notes — it's usually 48 hours. But if possible, you should write your notes the same day.

My colleague John Silipigni, a retired hospital social work administrator and social work professor who trains students and his employees, shared with me some tips for writing concise notes, and now I'm sharing them with you:

>> Check to make sure that you're documenting on the correct patient.

>> Write the date and time of your notes if you're not writing them electronically.

>> If you've documented in error, place a line through the note, write "error," and put your initials next to it.

>> Be clear, concise, factual, and brief, if possible.

>> Document what you see, hear, feel, or smell.

>> Be clear about the frequency and intensity of what you're documenting.

>> Consider the audience who will be reading your note.

- >> Write enough to tell the whole story with the understanding that someone else may read that story and comprehend it.

- >> Don't alter a record.

- >> Don't use biased language.

- >> Don't use vague language (for example, avoid the term *a lot*).

- >> Don't use slang, street language, jargon, or profanities unless in quotations.

- >> Don't include personal opinions without facts that back up those opinions.

- >> Don't use ambiguous terms that may cause someone reading your notes to think, "I wonder what that means."

- >> Don't write in code that no one will understand.

- >> Don't write about personal details that don't impact the case.

TECHNICAL STUFF

Three core documentation styles are routinely taught to human service providers. Agencies may use these documentation styles or, more commonly, create their own forms or reporting structures that adapt or mirror elements of these documentation methods. The three documentation styles are as follows:

- >> **Subjective, Objective, Assessment, Plan (SOAP):** The SOAP style looks at the subjective data (such as what the client is saying and reporting), the objective data (what the clinician observes), an assessment of the underlying issues, and the plan for the next session. This method is often used in clinical settings.

- >> **Data, Assessment, and Plan (DAP):** The DAP style looks at the data (both the subjective data and the objective data — see the preceding bullet), an assessment, and the plan. This method is often used in clinical settings.

- >> **Situation, Intervention, Response, and Plan (SIRP):** The SIRP style uses behavioral terms to describe what is happening in the session and is nondiagnostic. The notes describe the following:

  - • **The situation:** A brief explanation of what's happening during the session, including the setting and the events leading up to it

  - • **The intervention:** What the health-care professional does during the session to help the client, including the actions or strategies used

  - • **The response:** How the client reacts or behaves during and after the session, including their emotions or any changes

  - • **The plan:** Future actions or steps the professional suggests, considering what happened during the session

  This method is often used in behavioral health settings.

Chapter **16**

Facing Tough Situations

After starting their internships, one of the first things students want to talk with me about are the many ethical dilemmas and violations they encounter. They have to make decisions with competing systems, values, and clients — and they want me to tell them exactly what to do. The thing is, there are no clear lines — nothing is black and white. What's important is learning how to systematically think through these decisions and determine the best course of action for yourself, based on your training.

In this chapter, I discuss common ethical dilemmas that come up in social work practice and share a useful ethical decision-making process. I also outline what you can do when you face the dilemma of a client wanting to hurt you, themselves, or others.

All this talk can make social work seem like it's an ominous or dangerous profession. Social work is not for the faint of heart — we do look at tough situations and conditions, but our job is to make those things better. We can't do that if we shy away from them or only want sanitized "professional" settings. We get good solid training, so we know how to set ourselves and our clients up for success. We avoid being in conflicted spaces because we conduct ourselves in ways that leave very little room for avoidable mistakes. In fact, seasoned social workers are so good at managing ethical dilemmas that we almost forget it was a sticky situation in the first place. In this chapter, I share some of the tricks of the trade.

Addressing Ethical Dilemmas

Because social workers work with people and human-serving systems, they face complex situations that don't have clear-cut answers. Here are some examples of situations that may come up when working with clients and families. What would you do if you faced these situations?

>> A client invites you to their wedding, graduation, or other celebration.

>> A client invites you to connect with them on social media.

>> A client's child is in the same school as yours, and your kid wants to go on a play date with their kid.

>> A client wants advice on psychotropic medications.

>> A client offers you gifts as a gesture of gratitude.

>> A client's child acknowledges you in public settings, but the client does not.

>> A parent wants you to share your clinical notes on their child.

>> Your client's partner wants you to testify for them or against their partner (your client).

>> Your client shares that they want to hurt themselves or others and wants you not to tell anyone.

>> Your client passed away.

You may be thinking, "Why are these dilemmas?" Maybe you see them as black-and-white situations. But another person might feel just as strongly about the opposite point of view.

REMEMBER

These points and counterpoints are the reasons we discuss ethics. Ethical dilemmas ask us to consider two good or competing ideas that may be in conflict and decide on the best course of action. Ideally, you find a solution that honors *both* values. Other times, the values clash and you make a decision that may rupture the relationship.

Understanding boundaries within the work

Boundaries mark norms in professional practice and give guidance and sometimes overt instructions on what should and should not be done.

Boundaries are especially important in social work practice. They protect clients from being exploited or harmed. And they protect the social worker from conflicts of interests and from slipping into avoidable problematic situations.

DISPATCHES FROM THE FIELD

Early in my career as a social worker, I had a case where I worked with a family who had adolescent children. Of course, to no one's surprise, the teenagers were causing difficulties in the family. I was working with the whole family, and this was a family issue. I usually see the family for a few sessions, and then I see different family members individually at least once. In my session with the adolescents, they revealed that their parents were using excessively harsh punishment, including choking them. I asked for more information and got more contextual data that confirmed that this was happening often. After the session, I had to decide whether to report this incident as suspected child abuse or talk to the parents about it. I realized that if I made the report, it could cause big tensions in the home and with me.

However, because I was fresh out of school and my child abuse training, I made the decision to report the incident and talk to the parents about my report. They were very upset with me, and the family did not come back for more sessions. The parents told me that I was too young and easily manipulated by teenagers. I didn't get a chance to say goodbye to the children. I was devastated and felt like I put the children more at risk with my reporting.

I can reflect on this situation now and know I absolutely made the right decision. But at the time, it tore me up. It taught me a valuable lesson of *really* going over the limits of confidentiality and my professional obligations to report child abuse or neglect. I don't breeze through this section of the intake process. I make the boundaries of my role very clear. That way people know exactly what they can expect from me.

Some boundaries are very clear. Everyone knows that social workers should never engage in sexual relationship with their clients.

But what do you do if your client wants a hug? What if they're a child? Does the same stance apply? The Social Work Code of Ethics (see the nearby sidebar) states that social workers should refrain from physical contact that causes psychological harm. If we engage in any physical contact, we should set clear, appropriate, and culturally sensitive boundaries to govern this contact.

TIP

As a general rule, with young children I ask permission for high fives as my form of contact. With adults, I err on the side of caution and refrain from contact. But keep in mind that this is culturally informed. In some countries or cultures, refraining from physical contact may be seen as offensive or odd. Customary greetings may include a warm hug or sitting close to one another. If you refrain from these normative cultural customs, some clients may feel very uncomfortable.

THE SOCIAL WORK CODE OF ETHICS

The Social Work Code of Ethics was developed by a working group consisting of social work educators, researchers, and practitioners with the purpose of defining ethical standards for professional practice. The National Association of Social Workers (NASW), the largest professional organization for social workers in the United States, serves as the custodian of the Code of Ethics, making it available on their website.

Of particular significance for this discussion is the section of the Code of Ethics titled "Social Workers' Ethical Responsibilities to Clients." This section provides comprehensive insight into what a commitment to clients entails, outlines the rights that clients hold, specifies the responsibilities of social workers, and delves into crucial aspects such as rules regarding privacy, confidentiality, professional boundaries, recordkeeping standards, payment for services, and guidelines for termination. These standards are designed to address common ethical dilemmas encountered in practice and offer valuable guidance in these specific areas.

The code can be found at www.socialworkers.org/About/Ethics/Code-of-Ethics.

The CODES guidelines adopted by the profession as standards for practice. They're used for regulatory purposes and to protect the public. They're grounded in social work values that reflect the mission of social work. They outline the kind of relationship a social worker should have with their client, their colleagues, and the broader society. There are six core values that social workers use to guide their decision-making and practice behaviors:

>> Service

>> Social Justice

>> Dignity and worth of a person

>> Importance of human relationship

>> Integrity

>> Competence

REMEMBER

These values are guideposts for what to do. The Social Work Code of Ethics delineates ethical standards for practice based on these values. The Code of Ethics provides guidelines on a social worker's responsibilities to their clients. They state that a social worker's primary responsibility is to the well-being of their client and their right to self-determination. Clients should consent to treatment and be seen by competent social workers who are working within their scope of knowledge and skill. Clients should not be experimented on. If you don't have the expertise or time to work with the client, you should refer them to someone who does. The Code of Ethics also discuss that services should be set up clearly, fairly, and with minimal interruptions. When services end, they should end well.

Some social workers may think they are being fair when they don't collect fees or allow a client to accrue a huge debt, but this actually sets up a major imbalance in the relationship and opens up the door to problems. The client may barter with you and try to exchange services with you — they may offer to work on your house or your car, or try to give you something valuable to them. The problem is, this sets up a scenario where they feel indebted to you. You may capitulate to their offer so as not to offend them, but that can lead to conflict. What if your car breaks down after they fix it? Or what if they want that piece of jewelry back? You'll kick yourself for getting into this mess.

In the Code of Ethics, there is a considerable description of avoiding conflicts of interest and dual relationships. A *dual relationship* is a situation in which a social worker is in multiple roles with a client. These roles can involve both professional and personal aspects, and the intersection of these roles can create ethical challenges. Dual relationships can occur in various ways, such as when a social worker is not only a client's professional counselor but also has a personal relationship with the client outside of the professional context. For example, maybe the social worker attends the same religious institution as their client or the social worker's child is in the same class as the client they're serving. Dual relationships create the potential to harm or exploit clients, and they can be avoided.

TIP

Here are some tips on avoiding dual relationships:

» **Avoid networking or bartering when you can.** For example, "Thank you for offering to fix my car, but I think that will complicate things with us."

» **Be very clear about your duty to report abuse and the limits of confidentiality.**

» **Be clear about your role if you're seeing multiple members of a family or group.** I tell families I work with that, as a rule, I do not get involved in legal matters and will not testify in custody battles.

» **Don't be a social worker to your friends.** Instead, refer them to the best social worker you know.

» **Don't connect with your clients on social media.**

REMEMBER

In some helping professions, the professional and client are allowed to have a dual relationship after a period of time, usually one or two years, but that's not the case in social work. Once a client, always a client. Social workers must leave room for the client to come back for services if they need to. The relationship *always* centers the client and not the social worker. The best way to set yourself up for success is to have a good understanding of the values and principles of the profession and to operate with strong boundaries. It may feel rude or unkind to say no or to turn down nice offers, but you'll save yourself a lot of heartache (or formal sanctions!) by adhering to your boundaries.

What to do when there are competing values

Even though there are principles of practice and a Code of Ethics, sometimes you're faced with competing values, and you have to choose a course of action.

For example, when I was a school-based social worker, I ran into three scenarios repeatedly:

>> **Students would ask me to help them get pregnancy tests.** The school was very clear about sexual health education and what could and could not be given to children — no contraception.

>> **Students would share with me that they were pregnant, and ask me to not disclose it to their caregivers.** The school had no clear rules about disclosing information that students shared with social workers unless students were a danger to themselves.

>> **Students would wait and wait after school for a parent or guardian to pick them up and no one would come and get them — I would have to decide whether to leave them at school or give them a ride home.** The school had a rule about transporting kids — it was a big no-no because it put the school, the student, and the staff at risk. Could I just leave the student to wait for a parent in front of a locked school and drive off? What kind of social worker does that? But what about the rule against transporting kids in my car? What was I supposed to do?

Luckily, I had an excellent supervisor who helped me through these scenarios. We talked through each of the scenarios and the competing value and principles. Was there a clear right or wrong decision? Should I consider doing the most good? The least harm? Or make a decision based each individual issue, or what's called a *contingency-based ethical decision*.

It was clear that I shouldn't give pregnancy tests to middle-schoolers. There was a clear policy, and it wasn't causing the students harm not to get the test.

In the case of keeping an actual pregnancy a secret, the students had the right to privacy but not confidentiality. Our conversations were not confidential because I was not working as their therapist — I was a school-based social worker. That doesn't mean I could violate their wishes to not disclose that information. But it also doesn't mean I was breaking confidentiality if I needed to share that information with their parent. In these cases, I usually worked with the student on how to tell a trusted family member.

With the last scenario, I had to think about what was doing the least amount of harm. If the student lived close enough, I would walk them home. Other times, I would try every solution besides driving them home. But invariably, once a year, I would end up driving a child home and hope for the best. Leaving them unattended was too unsafe.

TIP

There is no exact formula for resolving ethical dilemmas. But there is a guiding framework and model that prominent social work ethicist Dr. Frederic Reamer outlines for social workers and other helping professionals. Most social workers use this model for practice, and it's taught as a frame of reference in schools of social work.

Here are the steps in the model:

1. Identify all the ethical issues that are in conflict with your situation.

2. Outline the course of action you might take and who would be involved.

3. Make a pros and cons list for each action and think about the Code of Ethics, legal issues, cultural considerations, social work principles, and your own values.

4. Consult with colleagues, supervisors, lawyers, and experts and get their advice on what you should consider.

5. Make the decision.

6. Document the decision.

7. Monitor and evaluate the decision.

Each of these steps will bring you closer to a wiser judgment. You'll be measured and non-impulsive in your decision-making process. Even if the pace of the job is fast, your decision-making process will be deliberate and thoughtful.

Being culturally responsive in ethical decision-making

REMEMBER

Ethical principles and guidelines are based on western and American standards, which often center the rights of the individual above all else. In other countries or collectivist cultures, the family is considered the primary and the individual secondary. It would be unthinkable — even unethical — not to share information with the family. Privacy, self-determination, dual relationships, and who's involved in client care are all negotiated through the lens of the culture.

Being culturally responsive in ethical decision-making also involves recognizing the culture and context of the organization. For social workers dealing with clients facing death and dying, like hospice or medical social workers, attending funeral services or visiting clients at the end of life at their request can be a common issue. Whether this is deemed a boundary concern or an acceptable practice depends on the specific agency and context. Cultural sensitivity and individual client and family wishes are paramount, with social workers respecting cultural variations in mourning and end-of-life practices, adhering to agency policies, seeking informed consent, and maintaining professional boundaries to ensure ethical and culturally responsive care in these sensitive situations. In international and cross-cultural contexts confidentiality, privacy, boundaries, and self-determination are not universal truths. They may even be out of step with how the culture views health and optimal outcomes. It's important to be humble, curious, and contextually adaptive.

With that in mind, in other countries, social workers may do the following as a typical part of their practice:

>> Attend their clients' weddings and celebrations.

>> Involve all family members in decisions for an individual.

>> Barter for services (clients feel it's a mutual exchange).

>> Value dual roles and feel more comfortable with someone who is a known.

>> Never decline gifts.

This list may look like it's telling you just to throw the rulebook out the window and do whatever you want, but that isn't the case. What it is saying is that decisions about what's right and wrong are culturally informed. What a social worker in Kansas does to be ethical and responsible will look different from what a social worker in Taiwan or India does because they live in different contexts. However, each of the social workers can use the ethical decision-making process to come to conclusions on what they should do. The ingredients to the recipe may vary, but the process is still the same.

When to quit your job

Sometimes even with the best of intentions, your work situation may repeatedly put you in situations where you're at risk. This may cause harm to your clients, or you may be injured.

This is different from having a job that's risky in nature. Even with risky jobs, there are measures put in place to minimize risk and maximize safety. I'm talking about situations where the organization is purely operating in survival mode or consistently disregarding or minimizing risk. In those cases, you don't need to be a martyr and stay in a dangerous situation. In fact, you may need to leave or stop your role in order to not violate ethical principles.

I sometimes supervise social workers as they prepare for their licensure. There have been times where I've told my supervisee that their work conditions are untenable and that they need to leave their job. There aren't sufficient risk management strategies in place for them to provide a sufficient standard of care.

REMEMBER

Sufficient care is defined as the ability of an employee to make sound decisions with reasonable information and resources. If you're in a workplace where the conditions are too stressed for you to provide a sufficient standard of care, it's best to leave. Otherwise, you're wide open for sanctions and lawsuits.

WARNING

You can't legally claim that your work condition didn't provide you enough support or supervision. You'll be held responsible for the work you did or did not do. Because of this very serious standard, you have to be conscious about situations where you're providing care to a vulnerable population with minimal support.

TIP

You should consider leaving your job if you encounter any of the following situations in your work environment:

>> Poor or no supervision and a complicated role

>> No process for clients' rights

>> Violations of confidentiality and privacy

>> Consent standards being violated

>> Poor boundaries

>> Disregard for clients or abandoning of clients

>> Fraudulent billing or falsifying of records

>> Minimal to no training

>> An impaired workforce (in which there are significant conflicting organizational values and personal values — for example, if you work in a social service agency that is tied to a religious institution, you may have legal but conflicting principles with you or social work practice)

These matters are very serious. You can't stay at a job just because you love the mission. You also have to be sure that you can *do* your job in a professional and ethical manner. Otherwise, you'll be complicit in harmful practices. And this has moral, social, and legal implications. Start drafting your termination letter. I bet all your friends and family members will sigh with relief when you leave that job.

Managing Crises with Clients

Crisis and social work almost go hand in hand. Social workers are trained to go *toward* crisis and to face tough situations. We have models and manuals to work in almost any crisis setting, and we're cool as a cucumber while doing it. This is part of the professional training we receive.

Now, that doesn't mean we're unflappable or immune to stress. It just means we have good training on what do in various crisis scenarios. Social workers are trained on what to do when clients want to hurt themselves, others, and, yes, even their social worker. This is foundational practice knowledge.

Sometimes the whole area of practice or specialty centers on one of these scenarios, meaning your work is solely on violence prevention, victim assistance, or acute psychiatric settings. Because I specialize in trauma and have worked in community-based settings, I have a high tolerance for crises and can quickly come up with creative solutions that stay within the risk management box.

In the following sections, I dive into some of these scenarios and talk about dicey situations you may face.

When your client wants to hurt themselves

Social workers who do direct practice work or work where they provide interventions on a one-on-one basis are trained to identify and respond to clients who endorse suicidal thinking or behaviors. Social workers are the number-one providers of mental-health services in the United States. Those who hold a license are mandated to receive training on suicide prevention and treatment. This training decreases anxiety about seeing clients who are struggling with suicidal ideation and gives tangible skills to assess for risk and plan for safety.

Training on suicidality usually covers these domains:

>> **Clarification of terms and policies,** including the definition of suicide, rates of suicide, policies and laws about social workers' responsibility, and involuntary commitments.

>> **Assessment of risk and protective factors through an interview process.**

>> **Exposure to assessment tools** such as the classic Columbia Suicide Severity Rating Scale (www.cms.gov/files/document/cssrs-screen-version-instrument.pdf).

>> **Evidence-based interventions and holistic treatment models** that work on safety plans as opposed to safety contracts. Examples include interventions like Mental Health First Aid or cognitive behavioral therapy for suicide prevention (CBT-SP).

Suicide is the tenth leading cause of death in the United States. It's the second leading cause of death among young people ages 15 to 24 years old. These alarming numbers have made suicide a national crisis. Given their expertise in mental-health work and crisis interventions, social workers are the ideal helping professionals to address this crisis. Social workers are trained to screen for suicidal ideation in various settings, such as health-care providers, community centers, schools, and places of worship.

Screening is the first part of the process. After identifying who is at risk, social workers must create holistic treatment plans with the population they're working with. If it's kids, they involve parents. If it's a faith community, they train elders and leaders of the congregation on how to identify and refer for services. If it's a hospital or mental-health setting, they provide the intervention themselves.

When your client wants to hurt you

Social workers work with clients who are victims of violence or in communities or settings where there is violence. In the course of their professional work, they may find themselves in unsafe or dangerous situations. This can be due to direct threats from clients or because the physical environment itself is unsafe (such as war zones or crisis situations). Or it can be because they face or work with clients who are impulsive, aggressive, unpredictable, or impaired.

The clients may display these behaviors because they live in chronically stressed environments, may be victims of violence themselves, are under the influence of substances, or are intentionally trying to be harmful. (Yes, even social workers believe that some people mean to cause harm and use violence as a weapon.) In other instances, the environment can feel unsafe because clients are hostile and verbally abusive.

Regardless of the reason for the violence, when helpers experience harm, it has a lasting effect. It can leave the worker on edge and make them constantly fearful of the next incident. It can make them less committed and less satisfied with their job.

Certain jobs — such as those dealing with child welfare or with intimate partner violence and those in emergency rooms — carry more risk than others. Child welfare workers walk into openly tense and potentially hostile situations every day. Hospitals or emergency shelters are open to the public and to people who are physically and psychologically impaired. Depending on their state of impairment and agitation, social workers must be very vigilant with their physical safety. Domestic violence shelter addresses are usually not publicly available because they need to keep their clients safe. Perpetrators of physical violence may turn up at the worksite and terrorize the workers and the clients.

WARNING

Social work jobs or settings that require social workers to visit a client's home often entail a higher level of risk as well. This holds true for roles in home health, aging care, and even probation services. The risk escalates when environmental factors come into play, such as when working in rural areas with limited cellphone service, higher rates of opioid use, or clandestine drug laboratories (commonly known as meth labs) or in neighborhoods that have higher rates of violence. It's essential to be aware that clients may have weapons in their homes, which further emphasizes the need for caution and proper safety protocols. Social workers in rural settings often use company cars equipped with tracking systems due to these safety concerns. The evolving political climate can also impact the context and potentially create safety issues, because social workers may be perceived as representatives of a government that some families prefer to avoid oversight from. These considerations underscore the importance of being cautious, especially when entering clients' homes, which is valuable guidance for students and new social workers entering the field.

In all these instances, it's the clients who are the origin of the danger. What should workers and worksites do? Should they employ more security guards, have more security gates, or give weapons and self-defense training to staff for self-protection? Probably not. These tactics are direct and may seem like they ameliorate problems, but what they end up doing is militarizing community centers and providers.

REMEMBER

It is *not* the sole responsibility of the worker to keep themselves safe. It is the job of the *organization* and its leadership to keep staff safe. Administrators should do environmental scans and ask workers what they see as threats and what makes them feel safe. They should also do physical scans of sites and take care of infrastructure issues. Locks should work, and people should have access to safe places. Staff should work in teams and as a unit so individuals aren't left alone to do site visits or work with unpredictable clients.

TIP

Worksites should get training in trauma-informed interventions so they understand the behaviors of their traumatized clients. That way, they won't be using excessive force with clients and make the place feel like it's a war zone for clients and staff. Staff should also get training on de-escalation and first aid mental-health training. These models will train workers on how to recognize and address risks before they become unmanageable. They also empower staff to plan and act when there are instances that demand social workers stay proactively ready. The combination of these factors will increase physical safety, keep clients safe, and protect staff's sense of well-being.

When clients want to hurt others

In certain cases, social workers face dilemmas where their clients threaten great harm or physical violence to a *third party* (another person). What do you do if your client directly discloses to you that they plan on harming another person? The target of the violence is usually a spouse, partner, lover, or coworker. This puts the social worker in a bind because they have the ethical principle of confidentiality, self-determination, and maintaining the therapeutic relationship butting up against preventing serious harm to third parties.

There is a famous legal case of *Tarasoff v. Board of Regents of the University of California*, in which a student disclosed to the campus psychologist that he was going to murder another student, Tarasoff. The psychologist notified the police. The psychologist and the police did not notify the intended target. Sadly, the client went through with the plan and murdered Tarasoff. The family of the victim sued the university and won the lawsuit. The California Supreme Court determined that clinicians have the duty to warn potential victims and disclose confidential information, to prevent serious harm to them. This set the precedent of what to do in cases like this.

TIP

So, when should the social worker break confidentiality and inform the third party? Under these four general conditions:

>> When there is evidence that the client poses a violent threat to the third party (by using force with a knife, gun, or other deadly weapon to inflict pain)

>> When the threat is predictable and foreseeable

>> When the threat is impending or imminent

>> When there is a known or problem victim

If these conditions are met, you should notify authorities, including law enfacement, and the intended victim. Because this is a delicate situation, you can't just call the target of the threat and say, "Hey, I just wanted to tell you that there is a threat against your life and you should probably lock your doors." A more comprehensive approach would entail your sharing the information, sharing the reasons you reached your judgment, and providing resources to the victim. Disclosing this information may escalate their impending harm, so have them take immediate precautions.

You also have the task of notifying your own client about breaking confidentiality. But because you're a diligent social worker, in your initial onboarding with the client, you were very clear about when you break confidentiality and about your duty to warn. You'll reference that conversation and talk with your client about what the next steps for their treatment are. They may need to enter intensive care or a higher level of care where they're closely monitored.

When you've made a mistake

Invariably in your work with clients, you'll make mistakes and hit bumps in the road. This is part of the process. You won't be a perfect social worker no matter how hard you try or how many Ivy League schools you attend. Mistakes can fall into the following broad categories:

>> **Misconduct:** Misconduct includes things like exploitation of clients, fraudulent billing, or boundary violations. Bad stuff.

>> **Impairment:** Usually, people have impairment in their professional lives because they're facing major personal stress — stress with the nature of their work, their family, financial troubles, health issues, legal problems, or substance use issues. These issues lead to an error in judgment and create harm for the worker and client.

>> **Ethical mistakes:** A mistake can have ethical implications, like leaving confidential materials exposed or forgetting an important part of the consent to treatment form.

What can be done to rectify mistakes, impairments, and misconduct? Read on.

Misconduct

Misconduct is the easiest issue to address because there is intent to deceive and cause harm. This is egregious with social work clients because they're often vulnerable. This exploitation doesn't just cause material harm — it's immoral and has generational impact.

I once had a coworker who was particularly nasty to me when I first started my job. She made the workplace unbearable. Beyond her treatment of me, the organization discovered that she was fraudulently billing for services for children and families she never saw. I'm talking kids and families who were under-resourced and dealt with a tremendous amount of challenges. This level of misconduct led to her license being suspended and being terminated from the job.

Impairment

For impaired professionals, there are a number of ways to address burnout. Worksites should provide good supervision, work-life balance, adequate compensation, and training and development.

TIP

In general, organizations can prevent risky behaviors from their staff and ethics-related lawsuits by conducting an internal ethics audit. This is a self-study of the organization where the organization addresses the following major ethical risk areas:

>> Clients rights

>> Privacy and confidentiality

>> Informed consent

>> Service delivery

>> Boundary issues

>> Documentation and client records

>> Use of technology

>> Fraud

>> Staff development

>> Practitioner impairment

In each area, the organization can assess for risk and determine if the current practice is acceptable or if it requires significant modifications. Finding the gaps or areas of work is the start of the process, not the end. Social workers at the site should tackle problems by prioritizing areas that create the most risk to clients and pose the most threat for lawsuits and ethics complaints.

Some of the improvements can be creating more updated and comprehensive confidentiality policies, creating new policies to address emerging technology, and creating training or staff. They can also create funding lines to hire legal or ethical consultants to help draft policies. They should have evaluation and monitoring policies and procedures so these practices are continuous and not a one-time fix.

In all of this, the company should document the processes they engaged in. This is good practice for self-reflections and can be helpful if there is an ethics-based lawsuit. The agency can prove that it cares about its practice policies. It engages in conscious ethical practices as a mission of the organization.

Ethical mistakes

Social workers, like all professionals make mistakes in their practice. You don't have to be a saint to be a social worker. And not all social workers consistently follow an ethical decision-making process. Common ethical mistakes made by social workers often revolve around issues such as inadequate boundary mainte-nance, errors in documentation (including failing to document contacts or protect confidential information), and engaging in practices that exceed their scope of competence.

Sometimes, in the face of a mistake, a social worker may feel defensive or over-whelmed, making it challenging to engage in a thoughtful decision-making pro-cess. They may be tempted to hide their error, deny responsibility, or even avoid addressing it altogether.

REMEMBER

However, it's important to remember that the ethical decision-making process exists as a valuable tool to help social workers navigate mistakes. It encourages transparency, accountability, and ethical reflection, fostering a culture of con-tinuous improvement and learning in the field of social work. People may deviate from this process at times, but the guide remains an essential resource for resolv-ing mistakes and upholding the profession's ethical standards.

TIP

When social workers make ethical mistakes, it's crucial for them to take proactive steps to address and rectify the situation:

1. **Acknowledge the mistake.**

   First, social workers should recognize and admit the mistake to themselves. Denial can hinder the resolution process.

2. **Engage in self-reflection.**

   Self-reflection helps a social worker to understand the underlying reasons that led to the mistake. Identifying the root causes can help prevent similar errors in the future.

3. **Consult with supervisors and mentors.**

   It's important to have an open and honest discussion with supervisors and mentors, seeking guidance and support. This can provide valuable insights and perspectives.

4. **Develop a correction plan.**

   Collaborate with supervisors and mentors to create a concrete plan for correcting the mistake. This plan should address the immediate consequences and how to mitigate them. It may also include addressing the issue with the client who was harmed or making boundaries much more overt and concrete.

5. **Prevent future mistakes.**

   Social workers should work with their supervisors and mentors to develop strategies and safeguards to prevent similar mistakes in the future. This may involve getting additional training, setting boundaries, or improving documentation practices.

6. **Continue to learn.**

   Recognize that making a mistake is an opportunity for growth and learning. Social workers should commit to ongoing professional development to enhance their ethical and practical skills.

By following these steps, social workers can not only correct their mistakes but also grow as professionals, ensuring that they provide the best possible care to their clients while upholding ethical standards.

Chapter **17**

Exploring Professional Development

hen you earn your degree(s) and start your first job, your professional journey is starting! After you get your feet wet and get some clients, projects, and maybe even an office, you'll get a sense of what you still need to do to keep growing and what you're doing well. The areas you need to grow in will need your attention — you can't ignore them. Maybe you just need more experience working through cases and projects. Or maybe you need more education and training.

Here's an example from my own career: I worked in a jail setting, where my role was to summarize therapeutic interactions with clients and talk to the attending psychiatrist about how the clients were responding to the medications they prescribed. I had minimal knowledge of medication and had chosen not to take the psychopharmacology course in college. (I mean, look at how many letters there are in the word alone! Why would I need to know medications in depth? I wasn't planning to be a hospital social worker.) But when I started my job at the jail, I discovered that knowing nothing about medications wasn't an option for me. So, I read books and enrolled in training on the topic.

In other work situations, there have been areas that I wanted to advance my knowledge and training because I liked the topic and the training hours counted toward my licensure hours.

If you acquire licensure as part of your educational and professional journey, you'll need to take continuing education to keep your license current. Each state's licensing board determines the number of hours you need annually or biannually (twice a year). You can use your continuing education training to develop your skills further.

Whether you're reading more books, getting continuing education credit, or just signing up for classes, you'll keep developing in the profession. This chapter covers all these topics so you never get complacent and continue to grow.

Taking Opportunities to Grow within Your Role

In the best-case scenario, you'll have a clear description of your duties and roles in your job. You'll also have a great supervisor who will mentor you and inspire you. And you'll routinely discuss your career track and aspirations. This kind of work situation isn't a pipe dream — I've had this happen (okay, it was only once, but it was really great!) — but you usually get *some* of the dream, not all of it.

Regardless of where you work, try to get a good handle on your current roles and duties. If it's a complex role with what seems like tons of moving parts and each part is important, talk to seasoned workers who seem to have a good grasp of the job. Look at their job management tools and see what you can replicate.

WARNING

You'll probably run across people whose management of their job role is more complicated than the job itself. They overcook things and will stress you out. Take what you can from them, but do what works for you.

REMEMBER

Another job opportunity you want to take advantage of is compensation for supervision toward licensure. Supervision for licensure happens on a weekly basis for two years, and you pay an hourly rate out of pocket for it. Employers commonly offer in-house supervision or pay for outside supervision. That's a nice perk, and you want to take advantage of it — it can save you thousands of dollars!

Additionally, your job will offer in-house training, especially if they stipulate that they do a particular mode of intervention. Say you're working at a place that uses cognitive processing therapy as the standard modality for care; your agency will train you on the treatment model. You want to take advantage of any in-house training offered — it's the best and most natural way to grow.

Some jobs have a clear path forward, and others don't. In the following sections, I walk you through your options for advancement, no matter what your role looks like.

When there is a clear promotional path

If you are thinking about getting into management or you're seeking a promotion, have that conversation with your supervisor or human resources (HR) rep. Ask what qualities they look for in leaders and what skill set you need. You don't have to become a new person — just look at what areas you need to grow in and plan.

I still do this, and I'm almost two decades into this line of work. I make a one-year plan and a five-year plan. When opportunities come my way, I see if they align with my goals and say yes if they do. Other opportunities I actively pursue.

TIP

Be intentional about your future, and go for it! Don't sit around hoping that someone notices you're a dedicated and diligent employee with potential. Often, very good people are overshadowed by the loudest person in the room.

Don't let this pattern deter you, though, even if you lean toward being more reserved, consider yourself an introvert, or firmly set your boundaries at work. There's no one-size-fits-all personality for effective leadership. So, don't disqualify yourself by thinking you don't fit the typical leadership mold. Keep being present and, in due time, muster the courage to seek that promotion while confidently showcasing why you'd excel as a leader. You might even team up with extroverted colleagues in your office, harnessing their unique strengths in a strategic manner, ultimately achieving remarkable results as a cohesive unit.

If your job is more bureaucratic, getting a promotion may be more clear cut. (This tends to be the case for federal and state jobs.) If you're working this kind of job, you still need good performance reviews — you can't just log your hours and expect to be promoted. The steps to a promotion are usually numbered. You move from level 1 to level 2 and so on, with pay raises and sometimes bonuses. You can't apply for supervisor role without having served in the appropriate roles in between.

In some cases, even when there seems to be a clear-cut trajectory toward leadership, the human service sector faces a unique challenge: a shortage of workers. This scarcity often results in people being handed leadership roles or promoted without the necessary training or adequate time in the field. People may see this as a compliment, suggesting potential for a significant leadership position, but elevating someone who isn't fully prepared can lead to a host of issues in the industry. It can foster burnout and even cause organizational trauma. In response, human service agencies are actively seeking remedies by establishing leadership institutes and incubators to support those who are promoted without all the essential skills in place. This approach offers a constructive route for these individuals to grow and develop into effective leaders.

Another way to get a "promotion" is to move to another employer. You may want to pivot and use the skills you developed in your current job to get another job at a higher position. This practice used to be frowned upon (people called it *job skipping*), but today people transition from one organization to another all the time.

WARNING

That said, you don't you want to be moving from one employer to another every six months or every year — that starts to look suspicious. Employers invest a lot of time and money in new hires. Make it worth their time and investment by sticking around and growing with them. Besides, when you're ready to move to a new job, you'll need references. You at least want a nice goodbye party!

When your job is unique or there appears to be no linear path

Sometimes you land a job where there's no clear path for moving up, no "next position," no obvious way to earn more money. For example, maybe your position is completely new for the agency you work for, maybe it's a time-limited contracted role, maybe you're working for a very small agency with few roles, or maybe you created the job you have.

What do you do in these cases? Just stick it out and hope for the best? Never. Always have a plan so you land on your feet. You can use each nontraditional job as a stepping stone for your next adventure.

In the following sections, I take it one scenario at a time and give you ideas for what you can do to grow professionally.

When you're in a new position with the agency

TIP

If your position is a new one for the agency you work for, take the following steps:

>> **Write a clear job description and go over it with your manager.** This is essential. *Job creep* (where people add things to the role that were never meant to be part of the job) is real, and you want to avoid that. A clear job description with delineated roles lets everyone know what your job is and what your job is not.

>> **Revisit your job description regularly and see if it needs to be tweaked.** It's usually good to revisit it after three months, after six months, and then annually after that.

>> **Keep a running list of what the job entails and what you're spending your time doing.** This information will help you quantify your efforts and make the case for more compensation in the future.

When your role is time limited and contracted

TIP

If you're working on a contract basis, do the following:

>> **Keep the end in mind and collect data so you can make the case for continuing the role or doing something enhanced with the role.** For example, the county where I was living had temporary funding for school-based social workers. I had a one-year contract. I collected metrics on what was important to the school district (truancy) and showed that my interventions had improved school attendance. That data helped me make the case for continuing the role, and they extended it by three years!

>> **Do a fantastic job in the role and use it to get more roles.** Have your next job in place before the contract ends.

When you work for a small agency with limited roles

TIP

If you work for a small agency and they don't have many roles, that usually means you're a tight knit team and it's all hands on deck. Have boundaries and don't be everything for everyone. (After all, you have to sleep at some point!)

On the other hand, you can probably be flexible and add to the role if you want. Use this opportunity to do big things that you wouldn't usually be allowed to do in bigger offices.

Finally, have a transitional plan or plan of succession when you're ready to move to the next job. Leave your team in good hands and train the next person if you can.

When you created the job

TIP

Yes, this can happen! Maybe you saw a need for a specific role in the agency and you tricked — I mean, convinced — the bosses to create the role for you. If so, follow these steps:

>> **Create a robust job description and job role.** This helps both you and the organization.

>> **Develop measurable outcomes and metrics so you know what success looks like.** This information will also help you prove to your manager that you're succeeding and deserve a raise!

>> **Join a professional group for people who do what you do.** That way, you'll a have network of people or mentors who can help you.

>> **Get a name plate that says, "Boss" and enjoy the ride!**

Pursuing Licensure

Social workers love acronyms and titles. You can be an MSW with an LCSW who specializes in CBT, EMDR, and DBT and belongs to the NASW and CSWE. You can get the whole alphabet after your name! So, what's the deal with all these titles, and what's the benefit of getting licensed or getting these training? Each acronym indicates that the person has advanced degrees and certifications (MSW and LCSW), has specialized training in an evidenced-based treatment (CBT, EMDR, and DBT), and belongs to major professional association groups for social work (NASW and CSWE).

In the following sections, I walk you through the different licenses, explain why they matter, dive into the importance of finding a good supervisor, and cover licensure exams. Read on if you're looking to add some more letters after your name (and get the valuable training that goes along with all those letters)!

Understanding the different licenses and their power

Social work is a profession of licenses. But licensure isn't just a series of hoops to jump through — it helps protect the public. Licensure is a social and legal contract. When you see someone is credentialed, that means they've gone through a training process. A social worker who wants to get a license must show entry-level competence by earning a social work degree from an accredited program, pass the licensure exam, and abide by the professional code of ethics.

Each state issues a license through a licensing board (with the exception of military social workers).

TECHNICAL STUFF

Social workers who are serving in the military can transfer (or *crosswalk*) their servicemember-level license into the state-level license. There are some procedural steps to do this transfer, but you aren't required to sit for a separate exam.

For all licensure types, you're required to abide by the licensing board's standards of conduct. Not all licenses are equal. Some indicate that you belong to a professional group and understand your profession's core competence. Others indicate that you belong to the profession *and* that you can practice independently and, therefore, receive insurance reimbursement.

Even though each state varies in the types of licensures, these are the usual categories:

>> **Bachelor's-level licensure:** Licensed baccalaureate social worker (LBSW). To get this licensure, you must pass an exam. You cannot go into private practice.

>> **Master's-level licensure:** For this licensure, there are two options:

- **Licensed master social worker (LMSW):** To get this licensure, you must pass an exam. You cannot go into private practice.

- **Licensed clinical social worker (LCSW):** To get this licensure, you usually must have the LMSW first (though this depends on the state), have a certain number of hours of clinical supervision (usually 2,000 to 3,000 hours) by a qualified supervisor (see the next section), and pass an exam. After passing the exam, you can go into private practice and you're eligible for medical insurance reimbursement.

The bachelor's-level of licensure is gaining more prominence, but it isn't available in all states. The social work profession likes having the LBSW because it increases public trust. The National Association of Social Workers (NASW) is advocating this to be a national standard.

Most master's-level social workers hold a license. It's the standard for the profession and employers prefer it. The highest level of licensure is the LCSW, which gives the social worker the highest level of independence.

For each license there is continuing education that is required to maintain the licenses. Continuing education ensures that the practitioner stays up to date on policies, standards of practice, and ethics. That's why the public trusts someone with a license. If you do something that violates the code of ethics or the licensing board standards, you'll face consequences.

REMEMBER

When you have a license, you're not just representing yourself — you're representing the profession and all the other people who practice. It's a collective identity. So, if you act like a fool or harm clients, be ready to face the music. You don't have to be perfect, but you're held to a certain standard.

Finding a good supervisor

If you're pursuing the LCSW licensure, you must find someone who holds an LCSW license, has a degree from an accredited school of social work, and has practice experience. Each state stipulates the number of years the supervisor should be practicing with their own LCSW license, but it's usually a minimum of three years and best practice is *at least* five years. You want someone with some years of experience who can help you with a wide range of cases. Obviously, they should also have no violations from the licensing board.

TIP

What qualities should you look for in a supervisor? Here's a checklist:

>> **A supervisor *must* have experience and expertise in the area that you're working with.** For example, if you're working in the area of addiction, find a supervisor who specializes in addiction. This is called *scope of practice* — your supervisor should have scope of practice in area of your practice.

>> **A supervisor must have knowledge and competencies in theory and treatment modalities.** They should be good at both theory and practice. *Remember:* They're prepping you for the exam (see the next section).

>> **A supervisor must be ethical and help you process ethical dilemmas.**

>> **A supervisor must be culturally sensitive and responsive.** They need to be sensitive to your identity and background and be able to guide you in how to do practice with an anti-oppressive framework.

>> **A supervisor should be able to address your strengths and challenges.**

>> **A supervisor should be organized.** They need to document your hours and sessions.

>> **A supervisor should be able to discuss boundaries, self-monitoring, and self-care practices.**

>> **A supervisor should be able to discuss workplace culture and stress.** When I'm serving as a supervisor, I'm always asked, "Hey, is this normal? Should this be happening at work?" The answer is usually, "No, it shouldn't, but it does."

>> **A supervisor should be someone you admire.** This relationship will be one of the most important and formative of your career. Make sure you like the person and find them inspiring.

TIP

How do you find a good supervisor? Sometimes your work provides a list of supervisors throughout the agency. Talk to people who have been supervisees of that person and get a sense of the pros and cons of working with that person.

WARNING

Your clinical supervisor shouldn't be your immediate work supervisor — that creates a dual relationship and can cause conflict. What happens if you want to discuss an issue you think they mishandled? You'll feel conflicted about bringing up this issue. You don't want to be doing these kinds of calculations. You need the supervision time to be a safe space for you to freely discuss what's troubling you.

TIP

If your workplace doesn't provide a list of supervisors for you, how do you find one? If you're a recent graduate, your university will likely have a list of people they recommend, or you can ask your professors for referrals. Get the names of at least three people and check out their backgrounds and expertise. If you aren't a recent graduate, your local chapter of the NASW has a list of local supervisors. (You must be a member of your local chapter to access the list.) Check out their profiles and contact at least three people.

Whether you're getting names of folks from word of mouth or from a list, talk to all the people you've identified as potential supervisors. Ask them questions about their theoretical orientation, their scope of work, how they work with diverse populations, whether they have experience supervising, how they like to structure supervision, their fee for service, and if they do group supervision (some folks will see you three times a month individually and once a month in a group setting — you may like that or you may not). The answers to all these questions will help you determine who's a good fit for you.

REMEMBER

The goal of supervision is to help you grow in your clinical skills and prepare to pass the licensure exam. It isn't personal therapy for you. It's there to further prepare you to practice on your own. When your supervisor offers you additional resources or makes training recommendations, follow up on them! They'll help you keep growing. Keep a log of your hours and a journal of your experience. Next to your graduate degree, this is one of the most significant investments you'll make financially, emotionally, and psychologically. It's a beautiful rite of passage.

Prepping for the licensure exam

Whether you're prepping for bachelor's- or master's-level licensure, you need to dedicate some time to prepare for the exam. There are two aspects of prepping for licensure exam:

>> Meeting the requirements to sit for the exam

>> Preparing for the content of the exam

Meeting the requirements to sit for the exam

Each state has a licensing board that sets the standard for each licensure level. The standard is usually a degree from an accredited school of social work. If you want a clinical social work license to practice independently, you'll need to complete supervised practice in addition to having an accredited degree.

Most licensure applications are done online. Find your state's licensing board website and submit your materials for the level of licensure you want to obtain. There is usually a fee to sit for the exam.

After you've been approved to take the exam, you can take it at an approved site. The exam is administered by the Association of Social Work Board (ASWB) and has 150 scored questions and 20 pretest questions that aren't scored (the non-scored questions are potential questions for future exams, and you don't know which ones they are).

The exam is administered online, and you'll get your results immediately. The ASWB does not provides an exact number for a passing score — they give a range instead: 90 to 107. Aim to get 107 correct. Most people pass the exam. If you don't pass the exam, you can take it again in 90 days.

Recently, the ASWB has gotten into trouble because, for the first time, it shared the passage rate for each state and the affiliated demographics. The results showed significant differences in passage rates by race for first-time test takers. Standardized tests of all types (for example, ACT, SAT, GRE, or GMAT) have historically pushed out people of color and have been instruments of a biased and racist system. Social workers are looking at these disparities in the LCSW licensure passage rates and are calling for action to remedy this gap, such as providing more support and resources for underrepresented groups and assessing the questions themselves to ensure they aren't biased.

Preparing for the content of the exam

TIP

The two years of supervision leading up to the final exam are the biggest way to prepare. Use your supervision time wisely! Apply theory to cases. Don't think that just because you're done with school that you can forget the academic information. Save your books from college. Use your supervision time to apply your academic information to what you're seeing.

Also, consider doing the following:

>> **Purchase licensure preparation manuals from the ASWB or NASW.** You can find the *ASWB Examination Guidebook* at www.aswb.org/exam/getting-ready-for-the-exam/aswb-examination-guidebook.

>> **Practice, practice, practice.** Set aside time, as you used to for school, and practice taking the exam. Buying a study guide isn't enough.

>> **Take a course on psychopharmacology.** Medications will be covered on the exam.

>> **Sign up for licensure preparation courses through your university or the NASW.** They're usually free or low cost and are worth it.

>> **Did I mention practice?**

Growing in Your Interest Area and Enjoying the Process

People choose to go into social work because they're passionate about helping people and feel called to the job. Getting a degree and even an advanced degree in an area you love is a privilege — but the degree is just the first part of the journey. Continuing to grow in the field by specializing increases your job and life satisfaction.

Having a scope of work and then having an even more specialized skill set within that scope increases your ability to effect change. Let me give you an example from my own life: In my early days as a social worker, my primary interest lay in the realm of mental health. However, it didn't take long for me to realize that, although I had a solid foundation in assessment skills and a general understanding of clinical issues, I needed more training to excel in this field. To bridge this gap, I took two essential steps:

>> I sought out a seasoned practitioner, my favorite professor, to serve as my supervisor for licensure.

>> I enrolled in targeted training programs that were relevant to the population I was working with, focusing on evidence-based approaches.

My supervisor played a pivotal role in guiding me toward the right certifications, and as a result, I became certified in motivational interviewing, structural family therapy, trauma-focused cognitive behavioral therapy (CBT), and exposure techniques for individuals dealing with anxiety. These certifications not only enhanced my competence as a practitioner but also helped me meet my licensure's continuing education requirements. I remain committed to ongoing learning, regularly participating in courses and training opportunities. Plus, I've had the privilege of sharing my expertise by providing training sessions in my areas of specialization.

Social work, as a profession, is truly remarkable because it promotes a lifelong journey of continuous learning while encouraging service and leadership. It allows us to evolve and grow as we simultaneously lead and serve others in our ever-developing craft.

If you're feeling stuck or bored, think about specializing or getting some more training! It will help you better serve your clients and make you feel better about yourself and your work.

REMEMBER

Continuing education is a requirement for people who obtain a licensure. Wise people take continuing education classes that line up with their interests and that may lead to a certification in a special treatment modality. The hours of training you do for the certification for treatment trainings can count toward your annual or biannual continuing education requirement — in other words, you can kill two birds with one stone.

Another way people get their continuing education credits is through conferences. If your work sends you to a conference, some of the sessions at the conference can count toward your license. (The conference will indicate if this is the case.) Other times, you may go to the annual NASW conference or a conference of the special subsection of social work practice you do (for example, the School of Social Workers of America conference), which gives you a chance to hear about the latest policy issues, network with some colleagues, and pick up some continuing education hours. And when you're seasoned enough, you may become one of the conference presenters with all your fancy credentials. You'll be the sage on stage telling the rest of us about the new way to do things.

4

The Part of Tens

Be inspired by pioneering and contemporary social workers.

Learn about the amazing jobs and professional tracks you can have as a practicing social worker.

Bake wellness into your job by practicing robust self-care through research-supported steps.

Chapter **18**

Ten Famous, Fabulous Social Workers

Social workers work on behalf of people and communities that need a voice and advocacy. We highlight the work and the people. In this chapter, I shine a light on the helpers themselves. I tell you about people who are hailed as heroes by the profession, people who are very visible and known, and contemporary social workers who are leading the profession today. All these social workers have lives and work that exemplify how much of a change social workers make. They're an inspiration and worth checking out!

Jane Addams (1860–1935)

There is no talk about notable social workers without talking about Jane Addams. That's because she was one of the founders of the social work profession and a Nobel Peace Prize winner in 1931.

Educated at the Rockford College for Women, Addams was the founder of the Hull House, a community center in the heart of Chicago. She created a social service model where the settlement house offered child care for working mothers, an art gallery, a library, music and art classes, a gym, a cooperative for working women, and a place for trade unions. Addams helped pass laws that addressed child labor and minimum educational standards for all children.

As important as the settlement homes and movements were, they focused on European immigrant and migrant families. Settlement houses ignored the needs of African-American migrants who were fleeing the South. Because of this issue, Black settlement houses were created by Black social workers.

Dorothy Irene Height (1912–2010)

Dorothy Height was a phenomenal social worker and someone who President Barack Obama called "the godmother of the civil rights movement and a hero to so many Americans." The U.S. Postal Service issued a stamp with her image on it.

Educated at New York University, Height held 36 honorary doctorates. She started as a social worker for the New York City Welfare Department and became a long-time national executive director of the YWCA and desegregated YWCA facilities nationwide. She was one of the first civil rights leader to highlight the need for women's rights and racial rights seamlessly. Height was president of Delta Sigma Theta, an international sorority of black women.

She was awarded the Presidential Medal of Freedom and the Congressional Gold Medal, the highest civilian awards in the United States. She worked with the "big six" civil rights leaders, including Martin Luther King, Jr. She was the unheralded seventh leader but was cut out or cropped out of the photos in history books. She deserves a bigger spotlight.

Francis Perkins (1889–1965)

Educated at Mount Holyoke and Columbia, Francis Perkins trained as a social worker at the Hull House in Chicago and was a professor at Mount Holyoke. She was the first woman to serve on the New York State Industrial Commission and served as the first female cabinet member, as Secretary of Labor for President Lyndon Johnson. Perkins was the woman behind the New Deal. The House of Representatives Committee on Un-American Activities (an anticommunist witch-hunt group) tried to impeach Perkins as a political move against the New Deal, but the House Judiciary Committee exonerated her.

She helped change the laws regarding minimum hours of the workweek and minimum wage; and helped draft the National Labor Relations Act, the Fair Labor Standards Act, and the Social Security Act. Her big dream was national insurance. Perkins was inducted into the National Women's Hall of Fame and the Labor Hall of Fame. The Department of Labor headquarters is named after her. The U.S. Postal Service created a stamp with her image on it.

Whitney M. Young (1921–1971)

Whitney M. Young's journey, marked by a stellar education that spanned Kentucky State College, the Massachusetts Institute of Technology, and the University of Minnesota, laid the foundation for his extraordinary career as a prominent social worker.

Young's career took flight when he assumed the position of executive director of the Urban League in 1961. He breathed life into the Urban League, significantly increasing its membership and budget, thereby making it a formidable force in the American Civil Rights movement. Through his visionary leadership, the Urban League became a pivotal and influential player in the quest for racial equality.

One of Young's most iconic achievements was the pivotal role he played in organizing the historic March on Washington, a momentous event that underscored his ability to bring people together in the pursuit of civil rights. By cosponsoring this seminal gathering, Young solidified the Urban League's position as a driving force in the fight for equal rights and justice.

Beyond his work with the Urban League, Whitney M. Young contributed to the field of social work as an esteemed professor and as the dean of the Clark Atlanta School of Social Work. His dedication to education ensured that the next generation of social workers was equipped with the knowledge and values necessary to carry the torch of social justice forward.

The significance of Young's life was duly recognized with the Presidential Medal of Freedom, a testament to his profound impact on civil rights and social work. However, his life took a tragic turn with a shocking and sudden death by drowning. His funeral, attended by more than 6,000 people, served as a poignant reminder of the legacy he left behind — a legacy that continues to inspire and guide those who follow in his footsteps, demonstrating the profound impact that dedicated social workers can have on the course of history.

Antonia Pantoja (1922–2202)

A true luminary in the realm of social work, this Afro–Puerto Rican leader's educational journey traversed Hunter College, Columbia University, and Union Institute & University. Her career and notable achievements, however, shine even brighter. As a fierce activist, she mobilized against labor violations and championed equity in education, leaving an indelible mark. Her founding of ASPIRA, meaning "to aspire," aimed to address the educational divide for non-English-speaking Puerto Rican students in public schools.

A watershed moment arrived when she filed a civil lawsuit against New York City Public Schools and emerged victorious, mandating the establishment of bilingual and English as a second language (ESL) support — a landmark ruling for bilingual students nationwide. Her remarkable efforts didn't go unnoticed: She became the first Puerto Rican to receive the Presidential Medal of Freedom and earned a place in the National Portrait Gallery.

Alice Walker (1944–)

Alice Walker is an author and social worker. She is best known for her book *The Color Purple*, which won the Pulitzer Prize and the National Book Award and was adapted for film and as a Broadway play. In her writing and life, Walker is an activist and humanitarian. She lends a voice for outsiders and makes the invisible visible. She is seen as a leader in in the literary and Black feminist community. She has worked as a social worker, teacher, and professor. Her books have sold more than 15 million copies and her work has been translated into 12 languages.

Recently, Alice Walker's support of an antisemitic author has been a serious challenge for her professionally. She has been asked to explain her endorsement of his work, and in a *New York Times* interview, she clarified that her criticism was not directed at Jewish people as a whole but rather at the state of Israel, along with the ancient texts and practices of various religions, such as Christianity, Islam, and Buddhism. She sought to distinguish between her critique of certain policies and practices and her stance on any particular group or ethnicity. Today, headlines about Walker describe her as icon *and* as someone who needs to clarify her stance on an antisemitic author.

Suze Orman (1951–)

Suze Orman is a personal financial expert who gained substantial visibility when she became a regular contributor on *The Oprah Winfrey Show* and her on own CNBC show, *The Suze Orman Show*. She holds a bachelor's degree in social work from the University of Illinois at Urbana–Champaign. and has deep respect for the practice of social work. She encourages people to have financial agency through living below their means, differentiating between needs and wants, and learning how to derive pleasure out of saving. I don't know how fun all of this sounds, but she has good points.

Orman has received Emmy Awards, was named one of *Time* magazine's most influential people, and has won multiple Gracie Allen Awards. She is a devoted supporter of her alma mater. Every year, a lucky student is awarded the Suze

Orman Award in which they're given support to pay off their student loan. Now *that* is a delightful surprise!

Brené Brown (1965–)

Brené Brown is a social work professor, researcher, author, and business owner, and she has one of the most viewed and popular TED Talks (www.ted.com/talks/brene_brown_the_power_of_vulnerability). She talks about emotions and, specifically, the topic of vulnerability. When I last checked, her TED Talk on vulnerability had been viewed more than 62 million times.

Brown's central message is that if you learn to embrace your flaws and live in vulnerability, you'll be more at peace and live a more connected life. Her work centers on connection and belonging — the things that disrupt it and the things that enhance it. Her message resonates with a global audience, and she is a highly sought-after speaker.

Brown trains clinicians and businesspeople. Her company is flourishing — it was referred to as an "empire" in a *New Yorker* profile. Her work has been celebrated by prominent people, including past presidents. She has received an endowed chair for research at the University of Houston and has won several local and national awards.

Larry Davis (1947–2021)

Dr. Larry E. Davis was a prominent figure in the field of social work. He began his academic pursuits by earning a bachelor's degree in psychology from Michigan State University and a master's degree in social work from the University of Michigan. He earned a second master's degree in psychology and became the first African American to obtain a Ph.D. through the University of Michigan's dual-degree program in social work and psychology.

Dr. Davis went on to become a professor, dean, activist, and public scholar. His remarkable career in social work was distinguished by his unwavering dedication to addressing issues of race and social justice at a time when these topics were not as widely discussed or embraced. He was a trailblazer in his unapologetic approach to "race work" and consistently utilized the term *race* in his research, long before it became a mainstream or palatable subject of discussion.

Dr. Davis eventually retired as the dean of the School of Social Work at the University of Pittsburgh. During his tenure, he not only led the school to a top-ten ranking but also founded the Center on Race and Social Problems, the first center of its kind in any American school of social work. His academic contributions were extensive, marked by a significant list of articles and the authorship, coauthorship, or editing of seven books. These works covered a wide range of topics related to race, ethnicity, and social inequality, addressing both professional peers and general audiences.

Dr. Davis's legacy extends beyond academia — he left an indelible mark on the field of social work, and his influence continues to resonate through the work of scholars and advocates who carry forward his vision. I consider myself lucky to have personally known him and to have been mentored by someone of his caliber.

Abolitionist Social Workers

Abolitionist is not the name of a cool new person you haven't heard of (but it could be the name of a band, right?). It's a movement. Contemporary abolitionist social work organizing and practice extend the early Black-led abolitionist movement of the 18th and 19th centuries that overthrew the institution of slavery. Modern-day social workers and thinkers who are a part of the abolitionist movement are folks who want to eliminate the use of excessive punishment, surveillance, imprisonment, and policing practices that oppress people. They don't just want to tear stuff down. Instead, they imagine a world where prisons, policing, surveillance, and punishment are obsolete or unthinkable. They want to build political and economic will to see a world where incarceration is not an acceptable form of social regulation, reform efforts are not about getting to build more harmonious relationship with prison systems (akin to having policies that would make enslavement less terrible), and reform efforts must include the people directly impacted by carceral states. They want to see a world where social service practices that are punitive are banned and replaced instead with institutions that give all people their basic human rights. They want it all, and they don't think it is impossible.

In the past, people couldn't imagine a world where enslavement wasn't the norm. Now slavery is seen as national atrocity. Abolitionists get a lot of eye rolls and are told that they want a utopian world that isn't possible. However, they correctly point out that the COVID-19 pandemic caused changes in social regulations that were once seen as impossible. Everyone gets federal support monthly and minimum wage is significantly higher? We can provide health care and education through the computer? For everyone? Yes, all that happened. There was public will and deep understanding that if these intense measures weren't taken, we would all be in jeopardy.

That's the mindset of abolitionists. Think big. Imagine a world where you dismantle and build at the same time. It's radical, indeed.

Chapter **19**

Ten Jobs You Didn't Know Social Workers Could Do

A re social-work jobs all about shuffling papers at your desk while eating a burger? Maybe the job switches it up sometimes, and you get to shuffle papers, eat burgers, and drink big sodas in your car while smoking? If your only exposure to social workers is repeat episodes of *Law & Order*, I have good news for you!

Social workers do some of the coolest jobs around, and in this chapter I tell you about ten of them. Whether you're interested in working with children, older people, animals, or veterans; whether you want to work at home or abroad, you're sure to find a job as a social worker that interests you.

Therapeutic Preschool Interventionist

If you enjoy working with kids in a school setting, think about working as a social worker in a therapeutic classroom. A therapeutic classroom (or what is known as *milieu therapy*) dedicates the whole classroom as a space for intervention. Children are not taken out of the classroom for an hour or so to get therapy or services. Instead, the entire class is designed to helping them learn social skills, emotional regulation, and problem-solving skills. Kids get individual plans and individual play therapy. Their parents get support, too, with parent education sessions or connections to family services.

In a therapeutic classroom, a social worker is part of an interdisciplinary team of psychiatrists, psychologists, and teachers. Kids who need this type of classroom tend to have developmental delays or are survivors of abuse who need lots of love to process their big stress. The classroom sizes are small (eight kids or so), and the team approach to work makes everyone mission-minded. Kids aren't labeled "good" or "bad" — they're all our kids, and we give them all the support they need.

Intensive Family Preservation Specialist

Researchers have found out that when families have complex, chronic problems, seeing a counselor once a week isn't enough. The intensive family preservation model provides up to 20 hours a week of counseling and life skills education for families who have children at risk of being placed in foster care. The services take place in the home or community of the client; they can also happen in a shelter. The intense intervention lasts four to six weeks.

As an intensive family preservation specialist, the social worker is a professional therapist and life coach for families who are in crisis. This role is a demanding one, where clients have access to you for emergency care. Therapists usually carry a small caseload of two or three families, at most. This is the type of job where you get to make a difference one family at a time. You become part of the family system because you could be spending four to five hours a day with one family. You see how they live their daily lives, give support to the parents about parenting in real time, and help the kids manage their emotions and lives, again in real time. At the end of your time with the family, they should be more stabilized and have services in place, like therapeutic preschools (see the preceding section).

Geriatric Transitional Care Planner

When older adults are hospitalized, they're extremely vulnerable and need a good transitional care plan so they don't end up being readmitted to the hospital. A transitional care social worker helps assess the health and social needs of the patient, facilitates a patient-centered continuity of care, and involves the family in treatment planning and in the creation of a health management plan. This job entails working with an interdisciplinary team of hospital providers who help older adults transition out of the hospital into the next level of care. You don't want people getting the runaround and feeling defeated and overwhelmed by the process. The goal is to decrease fragmented care by assigning them a social worker who can make sure they understand what's happening and get their questions answered.

I had an older family member experience an unexpected hospitalization, and I felt tremendously lucky that I had social-work skills. I made a spreadsheet of 15 different providers we interacted with and how we needed to follow up with each of them. Keeping track of my loved one's care was almost a full-time job. This could be *your* job, for patients in a hospital setting. You can help families like mine who need help so their loved one has a much better chance of recovery. My loved one recovered in an extraordinary way because of the continuity of care — you could provide that same service for patients.

Animal-Assisted Child and Family Therapist

This job is for folks who love to work with animals and people. In your clinical intervention as a therapist, you can use animals as part of your work. Some clients may be hesitant to work with humans but be more open to working on their struggles with an animal present. For example, you might offer equine (horse) therapy; to do this, you would typically join a farm or ranch that is offering this service. Or you could have a therapy animal (usually a dog) in the therapeutic space with you. You would intentionally use the animal to become a teacher, a co-therapist, or a facilitator in your work. You would train your animal to be a therapy animal who can tolerate intense emotions. The animal isn't just sitting as a companion to you or your client — they're *working* with you.

Sports Social Worker

Working with sports in social work can happen in two ways:

>> **You can be a social worker embedded as part of a professional or college athletic team.** Sometimes mental health or behaviors outside of the sport can jeopardize the athlete's career. In those situations, you can work with athletes on their well-being outside of athletics and provide individual or family support through counseling and life coaching.

>> **You can be a social worker who uses sports as your intervention.** The sport is the intervention and the method to engage the client in a nontraditional manner. You can do this with basketball, a ropes course, or clubs or community-based settings like the Boys & Girls Clubs of America or the YMCA. In these settings, social workers use sports activities to build connections with young people, as well as tools for emotional regulation. It can be as simple as talking about what's going on with them while shooting free throws. Or it can involve doing a ropes course for team building or something like teaching emotional management skills through yoga practice. Sports or recreational therapy is one of the oldest form of interventions in social work and one of the most effective.

Commissioned Officer in the Air Force

This job involves serving in the military as part of the health team called the Biomedical Sciences Corps (BSC). You start this process by contacting a recruiter in your area and sharing that you're interested in being a social worker as a service member. Educationally, you need a master of social work (MSW) degree and at least an entry-level license, like licensed master social worker (LMSW) or licensed social worker (LSW). It's preferred that you have LCSW licensure prior to applying. If you don't have the LCSW, there is residency program that allows you get your licensure; it's competitive but available.

To enter military service, you'll go through an extensive interview process; if approved, you can formally start active duty through the Officer Training School. After you complete that process, you'll rotate among three core areas as part of the health team:

>> Assessment

>> Mental health

>> Family advocacy

You'll have the opportunity to travel and have access to free housing, good health care, educational benefits, retirement, and sign-on bonuses. You'll also get leadership training.

Health-Care Social Worker, Pregnancy, and Women's Substance Use Recovery

This job is really about the last part of the job title. You'll be working with pregnant mothers who are recovering from using substances. The job is done in the hospital or health-care setting. In this role, social workers work with mothers who are using medication-assisted therapy to treat their dependence on substances. Medication-assisted treatment helps relieve cravings, blocks the euphoric effects of illegal drugs, and prevents withdrawal symptoms. The use of substances during pregnancy is a huge risk factor and can lead to infant mortality. In pregnancy, medication-assisted treatment helps to stabilize the womb, protect the fetus, and lower death rates.

Social workers who work in this area work with pregnant mothers and help provide prenatal care, care for the substance use, and mental health care. They give holistic treatment so that mother, baby, and family have the best outcomes. It's amazing what happens when you treat people with dignity and try to help them exactly where they are.

Diversity, Equity, and Inclusion Manager/Officer

Another growing area for social workers is to be a diversity, equity, and inclusion (DEI) officer/manager within a company. DEI managers help develop and implement organization diversity initiatives and foster and maintain an equitable work environment. Social workers have training in areas of diversity and justice. In this role, you bring that expertise to the organization's culture. For example, you would look at recruitment, hiring, and retention practices and ensure that those support the company's diversity goals. You would do an organizational climate and culture assessment and respond to issues that people raise as problematic or hostile. You would also get to do work that builds and strengthens the culture and climate of the space. This work is complex but makes a huge difference in the lives of staff and the people you serve.

International Social Worker

International social workers have a humans rights and global justice perspective. You can get a job through big known entities like the United Nations, the International Rescue Committee, the World Health Organization, or the State Department. You can also work with nongovernmental organizations (NGOs) that do humanitarian work with local governments.

If you're interested in the international population but you aren't able to leave the country, you can do international social work by working with international populations in your own city. For example, you might work with recent immigrants or people who've had to flee their country of origin and need relocation support.

International social work has a big scope. It encompasses work in environmental justice, child well-being and maternal health, human trafficking, child welfare, education, health, HIV prevention, and human rights. It spans from micro to macro. You need a heart for justice and a passport.

Traveling Social Worker

This job is for the folks who have a little bit of wanderlust. Its allows you to travel across the country (and sometimes outside of the country) and help systems that are very short staffed. Traveling social workers work in health-care settings, schools, and prisons. The majority of the work is in health care and, more specifically, in acute hospital settings. Typically, the hiring site wants experienced social workers, but they don't want to hire folks in an emergency and then train them on the basics of the job. They need help and they needed it yesterday.

The main draw for the job is the high income, flexibility, time-limited assignments (think: no work drama), and the opportunity to travel. You'll use a staffing agency, which will assign you to a recruiter who will connect you to a hiring manager. The hiring manager will be the staff person at the job site. You tell them what works for your schedule. Make sure it's all written out in the contract — how many days you'll work, if you'll work weekends, how many days you need in between shifts, and so on. If you need a particular day off to attend your cousin's wedding, make sure that's in the contract, too.

Chapter **20**

Ten Ways You Can Take Care of Yourself as a Social Worker

The work of helping others is personally and professionally satisfying, but the professional helping process is one-directional: You pour yourself and your energy into others. Your clients aren't expected to take care of you or make sure you're okay — that's your job. As you do this kind of work, you can inadvertently overlook your own needs and become taxed and drained.

WARNING

Not taking care of yourself has some serious hazards. If you don't take care of yourself, you may

» Have intrusive thoughts or flashbacks about disturbing things you've seen and heard

» Have dreams about disturbing things you've seen and heard

» Be easily startled or be on edge

» Become cynical and cold

>> Lose connections to people at work and in your personal life

>> Develop symptoms of post-traumatic stress disorder (PTSD)

To avoid this occupational hazard, you must intentionally take the time to tend to your own well-being. This is called *self-care* — the practice of attending to your well-being in a holistic way. Self-care is not selfish; it's a fundamental part of the helping process, and it helps you maintain connected to your work and have good outcomes with your clients. Self-care is prevention. It helps guard against burnout and increases your quality of life.

You are not doomed to becoming a weepy, cold person if you become a social worker! In fact, you can be an even *happier* human being who loves their work and life. Here are the benefits of having a good self-care plan:

>> Job satisfaction — you'll love your job!

>> Longer retention at work — you'll want to stay at your job!

>> Increased connection to yourself.

>> Increased connection to others.

>> Increased satisfaction in life over all.

In this chapter, I offer specific steps you can take to make self-care part of your daily life.

WARNING

Sometimes a self-care plan isn't enough. If you have symptoms of PTSD, it's time to get formal help and see a therapist. And maybe consider taking some time off, too.

Fuel Up

I cannot stress enough the importance of attending to the basic things all humans need to function, starting with eating. You must pay attention to your nutritional needs and recognize that living a harried life, where food is an afterthought, will not serve you well. Consume foods that are nourishing and energizing. I don't mean the nonsense fad of labeling certain foods as "good" and others as "bad" — I mean eating a well-balanced meal that includes a balance of carbohydrates, proteins, and fats.

TIP

Some simple things can have a big impact:

>> **Eat three meals a day.** Are you guilty of grabbing a snack from the vending machine or scarfing down food from the drive-thru on your way from point A to point B? Taking time to sit down at a table and eat a meal without distractions can go a long way toward nourishing your body.

>> **Drink enough water.** You'll find different "rules" about how much water you should drink — one common one is to drink eight 8-ounce glasses a day. I don't know about you, but I'm not walking around with an 8-ounce glass everywhere I go. Instead, bring a refillable water bottle with you and make an effort to drink several bottles of water a day.

Get Enough Sleep

When I talk about self-care, people often imagine elaborate rituals to help them center themselves and feel good. But it doesn't have to be that complicated. The most fundamental self-care step you can take is getting enough sleep. Sleep allows your body to rest and digest. Not only is sleep delightful, but it's critical for humans to function. That's why sleep deprivation is used as a torture tactic. Without adequate sleep, your body will fall apart.

TIP

Adults typically need a solid six to eight hours of sleep every night. You can't "bank" sleep by getting a ton of it on the weekends and expect it to last you all week either. Start paying attention to how you feel after getting six hours of sleep, seven hours of sleep, eight hours of sleep. How much sleep does it take for you to feel your best? When you know the answer to that question, make it a priority to make sure you get that much sleep *every night*.

Move It

Exercise offers tremendous psychological and emotional benefits. It not only helps you live longer but also makes you feel better. The key to engaging in physical activity is doing something you genuinely enjoy. Many people mistakenly associate physical activity solely with going to the gym or running, which may sound torturous to you.

Instead, find an activity you genuinely enjoy, something that connects you to yourself. Whether it's taking a leisurely walk with your dog, hiking, swimming, or even tending to a garden, as long as you're moving your body to the best of your ability, it's beneficial. This investment in your physical well-being will yield long-term rewards.

TIP

Get at least 150 minutes of activity every week. That doesn't mean you have to do 150 minutes of a heart-pounding workout. You can spread those 150 minutes throughout the week however works best for you (for example, you can do it in ten-minute chunks), and you can incorporate it into your daily life. Park farther away, take the stairs, or take the dog for a walk.

Spend Time in Nature

Spending time in nature is an important form of self-care. "Forest bathing," inspired by the Japanese practice of Shinrin-yoku, involves immersing yourself in a forest environment to reduce stress, lower blood pressure, and improve overall well-being, as supported by scientific research. This can be extended to include all of nature — flowers, plants, fields, plains — so even if you don't live near a forest, you can "forest bathe."

Beyond the health advantages, spending time in nature allows you to appreciate the natural beauty of the world. It serves as an opportunity to unplug from your digital devices and detach from the world's problems. In nature, you can tap into something larger than yourself and get a little lost.

REMEMBER

Spending time in nature doesn't have to mean taking an elaborate 3-mile hike. Something as simple as eating your lunch outside or near something green is good. Try to incorporate nature that is accessible or near you, like in your neighborhood or near work. The easier and closer it is, the more likely you are to access it. And remember to unplug while in nature. Listen to the natural sounds and notice the changing seasons. Don't listen to music or podcasts. Really unplug.

Focus on Relationships

Relationships play a central role in our human experience. Being part of a community is not only important but also something that social workers can sometimes overlook when they're immersed in their demanding work, addressing challenging issues day in and day out. Instead of neglecting these relationships, make a concerted effort to consistently connect with others. This effort not only benefits you but also enhances the support and care you can provide to the people you serve.

TIP

Here are some tips for focusing on your relationships:

>> **Connect consistently with friends and family.** Maybe you can meet your best friend for coffee once a week, or maybe you and your family can have a weekly game night.

>> **Find at least one person you connect with at work.** Make sure this relationship is a healthy one and not part of a negative group. Having support at work can be a key part of self-care.

>> **Get good supervision or a mentor at work.** If it's not your immediate supervisor, find someone else who can serve as your mentor. Having strong supervision increases your sense of belonging and job satisfaction.

>> **Join a group.** Meet new friends by joining a group. Like to hike? Join a hiking group, and you'll get out in nature, move your body, and meet new people, all at the same time! Do you enjoy competition? Join a softball team, a pickleball club, or a bowling league! Meetup (www.meetup.com) is a great place to find people interested in everything from archery to Zen.

Feed Your Mind

Continuous learning is a fundamental aspect of social work. It's an ongoing journey that invites you to nurture your curiosity and explore areas of interest, whether or not they're directly related to social work. The key is not to remain stagnant and to constantly challenge yourself. Embracing this process of lifelong learning is one of the many joys of life and a rewarding aspect of growing older.

TIP

If learning new things and challenging your brain makes you feel energized or happy, you can incorporate that into your life as a form of self-care. For example:

>> **Learn a new language.** Have you always wanted to travel to Italy? Sign up for an Italian language course at your local community college or online.

>> **Take a writing class.** Maybe you'll start writing the Great American Novel (or the Great American Short Story). Maybe you'll find poetry is your jam. Or maybe you'll write the screenplay for the movie you wish Hollywood would make. Writing is a great way to exercise your brain!

>> **Learn a new skill for your job or specialize in an area of social work that interests you.** Maybe you'd really like to work more with kids, or with the LGBTQIA+ community, or with older people. Take courses to help shift the focus of your practice, and you'll not only work your brain but also improve your happiness on the job!

>> **Take the course you wish you'd taken in college.** Maybe you never got around to taking that astronomy course everyone was raving about, or maybe you wish you knew more about women's history. Feed your brain — and practice self-care in the process — by studying a subject that's always interested you.

>> **Join a book group.** You'll read books you might not have picked on your own and get to discuss them with interesting people in your community. Local bookstores often sponsor book groups. If you can't find one in your area, start your own!

Get Spiritual

Spirituality takes on a variety of forms in our lives. It can manifest through organized religion and affiliation with a specific group, stand alone as an unaffiliated and purely spiritual experience, or simply involve the act of introspection and the practice of gratitude.

Spirituality has been shown to be a valuable tool in a variety of ways. It can help you find meaning, offer comfort, help you adapt to change, and help you cope with challenges. Regardless of your personal beliefs or experiences, consider incorporating spiritual practices in your life in order to nurture this essential aspect of yourself.

TIP

You don't have to be religious to find self-care in spiritual activities. Here are some activities or practices you can do to nourish your spirit:

>> **Meditation:** Engaging in meditation involves setting aside dedicated time to quiet the mind and focus on breathing or a specific thought, allowing for relaxation and inner peace. Some religious practices can give you specific tools to do this. But you can also download an app on your phone (Headspace is a good one) if you don't know where to start.

>> **Self-reflection:** Self-reflection is the practice of taking a step back to contemplate your thoughts, actions, and experiences. It often involves capturing this process in a medium such as journaling or taking pictures.

>> **Mindfulness:** Mindfulness is the act of staying fully present in the moment and being observant through simple activities like eating, walking, or just breathing. By cultivating mindfulness, you can reduce anxiety, manage your reactions to stressors, and appreciate the richness of daily life more fully.

Practice Radical Self-Acceptance and Healing-Centered Practices

Radical acceptance and healing-centered practices to self-care are transformative practices rooted in the principles of dialectical behavior therapy (DBT) and healing-centered engagement. These concepts emphasize looking beyond what has happened to you and instead focusing on what's right within you.

Radical acceptance involves acknowledging and embracing life's realities, both positive and negative, without judgment or resistance. Healing-centered practices are a holistic approach to well-being that nurtures your emotional, mental, and spiritual health. Social workers often encourage clients and communities to use these principles, but these principles are also profound when applied to your own life.

TIP

To incorporate radical acceptance and a healing-centered mindset into your self-care routine, consider these three key tips:

>> **Embrace the present moment.** Begin by grounding yourself in the present. Acknowledge your thoughts, emotions, and physical sensations without judgment. Practice mindfulness to become more attuned to your inner experiences. When you fully accept and acknowledge your present state, you can better understand your needs and take proactive steps toward self-care.

>> **Cultivate self-compassion.** Show yourself the same kindness and understanding you would offer to a dear friend. Recognize that you're doing the best you can with the resources and knowledge you have. Self-compassion is a vital component of healing-centered self-care, allowing you to forgive yourself for past mistakes and work toward personal growth and transformation.

>> **Identify your strengths and resources.** Shift your focus from what has happened to you to what is right within you. Recognize your strengths, skills, and internal resources that have enabled you to navigate life's challenges. Develop a gratitude practice to appreciate the positive aspects of your life. This not only promotes healing but also enhances your resilience and ability to move forward.

Play

Social work often involves grappling with intense and occasionally distressing subjects. Therefore, it's crucial for social workers to infuse some lightheartedness into their lives, which I like to call "play." This entails engaging in activities that bring joy, spark laughter, and add brightness to your existence. These activities can encompass escapism, like taking a relaxing vacation, or become an integral part of your daily routine, such as baking. Regardless of the activity, the key is to make sure they don't contribute to stress or resemble work. The focus should simply be on relishing the experience.

TIP

Here are three straightforward strategies for embracing play and cultivating joy in your life:

>> **Embrace escapism.** Dedicate time to indulging in activities that allow you to detach from the demands of your profession. This may include watching mindless TV shows or reading a page-turner — whatever offers you an opportunity to unwind and escape into a world of whimsy.

>> **Explore comedy and entertainment.** Attend improv shows, standup comedy, or live performances that specialize in humor. Laughter is an excellent way to lighten your spirits and find amusement in the absurdities of life.

>> **Tell stories and jokes.** Invest quality time with friends and loved ones and share stories and laughter. This provide a welcome respite from the emotional challenges of social work, helping you recharge and uncover moments of joy in human connection.

By incorporating these practices into your life, you can effectively maintain a well-rounded work-life balance and enhance your overall well-being as a social worker.

Create a Self-Care Plan

Taking care of yourself doesn't happen in a vacuum. In fact, what often happens is that when you're most stressed, you'll neglect yourself until you have a breakdown. In order to prevent that from happening, you need to *plan* to make self-care activities part of your daily life. That way, when your life gets hectic, these activities will be reflexive or automatic for you. Then, when you notice yourself feeling irritable and tired, you'll think, "Let me make sure I'm eating right and calling a friend over for dinner."

TIP

After you figure out what you need (see the previous sections), figure out what you can do to incorporate those activities into your life. Maybe you know you need to get more sleep. Great! Now get specific. How many hours of sleep do you need? What time do you have to wake up in the morning? What time will you need to be in bed in order to get enough sleep? For example, instead of setting a goal to "get more sleep," set a goal to "be in bed by 10 p.m. and turn the lights and all devices off by 10:30 p.m. at least four nights a week."

Making changes takes time. Don't beat yourself up or totally give up if you have trouble sticking to your self-care plan. Undoing old habits and building new habits will take time. Practice radical acceptance as you do this. You aren't looking for perfection.

TIP

You don't need to do just one thing, but I recommend starting with one goal and adding more. Try not to overwhelm yourself with too many goals. Also, look for ways to kill two or three birds with one stone! Maybe you like nature, friends, and working out. You could get a great workout by going for a weekly hike in the woods with your best friend!

REMEMBER

Add the plan to your schedule like it's an appointment. Tell someone about it so they can hold you accountable.

Index

A

AA (Alcoholics Anonymous), 176, 192, 254

ability/disability, 106–116

  ableism, 106, 109–113

  Americans with Disabilities Act, 110, 112–114, 222

  anti-ableist activism, 113–116

  disability/intersectional model, 108–109

  explanatory legitimacy model, 107

  medical model, 107–108

  person-first language, 114

  social model, 107–108

ableism, 109–113

  anti-ableist activism, 113–116

  defined, 106

  individual level, 110–111

  institutional and cultural level, 111–113

abnormal psychology, 12

abolitionist social workers, 340

absenteeism, 228–233

  cost of chronic, 229–230

  engaging family members, 231–233

  increasing school connection, 231–233

  intervention approaches, 228–229

  root causes of, 230–231

  truancy, 229–230

accommodationist approach, 241

ACE (Adverse Childhood Experiences) Study, 157–158

ACEs (adverse childhood experiences), 157–158, 213

ACHIEVA, 114

acute-care settings, 200, 206

ADA (Americans with Disabilities Act), 110, 112–114, 222

Addams, Jane, 335–336

addiction. *See* substance use and addiction

Administration of Children & Families, HHS, 262

administrative specialists, 29

Adverse Childhood Experiences (ACE) Study, 157–158

adverse childhood experiences (ACEs), 157–158, 213

adverse life experiences, 131

alcohol, 171, 182–184. *See also* substance use and addiction

Alcoholics Anonymous (AA), 176, 192, 254

Alinsky, Saul, 243

American Association of People with Disabilities, 114

American Council of the Blind, 114

American Psychiatric Association (APA), 140–141

American Psychological Association (APA), 12

Americans with Disabilities Act (ADA), 110, 112–114, 222

animal-assisted child and family therapists, 343

applied learning, 10

Arc, The, 114

asexual, 89, 102. *See also* LGBTQIA+ individuals

assertive community treatment, 147

assessment phase, 22, 51–53

  bachelor of social work degree, 28

  community organization, 245–246

  diagnoses, 52

  dynamic process, 53

  holistic perspective, 53

  information sources, 52

  mental health and wellness, 139–144

  as process and product, 51

  screening instruments, 52

  structured interviews, 51–52

  substance use and addiction, 194–195

asset-based community development, 243

associate's degree, 26–27, 37, 84

Association of Social Work Board (ASWB), 330

B

bachelor of social work (BSW) degree, 11, 27–31
  advanced standing, 31
  career opportunities, 27–31, 37–39, 42–44, 46
  educational requirements, 27–28
  income, 30–31
  international social work, 283
  internships, 28–29
  licensure, 327, 329
barbiturates, 186
BDSM (bondage, discipline, sadism, and masochism), 103
beauty and aesthetics
  ableism, 110, 116
  gender socialization, 94
  privilege, 72
  racism, 80
behavior health facilities, 200
behavior health workers, 38, 44, 137, 200
Bem, Daryl, 99
benefits specialists, 29
benzodiazepines, 186
binge drinking, 183
Biomedical Sciences Corps (BSC), 344
biopsychosocial history, 139
biopsychosocial theories of sexual development, 99
bisexual, 88–89, 101. See also LGBTQIA+ individuals
block placements, 29
BLS (U.S. Bureau of Labor Statistics), 14
bondage, discipline, sadism, and masochism (BDSM), 103
Brandt line, 268
Brown, Brené, 338–339
BSC (Biomedical Sciences Corps), 344
BSW. See bachelor of social work degree
bullying, 218, 226–228
burnout, 28, 80, 164, 168–169, 292, 317, 323, 348

C

cannabidiol (CBD), 188
cannabis, 180, 188–189. See also substance use and addiction
care coordination, 200
career opportunities, 26–31, 36–46, 341–346. See also names of specific jobs and careers
case manager aides, 27
case managers and caseworkers, 29–30, 43–44, 200
CBD (cannabidiol), 188
CBT (cognitive behavioral therapy), 147, 162
Centers for Disease Control and Prevention (CDC), 158, 183
chain migration, 280
change process, 9. See also helping process
Charity Navigator, 261
chattel enslavement, 278
check and connect model, 55, 232
child removal and placement, 15–16, 69, 294
child welfare workers, 16, 29, 31, 43–44, 219, 291, 294, 314
Christian normativity, 116, 120–122
Christian privilege, 120–123
chromosomes, 93
cisgender, 71, 91
cisnormativity, 97
cissexism, 96–97. See also LGBTQIA+ individuals
Civil Rights Act, 77, 222
class inequality, 81–85
  defined, 82
  disassociation of economic security with happiness, 82
  educational access, 84–85
  family assets and wealth, 83–84
  life chances, 83–85
  measuring class, 81–82
  social class, defined, 81
  work access and success, 85
client-centered approaches, 49, 53, 55, 58, 145–146, 202
clinical psychologists, 12
cocaine, 182

D

Data, Assessment, and Plan (DAP)
documentation style, 302
Davis, Larry E., 339–340
decision tree mapping, 294
Declaration of Independence, 18
Defense of Marriage Act, 102
DEI (diversity, equity, and inclusion) work, 135,
295, 345
demisexual, 102
developmental models
micro-level social work, 60
schools, 215–216
sexual development, 99
*Diagnostic and Statistical Manual of Mental
Disorders* (DSM), 132, 140–143, 173–174
dialectical behavioral therapy, 147, 163
dignity and worth of the person, 17–19, 47, 49,
105, 125, 176, 208, 274, 299, 306, 345
direct practice, 32, 59–61, 191, 212, 312.
See also micro-level social work
disability. *See* ability/disability
disability studies, 107
disability/intersectional model, 108–109
diversity, equity, and inclusion (DEI) work, 135,
295, 345
doctorate degrees, 13, 35–36
career opportunities, 37–39, 41–44
doctor of philosophy (PhD) in social work, 35–39,
41–44
doctor of social work (DSW) degree, 36–39,
41–44
educational requirements, 35–36
income, 36
Doctors Without Borders (Médecins sans
Frontières), 285
documentation. *See* paperwork
"Don't Say Gay" law, 74
dopamine, 184
DSM (*Diagnostic and Statistical Manual of Mental
Disorders*), 132, 140–143, 173–174
dual diagnosis (co-occurring disorders),
138–139, 147
dual relationships, 307–308, 329

E

eco maps, 142
ecological model, 49
Economic and Social Council (ECOSOC), 273
elected office, 249
emergency shelter case managers, 30
emotional intelligence, 50, 263–264
emotionally focused therapy, 147
empowerment framework, 49
endorphins, 186
enforcement officers, 219
engagement phase, 21, 50–51
building rapport, 51
considerations before meeting clients,
50–51
intakes, 27
warmup conversations, 51
enslavement, 77–78, 278
equity and justice, 67–85
anti-oppressive practice stages, 68
class inequality, 81–85
color-blind (neutral) stance, 67
defined, 67
health care, 203–205
layers of identity, 68
oppression, 73–75
power, 75–77
privilege, 69–73
race and racism, 77–81
social justice, 67
essentialism, 106
ethical dilemmas, 304–312
boundaries, 312–319
competing values, 308–309
contingency-based ethical decisions,
308–309
culturally responsiveness in decision-
making, 310
deciding to quit, 311–312
dual relationships, 307–308
Social Work Code of Ethics, 305–307
ethical mistakes, 316, 318–319

European Institute for Social Work, 285
evaluation process, 57–59
  accountability, 58
  families and groups, 58
  individuals, 58
  informal versus structured evaluations, 58
  nonprofit programs, 171–172
  organizations, 59
  personal narratives and insights, 58
evidence-based practice, 64–65
  defined, 64
  self-harm and suicidality, 313
  social problems addressed by social workers, 65
  social workers as scientists and researchers, 64–65
explanatory legitimacy model of disability, 107
exposure therapy, 146–147, 162
externalizing behaviors, 225
eye movement desensitization and reprocessing, 147, 163

F

family advocates, 30
family caregiver development specialists, 30
Family Educational Rights and Privacy Act (FERPA), 222
FDA (U.S. Food and Drug Administration), 188
feminist organizing model, 243
fentanyl, 187
financial ratios, 261

G

gambling disorder, 174
gay, 88–89, 102. See also LGBTQIA+ individuals
gender development, 92–94
gender dysphoria, 94
gender expansive, 91. See also LGBTQIA+ individuals
gender expression, 92, 97–98
gender fluidity, 102. See also LGBTQIA+ individuals
gender reveal parties, 92

General Assembly, UN, 272–273
general systems model, 49
generalist approach, 64
genitalia, 93
gentrification, 239
geriatric social work, 61–62
geriatric transitional care planners, 343
G.I. Bill, 72
Global Impact, 285
Global North and Global South, 269–270
Global Social Service Workforce Alliance, 285
goal-setting (planning) phase, 22, 53–54
  advocacy for change, 251–252
  client-centered approach, 53
  community organization, 246
  mandated treatment, 54
  nonprofit leadership, 258
  for patient-centered health care, 208–209
  voluntary treatment, 54
gonads, 93
Grand Challenges for Social Work, 65
grassroots organizing model, 243
group work
  bachelor of social work degree, 28
  benefits of, 63
  trauma, 163
  types of groups, 63

H

halfway houses, 193
healing-centered practices, 353
Health Resource and Service Administration, 15
health-care access, 197
  barriers to, 205
  disparities in health outcomes, 202
  importance of, 199
health-care settings, 197–210
  ableism, 112
  addressing social problems, 206–207
  disparities in health outcomes, 202–205
  engaging family members in care, 210

MSW. *See* master of social work degree

multisystemic therapy, 147

mutual aid, 256

N

naloxone, 187

Narcotics Anonymous (NA), 192, 254

narrative therapy, 162

National Association of Social Workers (NASW), 248–249, 327, 331–332

  mission of social work, 8

  Social Work Code of Ethics, 18, 20, 274, 297, 299, 305–307

National Association of the Deaf, 115

National Center for Drug Abuse Statistics (NCDAS), 171

National Center for Educational Statistics, 84–85

National Conference of State Legislatures, 15

National Council on Disability, 115

National Institutes of Health (NIH), 158

neutral stance, 67

nonprofit managers and executive directors, 45, 253–266

  advantage of organizations over individuals, 255–257

  central goal of nonprofits, 254

  funding for nonprofits, 255

  good leadership, 263–264

  human service nonprofits, 255

  mission creep, 257

  mission statements, 257

  motivating people to change, 264–265

  number of nonprofits, 253

  organizational culture, 265–266

  program development and implementation, 258–260

  program evaluation, 260–262

  public good and benevolence, 256

  role of, 262–266

  strategic planning, 258

  theories for existence of nonprofits, 256

  values, 258

  vision, 258

O

Obama, Barack, 77, 336

online resources

  ACHIEVA, 114

  Adverse Childhood Experiences Study, 158

  American Association of People with Disabilities, 114

  American Council of the Blind, 114

  American Psychological Association, 12

  Americans with Disabilities Act, 114

  Arc, The, 114

  Association of Social Work Board licensure preparation manual, 330

  Brené Brown's TED Talk, 339

  Charity Navigator, 261

  Cheat Sheet (companion to book), 4

  Columbia Suicide Severity Rating Scale, 313

  Council on Social Work Education, 12, 31, 285

  European Institute for Social Work, 285

  Global Impact, 285

  Global Social Service Workforce Alliance, 285

  Grand Challenges for Social Work, 65

  International Association of Schools of Social Work, 285

  International Council on Social Welfare, 285

  International Federation of Social Workers, 267, 285

  International Rescue Committee, 285

  logic model template, 262

  Médecins sans Frontières, 285

  National Association of Social Workers, 8

  National Association of Social Workers Social Work Code of Ethics, 297, 306

  National Association of the Deaf, 115

  National Council on Disability, 115

  Save the Children, 285

  UN Sustainable Development Goals, 275

  United Nations, 285

  U.S. Agency for International Development, 285

  U.S. Bureau of Labor Statistics, 14

  U.S. Census Bureau homeownership data, 79

  U.S News & World Report school rankings, 31

opiates, 186–188. *See also* substance use and addiction
opioids, 172, 186–187
oppression, 73–75
  defined, 73
  discrimination, 74–75
  dual, 95
  harassment, 74
  robbery, 75
  violence, 75
organizational culture and climate, 265–266
organizing model for schools, 216
Orman, Suze, 338–339
outpatient care facilities, 193, 199

P

painkiller misuse, 172
palliative care facilities, 200
pansexual, 102
Pantoja, Antonia, 337–338
paperwork, 296–302
  clients' rights, 299–300
  confidentiality, 299–300
  documentation styles, 302
  electronic versus paper, 301
  importance and purposes of, 296–299
  requirements for, 297–298
  tips and considerations, 301–302
paraphilia, 103
paraprofessionals, 26, 37, 42
pathologizing
  gender narratives, 94
  substance use and addiction, 172
patient advocates, 26
patient-centered health care, 207–210
  creating plans for, 208–209
  engaging family members in, 210
patriarchy, 95–96
Perkins, Francis, 336
personality-based leadership models, 264
person-first language

ability/disability, 114
  substance use and addiction, 173
person-in-environment (PIE) framework, 216
Pew Research Center, 118–119
planning phase. *See* goal-setting phase
polyamorous, 102
post-traumatic stress disorder (PTSD), 141–142, 152–153, 190
power, 75–77
  categorizations, 76
  community organization, 241–242
  defined, 75
  legislative and political action, 250–251
  sources of, 75
principles of social work, 17–19
privilege, 69–73
  Christian privilege, 120–123
  defined, 70
  individual dimension, 71–72
  institutional dimension, 72
  myth of meritocracy, 70
  societal dimension, 72
process addictions, 174
professional development, 321–332
  clear promotional path, 322–323
  contract work, 325
  licensure, 326–331
  limited roles in small agencies, 325
  new positions, 324–325
  preparing for exams, 329–331
  requirements for exams, 330
  self-created roles, 325–326
  supervision for licensure, 321, 328–329
  supervision structure, 294–295
program specialists, 30
psychedelics, 190. *See also* substance use and addiction
psychologists, 12–13
PTSD (post-traumatic stress disorder), 141–142, 152–153, 190
punitive approach to school absenteeism, 228–229

Q

queer, 89–90. *See also* LGBTQIA+ individuals

questioning, 89. *See also* LGBTQIA+ individuals

R

race and racism, 77–81
  bullying, 227
  disparities, 77
  dual oppression, 95
  enslavement, 77–78
  health care, 204–205
  institutional racism, 78–80
  internalized racism, 80–81
  interpersonal racism, 78
  mental health and wellness, 134–135
  social construction, 77

radical self-acceptance, 353

Reamer, Frederic, 309

recovery model for mental health and wellness, 132–133

rehabilitation facilities, 193, 200

religion and spirituality, 116–125
  changes in religious identification, 118–120
  Christian privilege, 120–123
  defined, 117
  faith-based organizing model, 243
  intrinsic versus extrinsic religiosity, 117
  religious affiliation in the US, 118
  religious oppression, 120–123
  screening tool, 142
  self-care, 352
  social work practice and, 116, 123–125

reparative justice, 277

research assistants, 30

residential case managers, 30

residential facilities, 193

restorative approach to school absenteeism, 228–229

Rothman, Jack, 242–243

S

safety plans, 22

Save the Children, 285

School Social Worker Association of America, 34

schools, 211–233
  ableism, 112
  absenteeism and truancy, 228–233
  behavioral, therapeutic, and emotional supports, 225
  boundaries, 219
  bullying, 226–228
  disparities in educational outcomes, 215
  educational policies, 220–225
  individualized education plans, 223–225
  institutional racism, 79
  interprofessional work, 217
  models and approaches, 215–216
  patriarchy, 96
  as places for social support and interventions, 212–219
  privilege, 72
  public right and institutions, 213–214
  school counselors, 219
  shaping gender socialization, 94
  social workers' role, 30, 42–43, 216–219
  socialization and emotional learning, 214–215

scientific approaches, 47–48

SDGs (Sustainable Development Goals), 271, 274–275

SDOH (social determinants of health), 201, 206, 210

secondary trauma (vicarious trauma; compassion fatigue), 152, 164, 169

sedatives, 185–186. *See also* substance use and addiction

self-care, 163–169
  continuous learning, 351–352
  creating plans for, 165–168, 354–355
  defined, 348
  diet, 348–349
  exercise, 349–350

About the Author

Dr. Yodit Betru holds a doctorate in clinical social work from the University of Pennsylvania and earned MSW and BA degrees from the University of Oklahoma. She is currently the director of the MSW program at the University of Pittsburgh, where she is a clinical assistant professor. As an educator, Yodit trains students on critical issues that impact identity and community, including race, gender, sexual orientation, and gender identity expression.

Her extensive clinical experience — including work in schools, shelters, jails, public child welfare programs, and community and private practice settings — provides the foundation for Yodit's research and work. Her expertise includes trauma-informed treatments, race-conscious practices, and homelessness. Yodit frequently speaks and publishes on these issues at national conferences, schools, and universities. Her trauma-informed curriculum for case managers has been used extensively across the United States to inform practice, policies, and legislation.

As a committed community advocate, Yodit serves on the board of directors for local community agencies. She also continues to see individuals and families for therapy in a private practice setting to keep abreast of contemporary issues in practice.

Dedication

This book is dedicated to my family. I am immensely loved, supported, and blessed. I can do my work, my life, and this project because of their constant and abiding love.

Author's Acknowledgments

This work is the result of many hands and hearts. I thank the *For Dummies* team for their contributions and support, especially Jennifer Yee, who saw my potential and gave me this opportunity. I thank Dr. Shiloh Erdley for her insight and feedback.

I want to acknowledge that the field of social work is built on the shoulders of incredible pioneers and people with radical hope. I want to especially acknowledge pioneering Black social workers, who are often left out of the narration of social work history. They were committed to the work with insight, vision, and passion, despite being locked out of the systems that were meant to help all people. It is my hope that this book exposes people to what social work can do as an homage to their legacy.

Publisher's Acknowledgments

Senior Editor: Jennifer Yee

Senior Managing Editor: Kristie Pyles

Editor: Elizabeth Kuball

Technical Editor: Shiloh Erdley, MSW, DSW

Proofreader: Debbye Butler

Production Editor: Tamilmani Varadharaj

Cover Image: © FatCamera/Getty Images